THE REMINISCENCES OF

Rear Admiral Charles Elliott Loughlin U.S. Navy (Retired)

INTERVIEWED BY

Dr. John T. Mason, Jr.

U.S. Naval Institute • Annapolis, Maryland

Copyright © 1982

Preface

It is one of the ironies of life that Rear Admiral Loughlin will probably always be best known for something he shouldn't have done and was not really blamed for--the sinking of the Japanese ship *Awa Maru* in 1945 after the vessel had been given an assurance of safe passage by the U.S. Government. That one sensational event--which Loughlin explains in the recollections that follow--has for the most part overshadowed the rest of a naval career that was marked by solid achievement.

As a midshipman in the class of 1933 at the Naval Academy, Loughlin was a superb athlete, excelling at both tennis and basketball. He was an All-America in basketball, an achievement which stood him in good stead more than 20 years later when he returned to the Naval Academy as director of athletics. As a junior officer, he spent more than four years in the battleship *New Mexico*. While on board, he served under Lieutenant Hyman Rickover, whom he recalls with a good deal of admiration. Then it was on to submarine school in a class which contained a number of men who would be top skippers in World War II. During the war, he commanded the *S-14* in the Atlantic and the *Queenfish* in the Pacific. In his eight war patrols, he was credited with sinking 12 ships with a combined tonnage of more than 100,000.

Afterward, he advanced up the hierarchy of submarine leadership positions: executive officer of a tender, division commander, and squadron commander. Ashore, in addition to the billet as athletic director, he commanded the naval station at Annapolis, served in the antisubmarine warfare directorate of OpNav, and in the plans section of the SACLANT staff. He commanded the fleet oiler Mississinewa and the heavy cruiser Toledo prior to his selection for flag rank. While a rear admiral, he commanded a submarine flotilla during the buildup of the Polaris fleet and later was Commandant Naval District Washington. In an epilogue to the recollections of his active duty naval career, Admiral Loughlin provides a valuable explanation of the work of the Naval Academy Foundation from his vantage point as executive director.

The transcript depicts the interviews essentially as they took place between Admiral Loughlin and Dr. John T. Mason of the Naval Institute. The admiral has made some changes in the interests of accuracy. For scholars with an interest in U.S. submarine operations or Naval Academy athletics, this memoir is an especially useful one.

Paul Stillwell
Director of Oral History
U.S. Naval Institute
December 1982

REAR ADMIRAL CHARLES E. LOUGHLIN, UNITED STATES NAVY, RETIRED

Charles Elliott Loughlin was born on February 19, 1910, in Wilmington, North Carolina, son of the late Colonel Joseph J. Loughlin, U. S. Army (killed during World War I, November 9, 1918) and Mrs. Eleanor (King) Loughlin. He attended Episcopal Academy, Philadelphia, Pennsylvania, before his appointment, at large, to the U. S. Naval Academy, Annapolis, Maryland, in 1929. As a Midshipman, he played tennis (Captain, 1933; received inter-collegiate ranking 1932 and 1933); basketball (All American, 1932 and 1933); and was awarded the Thompson Trophy in 1933 (awarded to the member of each graduating class who has done the most for promotion of athletics at the USNA). Graduated and commissioned Ensign on June 1, 1933, he subsequently attained the rank of Rear Admiral, to date from July 1, 1961.

Following graduation from the Naval Academy in 1933, he joined the USS NEW MEXICO, and served in that battleship until December 1937, when he was ordered to the Submarine Base, New London, Connecticut, for submarine training. Designated a submariner in June 1938, he reported, the next month, aboard USS S-35. Detached from that underseas craft in October 1940, he was assigned in November, to the USS S-14, and later commanded her until August 1943, during which time the S-14 was based in Panama, engaged in training and defensive War Patrol operations.

He had temporary duty under instruction at the Submarine Prospective Commanding Officers School, Submarine Base, New London, and in September 1943, reported for fitting out duty in USS QUEENFISH (SS 393), at the Navy Yard, Portsmouth, New Hampshire. Upon the commissioning of that submarine on March 11, 1944, he assumed command, and for his outstanding service while in that capacity, was awarded the Navy Cross, a Gold Star in lieu of the Second Navy Cross, the Silver Star Medal; and the Bronze Star Medal with Combat "V." The citations follow in part:

Navy Cross: "For extraordinary heroism...during the First War Patrol of (QUEENFISH)...from August 4 to October 3, 1944...(He) penetrated enemy escort screens to launch damaging torpedo attacks against enemy Japanese shipping which resulted in the sinking of a 1,300-ton enemy destroyer, two large tankers, a large freighter and two large transports for a total of 48,000 tons. Participating in the rescue of eighteen British and Australian prisoners of war who were survivors of a Japanese ship which had been sunk, he provided care and treatment for the sick and wounded survivors and skillfully evaded enemy countermeasures to bring his ship to port without serious damage..."

Gold Star in lieu of the Second Navy Cross: "For extraordinary heroism as Commanding Officer of USS QUEENFISH during the Second War Patrol of that vessel...in the Pacific War Area from October 27 to December 2, 1944..." The citation further stated that due to his skill and aggressive leadership, the QUEENFISH succeeded in sinking a total of 55,300 tons of hostile shipping and in damaging 10,000 tons.

R. Adm. C. E. Loughlin, USN, Ret.

Silver Star Medal: "For conspicuous gallantry and intrepidity... during the Third War Patrol of that vessel in...waters in the Formosa Straits and waters adjacent to the China Coast, from December 29, 1944 to January 29, 1945...As group Commander, he contributed materially to the success of his command in sinking eight enemy ships totaling 60,000 tons and successfully evaded strong enemy antisubmarine measures..."

Bronze Star Medal: "For meritorious service...during the Fourth War Patrol (of QUEENFISH)...from February 24 to April 14, 1945...Commander Loughlin carried out the successful rescue of thirteen downed aviators and brought his vessel safe back to port..."

He is also entitled to the Ribbon for, and a facsimile of the Presidential Unit Citation awarded to USS QUEENFISH for attacking and sinking a Japanese carrier, in a brilliantly executed periscope attack against heavily escorted convoys and for rescuing eighteen British and Australian prisoners of war from the sea during a tropical typhoon.

Detached from command of the QUEENFISH in March 1945, he had a month's duty with Submarine Division TWO HUNDRED EIGHTY TWO, after which, during May and June 1945, he served as Assistant Tactical Officer and Training Officer on the Staff of Commander Submarine Force, U. S. Pacific Fleet, aboard USS POGY. In July, he joined the Staff of Commander Submarine Force, U. S. Atlantic Fleet, as Operations Officer, and continued to serve in that capacity for two years, when in July 1947, he became Executive Officer of the USS ORION. In July 1948, he assumed command of Submarine Division SIXTY-TWO, continuing to serve as such until ordered to return to the United States.

In June 1949, he reported as Executive Officer of the Naval Station, Annapolis, Maryland. In January 1951, he became Commanding Officer of the station, and of the historic station ship USS REINA MERCEDES. He served in this command until July 1952. He was Chief Staff Officer to Commander Submarine Flotilla ONE until July 1953, after which he had duty in command of Submarine Squadron THREE.

Returning to the Naval Academy in July 1954, he served as Head of the Physical Training Department and Director of Athletics until August 1957, when he assumed command of the oiler MISSISSINEWA (AO 144). The MISSISSINEWA underwent conversion to the Flagship of Commander Service Force, SIXTH Fleet, and in April 1958, rejoined the SIXTH Fleet in the Mediterranean with homeport in Naples, Italy. In August 1958, he became Commanding Officer of the USS TOLEDO (CA 133). Following local operations on the West Coast, TOLEDO deployed to the Western Pacific in June 1959, serving with the SEVENTH Fleet until its return to Long Beach, on November 25, 1959. Detached from command of that cruiser in November 1959, he next served as Deputy to the Anti-Submarine Warfare Readiness Executive, Office of the Chief of Naval Operations, Washington, D. C.

R. Adm. C. E. Loughlin, USN, Ret.   Page 3

On August 10, 1960 he was assigned as Director for Plans to the Supreme Allied Commander, Atlantic and in October 1961 assumed command of Cruiser-Destroyer Flotilla NINE. In November 1962 he reported as Deputy Chief of Staff and Deputy Chief of Staff for Plans, Policy and Operations, to the Supreme Allied Commander, Atlantic and served as such until August 1964 when he became Commander Submarine Flotilla SIX. "For exceptional meritorious achievement...(in that capacity) from August 24, 1964 to September 24, 1966..." he was awarded the Legion of Merit. The citation further states:

"...Rear Admiral Loughlin exercised military and operational command over a major portion of the Submarine Force, U. S. Atlantic Fleet during a period of unprecedented growth. In particular, he supervised the post construction and post overhaul pre-deployment training, Demonstration and Shakedown Operations (ASO) and tactical load out periods for the Fleet Ballistic Missile Submarines in an exemplary manner. By virtue of dynamic leadership and outstanding professional knowledge, he ensured the successful operations of two SSBN replenishment sites and the effective functioning of off crew support operations at Charleston, South Carolina. Rear Admiral Loughlin further has proven to be a most articulate and impressive spokesman for the Navy. In carrying out all of the foregoing duties, as well as the additional NATO duty of Commander Submarine Force, Eastern Atlantic Area (Designate), (he) has demonstrated the finest degree of judgment and an inspiring devotion to duty which has been fully in keeping with the highest traditions of the United States Naval Service."

On October 4, 1966 he reported as Commandant of the Naval District, Washington, D. C., and served as such until relieved of active duty pending his retirement, effective August 1, 1968. "For exceptionally meritorious service from October 1966 to June 1968..." he was awarded a Gold Star in lieu of the Second Legion of Merit. The citation further states in part:

"...Rear Admiral Loughlin successfully directed and supervised the efforts of the large, diversified complex of naval activities that comprise his command, all of which are dedicated to the mission of Fleet support. Under his command, military-civilian relationships have been enhanced, leading to an increased awareness of the important role played by the Navy in the community. Rear Admiral Loughlin maintained close contact with civilian leaders in his area of coordination with a resultant increase in integrated off-base housing for military personnel. Further, he coordinated the Navy Youth Opportunity Program in the Washington, D. C. area and was instrumental in the development, coordination and implementation of the Navy Equal Employment Opportunity Program and the Civil Disturbance Plan for his area of command. He established policies which encourage, and has personally fostered, the closest cooperation among the Navy and the other services as well as with civilian groups..."

In addition to the Navy Cross with Gold Star, the Silver Star Medal, the Legion of Merit with Gold Star, the Bronze Star Medal with Combat "V," and the Presidential Unit Citation Ribbon, Rear Admiral Loughlin has the American Defense Service Medal, Fleet Clasp; American Campaign Medal; Asiatic-Pacific Campaign Medal; World War II Victory Medal; National Defense Service Medal with bronze star; Korean Service Medal; and the United Nations Service Medal.

His official home address is R. D. 1, Brockport, Pennsylvania. He is married to the former Marjorie Angela McGurn of Brockport, and has three daughters, Mrs. Edmee Kaye Ryan; Mrs. Lynn Elliott Higgins, and Mrs. Gay Kulpe. His brother, Lieutenant (jg) Joseph J. Loughlin, Jr., USN, Naval Academy Class of 1932, was killed on April 6, 1937, in a plane crash while attached to aircraft carrier LEXINGTON.

Navy Office of Information
Internal Relations Division (OI-430)
3 October 1968

DECLARATION OF TRUST

The undersigned does hereby appoint and designate as his (her) Trustee herein, the Secretary-Treasurer and Publisher of the United States Naval Institute to perform and discharge the following duties, powers, and privileges in connection with the possession and use of a certain taped interview between the undersigned and the Oral History Department of the United States Naval Institute.

1. Classification of Transcript.

   (X)a. If classified OPEN, the transcript(s) may be read or the recording(s) audited by the qualified personnel upon presentation of proper credentials, as determined by the Secretary-Treasurer of the U.S. Naval Institute.

   ( )b. If classified PERMISSION REQUIRED TO CITE OR QUOTE, the user will be required to obtain permission in writing from the interviewee prior to quoting or citing from either the transcript(s) or the recording(s).

   ( )c. If classified PERMISSION REQUIRED, permission must be obtained in writing from the interviewee before the transcribed interview(s) can be examined or the tape recording(s) audited.

   ( )d. If classified CLOSED, the transcribed interview(s) and the tape recording(s) will be sealed until a time specified by the interviewee. This may be until the death of the interviewee or for any specified number of years.

2. It is expressly understood that in giving this authorization, I am in no way precluded from placing such restrictions as I may desire upon use of the interview at any time during my lifetime, nor does this authorization in any way affect my rights to the copyright of my literary expressions that may be contained in the interview.

Witness my hand and seal this 29th day of JUNE 1982.

Interview No. 1 with Rear Admiral Charles Elliott Loughlin, U.S. Navy
(Retired)

Place: Annapolis, Maryland

Date: Tuesday, 19 August 1980

Subject: Biography

By: John T. Mason, Jr.

Q: I suppose I should start with those words, "At long last." Who was it said that? Edward the VIII, "At long last."

Adm. L.: My fault too.

Q: We're trying to sit down with a tape recorder and have an account of your interesting and very remarkable Naval career. Now this is a talking biography; would you begin in a proper way and tell me the place of your birth and something of your family background.

Adm. L.: I was born in Wilmington, North Carolina on the 19th of February 1910. My father was a North Carolinian. My mother was a transplated Pennsylvanian.

Q: Your father was military, wasn't he?

Adm. L.: My father during World War I at the age of thirty-eight with three children volunteered. In retrospect it was, perhaps, stupid, but in this day and age I think loyalty to one's country

Loughlin #1 -2-

is to be admired. Unfortunately he was killed by a German sniper two days before armistice in World War I, leaving my mother and three children. I was eight at the time, my brother was nine and my sister was five. She didn't learn about it until mid-December. This happened on the ninth of November so it was quite a terrible experience for her, I'm sure.

She never remarried although she had frequent opportunities and was a very attractive lady.

We remained in North Carolina until 1924. She had three sisters in Philadelphia. She came from a very large family. I think there were eleven children in the King family. Then we moved to Philadelphia. I went to school in Philadelphia after having gone through the freshman year in Hanover High School in Wilmington.

Q: Now, your father's death, did that make a hardship for the family?

Adm. L.: Yes it did. She only had, really, what the government gave her and an insurance policy. My brother worked and went to the Severn School in order to go to the Naval Academy. He preceded me by a year. I worked during the summers and went to three different high schools in the Philadelphia area before I came to the Naval Academy.

Q: Were you always prepping for the Naval Academy?

Adm. L.: No. This is, perhaps, an interesting point. After having finished Lansdowne High School in 1928 I went to Episcopal Academy which is really a fine prep school.

Loughlin #1 -3-

Q: Is that a military academy?

Adm. L.: No, it ranks with the Hill School in Lawrenceville and all of those schools. I went there with the intention of going to West Point. My father had been in the Army. He had gone to OCS and was a major when he was killed. I had an uncle who also went to OCS and got through the war and ended up as a career Army officer with thirty-five years service. My tendency was to the Military rather than the Naval.

But, my brother came home Christmas leave his Plebe year and said, "You're not going up to the Military Academy; you're going to the Naval Academy.

Q: He liked it so well.

Adm. L.: And, I think this is an interesting fact, at that time, my brother entered in 1928 and I entered in 1929, at that time there were few people in the service of World War I, that had been in World War I who had had sons who were old enough to qualify for entrance to either the Military Academy or the Naval Academy. As a matter of record and interest I had Ed Heise look this up for me. My brother was the third midshipman to enter the Naval Academy under the Sons of Deceased Veterans and I was the fourth. The other three are dead so I am the oldest living Naval Academy graduate who entered the Naval Academy under the Sons of Deceased Veterans.

Q: That is a landmark and something to observe.

Loughlin #1 -4-

Adm. L.: So, that's the reason I had my choice of whether I wanted to go to West Point or the Naval Academy. I could go to either one.

Q: Then you had no problem with an appointment.

Adm. L.: It was automatic. All I had to do was pass what they used to call the Substantiating Exam. If you passed that, you were automatically in. So, as I said, there was really no problem for me to go to either one or the other. My brother said, "I think you'll like the Naval Academy better." So, I came to the Naval Academy.

Q: Well, that's great. His enthusiasm carried over to you then I take it?

Adm. L.: Yes. He was my older brother. I was primarily intereste in the athletics, having achieved quite a bit of success in high schoool.

Q: What particular sports were you involved in in high school?

Adm. L.: The same as the Naval Academy; tennis and basketball. I was a state champion in tennis. I had a national ranking in tennis and made all city and all state, not all state, but all city in basketball. I primarily wanted to go some place where I could play tennis and basketball. At that time a career was the fartherest thing in my mind.

Loughlin #1 -5-

Q: Was your brother an athlete too?

Adm. L.: He was on the varsity wrestling team and won his letter three years in varsity wrestling. A very fine young man with an enviable reputation. He was killed in a peace time aircraft back in 1937.

Q: Your scholastic record must have been pretty good too.

Adm. L.: Yes sir. I stood very high in high school and, in fact, I stood number two at the Episcopal Academy, but I was not a four year person. I think I skipped graduation in order to come down and visit my brother in June week here at the Naval Academy. So, I didn't get the salutatorian. I would have had that if I had been a four year student.

Q: That's a very unusual combination to have- a high scholastic standing and be an outstanding athlete as well. Maybe you can equate that with your experience here at the foundation.

Adm. L.: I think it is in these days. I don't think it was in those days. I think most of us went to school to get an education. We had to study, at least our parents made us study. There were no drugs, there was no drinking, or little drinking and no smoking. I just think we lived in entirely different conditions.

Q: Your mother must have been very happy at the prospect of the two of you.

Adm. L.: Yes. She maintained her home in Lansdowne until I graduated. Then she kind of followed --my brother went to flight training and she went there. I went to the submarine force. I went out to Pearl and she came out there. Several years after my brother died, her heart was broken and she just, really, gave up the ghost and died in 1941. Really of a broken heart, I think, more than of anything else.

Q: You entered the Naval Academy in 1929 all prepared for a career in athletics.

Adm. L.: A career in athletics, but not a career in the Navy.

Q: Tell me about the impact that it made on you.

Adm. L.: I hesitate to say this, but I'm probably one of the few and maybe the only midshipman who ever graduated who was sorry to graduate. I liked the Naval Academy so much that I just wanted to stay here. That is an honest true statement. Of course, athletics played a great part in that.

Q: And your success in athletics.

Adm. L.: Yes. I seriously considered going in the Supply Corps in order to maintain my tennis career. That's stupid, but---

Q: Well, no, there certainly is a career in the Supply Corps.

Adm. L.: I know, but I knew I would have shore duty and could continue tennis.

Q: How did you take to the regimentation in those days?

Adm. L.: Just like ninty-nine and a half percent of the other Plebes, I thought Plebe summer was atrocious. I mean Plebe year.

Loughlin #1 -7-

I didn't like many of the things that were done, but as I tell all the young people we sponsor here, I've never really seen a Plebe yet that enjoyed Plebe year, and I've never seen anyone yet who graduated from the Naval Academy who didn't think Plebe year was necessary. It is just something you had to go through and just maintain your composure and get through it.

Q: It's a part of growing up I suppose?

Adm. L.: I think so.

Q: If one can assume that perspective.

Adm. L.: I think so. Growing up and you take all the diverse backgrounds of young men and, now women who come here and in a matter or five or six weeks get them into a coordinated unit. If you saw the Plebe parade on Sunday it is just amazing what the Naval Academy has done in five and a half weeks.

Q: Yes how quickly they---

Adm. L.: Absolutely amazing. Fantastic is a better word for it.

Q: Tell me about some of the outstanding experiences in classes during your four years.

Adm. L.: In classes?

Q: Yes, other than athletics.

Adm. L.: Well, second class summer, which would be the summer of 1934 we were told, fortunately, that there was a law on the books that only the top half of the class would be commissioned. You see this was in the midst of the depression.

Loughlin #1 -8-

Q: Yes.

Adm. L.: And I stood very poorly in my Plebe and Youngster year. I wasn't in danger of failing but I didn't stand in the upper part of the class. So, not having any money and knowing that my mother was dependent on my brother and myself when we graduated I really hit the books and made a dramatic increase in my standing during my junior and senior year.

Q: It's obvious from the record.

Adm. L.: From four hundred and something to a hundred and forty in the last two years. I stood number two, I think, in English and pretty high in navigation and pretty high up in ordnance, but not very well in "juice" and math. In other words, I studied for the subjects I liked and tended to just get by in the subjects I didn't. And sure enough when we graudated only the top half of the class was commissioned.

Q: What impact did that bit of news in 1931 have on the class as a whole?

Adm. L.: I don't know. I can only speak for myself. I really started to study and really hit the books. What other people did, I don't know. I can't answer that honestly.

Q: Tell me about the summer cruises.

Adm. L.: Well, again during the depression days we only had, well we still had only two, as they do now. Both were in the battleships the BB WYOMING and the BB ARKANSAS, I guess. I wasn't too impress with the cruises. I don't think they utilized--you really didn't have anything to do. Maybe that was my fault. I remember the first cruise as a Youngster Ernie Lee Jahncke whose father was a former Assistant Secretary of the Navy and Draper Kauffman and I were compartment cleaners. We spent three quarters of our cruise, we took great pride in cleaning compartments, so they kept putting us on compartments. My Youngster cruise other than going to Kiel, Germany and Edinburgh and Cherbourg, where I played tennis in all three places, my Youngster cruise is really reminiscence being a swabbie.

Q: Your status improved with the next cruise didn't it?

Adm. L.: It did. The cruise was divided into two parts. I think we had the second part on one ship, the BB WYOMING, I guess. We went to the Azores and we went up to Halifax. They were the only two ports. Than we ran into a terrible hurricane coming from Halifax back to Annapolis. I thought the ship was going to capsize and Captain Dutton was the Skipper and I think he thought it would too. They had taken out the turrets aft and we just had a barbette there. The ship was really not stable. We rolled more than any battleship has ever rolled in history in that hurricane. I think everybody including the Skipper was glad to get back in Norfolk.

The memories of the cruise, I just don't think the midshipmen were utilized as they are now. I din't think we learned too much. Perhaps it was my fault.

Loughlin #1 -10-

Q: Then as you reflect on your cruises in battleships and compare them with what the midshipmen do today you would come down in favor of the present policy?

Adm. L.: Oh, absolutely, absolutely. Throughout our whole class, we had about six hundred in our class. I guess six fifty to start with. Maybe on the Youngster cruise five hundred and some and in the First Class you would probably have five hundred and some. When you put that number of people plus the Second Class as a Youngster plus the First Class you would probably have around a thousand people or eight hundred people on the darned ship. There just wasn't enough to do on the ship. Now they're scattered as you well know, throughout the whole world on submarines, destro carriers, LSD's, everything. I think this system is infinitely better than the old system.

Q: There are some men who talk about the value of the whole group going together, being together, having the same experiences.

Adm. L.: You're together here for four years except for the cruis I don't subscribe to that theory personally.

Q: Now, tell me about the athletic career in the Naval Academy.

Adm. L.: I guess this is going to sound like bragging, but the record is there so you can check it. I only lost three dual tenni matches in four years here which I think, except for Joe Hunt who was a National Champion before he came here, is unexcelled by anyone here at the Naval Academy. I received a national inter-scholastic inter-collegiate ranking my last two years.

In basketball I played regular every game my three seasons here. You know we didn't play Freshman then. I set scoring records which stood up until, one was broken in 1948 or 1949 and the other was broken in 1951 or 1952. Now, we played basketball with the center jump, so when they did away with the center jump the playing time, roughly, increased fifteen to twenty to twenty-five percent. I made second team All American my Second Class year and first team my First Class year.

Q: A remarkable record.

Adm. L.: I also won the Thompson trophy upon graduation. As you know, one of the two athletic trophies awarded each year.

Q: Yes. Well, in that day, I suppose, the temptation wasn't as great to think in terms of a professional career?

Adm. B.: There wasn't any professional basketball in those days and no professional tennis. I was good, but I wasn't that good. I would have never gotten a first team ranking in the country.

Q: Who was the ranking man then, Tilden?

Adm. L.: Tilden was when I was a midshipman. I remember seeing the Davis Cup matches about four or five years in Germantown Cricket Club because my home was then in Germantown. As a matter of fact, I was an usher for three years as a midshipman. I actually saw France beat the United States in a Davis Cup match. I remember seeing La Coste, Borotra Cochet beat Billy Johnson, from California, Norris Williams and Tilden in a three, two match.

But amateur was the thing. There was no such thing as pro-tennis. There was no such thing as pro-basketball.

Q: You almost had to be of gentlemen standing, I mean financial backing to really have a career then.

Adm. L.: Yes. As a midshipman I played in various state tournaments during leave. I would usually stay with private families who extended their hospitality. You had to have money to play the circuit. And, very few poor people did play the circuit. I don't think Bill Tilden had any financial worries. Vinnie Richards didn't and neither did Norris Williams.

Q: The women were coming along in those days. Helen Wills--

Adm. L.: Helen Wills was there. As a matter of fact, I saw Helen Wills play Wilmer Allison an exhibition match the year after we lost the Davis Cup when we had a Britsh and American team match. Allison gave her one game. He beat her six-love and six-one.

Q: You can remember Suzanne Lenglen?

Adm. L.: That was a little bit before. She was playing in 1928 or 1929, I think, Helen Wills and Helen Jacobs were the two top gals when I was a midshipman. Suzanne, I think, was a couple years before that. I saw her play, so it had to be a couple of years before that.

Q: Your success in athletics must have given you some luster in the eyes of your classmates?

Adm. L.: Well, it's, again, hard to say. I don't think it aroused any envy. I mean, the record was there and I don't know that anybody really objected to my getting the Thompson Trophy.

Q: I wouldn't think so.

Adm. L.: There were other very worthy midshipmen, Ray Thompson was on the Olympic swimming team, you know. He swam in the 1932 Olympics. He got to the finals in the one hundred meter, one hundred yard dash and at the end of fifty yards he was ahead of the field. He faded and finished sixth out of six, but he was among the top six in the world of swimming. Bill Kane won the sword. He was the only one to letter in three sports. Bill was never a particularly outstanding athlete in any of his three sports. He was good. So, I would say that Ray would have been the only other--well Tom Connolly was an Olympic rope climber.

Q: He's another I should add to the list.

Adm. L.: He's in Washington.

Q: Please say something about the kind of hazing that took place at the Academy in those days.

Adm. L.: For historical purposes, my basketball career was damned near ruined because of, and his name I won't mention, in those days, and they still may do it, but I doubt it now when you get up into the seventies and eighties, I was always relatively slight physique. I mean I weighed a hundred and forty-five or a hundred and fifty and wasn't well developed. It was a first classman who made me do push ups until I could do thirty-three. I'd go out to basketball practice and I would actually be dead. I couldn't even shoot the damned ball.

Q: Your muscles were so strained.

Adm. L.: Yes sir, it was horrible. Everyday before practice I would have to go to this first classman's room and do these push ups. Finally I was able to do thirty-three of them. But, for the life of me, I don't really see the benefit of it yet.

However I was able to complete the 33 pushups before the end of plebe basketball season and in our final game against a good high school, I scored 39 points, a total unheard of in those days, a school record for years and a sports item noted throughout the country.

Q: What was his rationale?

Adm. L.: It was just part of the hazing process. There was quite a bit of broom beating in those days. That was the only physical hazing. There was hazing at the table which was quite distasteful. One First Classman had the nickname "Foo". A First Classman at my table would make me go over and address him as Foo. Then he would pour a whole tureen of hot coffee or chocolate down your sleeve and ruin a damn uniform, ruin your shirt and you would have to go and change clothes. Things like that, I just---

Q: Just stupid things?

Adm. L.: I don't think they accomplished anything. They didn't accomplish any sense of discipline. All it did was arouse anger and resentment.

Q: Did you also go through the routine of memorizing all sorts of silly things?

Loughlin #1 -15-

Adm. L.: Oh, yes.

Q: As Bill Mack calls them, "Silly things."

Adm. L.: Well, one good thing, a fellow by the name of Todd, Butch Todd--I had to come out with a nautical expression every meal. That's fine.

Q: That's something you would use?

Adm. L.: Sure, it made you do some research. That I had no objection to what so ever. But, some of the other things, I think, were pretty ludicrous. Matter of fact, I don't think the class of 1930, I hope no one from the class of 1930 ever listens to this, but I don't think the class of 1930 was one of the better classes. We loved 1931. We were the second class to go through Second Class Summer, as Plebes. 1931 was our Second Class when we were Plebes. We always, for some reason or other, we, when we were Plebes we always maintained good relations with the class of 1931. But, 1930, I didn't have too much respect for.

Q: Were you tempted with aviation. Your brother being an aviator.

Adm. L.: Artie Doyle who became Vice Admiral, and I'm sure you remember Artie?

Q: I've been talking to Artie.

Adm. L.: Artie was flying these big flying boats down here and during our Second Class summer, you remember, not the Yellow Perils, but the big flying boats. Artie was a tennis player and I used to work out with him. He just tried his best to get me into aviation.

I said, "Lieutenant Doyle, I just don't want to fly. I'm not afraid." I said, "I just don't want to fly. I have no desire to fly."

Q: He was a pretty persuasive guy.

Adm. L.: Yes, he was. But, I ended up, I could have gone, I was still qualified for aviation. When I graduated I didn't know what I wanted to do. I was ordered to the BB NEW MEXICO. I started to grow up, I think, after I got aboard ship. I'll come to that later. The influence of Mr. Rickover as I called him.

Q: Did you have any experience with Tommy Hart who was--?

Adm. L.: He was superintendent here. He relieved Admiral Robison. He was a very straight laced person. He wore a high collar. Very impersonal. I had no personal contact with him. I think he was respected. I don't know whether he was admired or not, but he certainly was respected.

Captain Snyder was the Commandant. I think he was well liked because, Jane, his daughter was such a beautiful young girl. Poco Smith was the Exec. I have very, very sad memories of him because of what he did to me as a First Classman. Are you interested in that?

Q: Yes. Yes.

Adm. L.: I went to a football game First Class year after my brother graduated. He was in Annapolis. He and my mother and sister had come to the Penn game up in Franklin Field, I sat, as I was supposed to sit during the first half and during the half time intermission I went around and joined my mother and sister and brother and before the second half kickoff returned to my seat.

On Monday I got back and found that I was on report for sitting with friends during the second half of the football game and chewing chewing gum. Well, I couldn't combat the chewing gum because I was. And, Poco Smith, himself, had put me on report. So, I submitted a statement which was not very diplomatic, but, I said-

Q: Well couched in English.

Adm. L.: Well, in fact, I just said, "Commander Smith, you're not telling the truth." In effect I said that. I said I was chewing chewing gum and I left my seat at the end of the first half and I sat with my mother and my sister and brother and before the second half kickoff I returned to my seat and sat in the midshipmen's section the entire second half.

Well, the class A was dropped and I got fifteen or thirty demerits for chewing chewing-gum at a football game in the first half. That's one of my memories.

Q: It rankles?

Adm. L.: It rankles.

Q: Did you have any other demerits?

Adm. L.: This sounds like sour grapes, but I had a run-in with my company officer who is dead now, Lieutenant Swanston. He was called Square Shooting Bill because of he knifed everybody in the back. The run in cost me quite a bit of class standing and perhaps some---, perhaps most of it was my fault. For example, the Second Class summer my roommate was a football player and he had early leave. I was an avid ping pong player, so rooming by myself I moved a table in from one room to another in order to play ping pong at authorized hours. Well, when I came back to the room one afternoon the mate of the deck said Lieutenant Swanston said to get rid of that second table. Well, this was my fault. I was just stupid. Instead of just getting rid of it and then going down, he wasn't even my company officer, I went right down to my company officer and requested permission to have the second table in my room. Swanston threatened to give me a general court-martial. If I had gotten rid of the darned thing first, but this was my fault see. But, that started off a very, very bad relationship between Mr. Swanston and me. As a Second Classman my brother happened to be my platoon commander and the company officer was from Philadelphia, Bud Leeds. He was a very close personal friend of mine. I made a vow to myself that I would be the most regulation Second Classman in the Brigade or at that time the Regiment because of my brother and Bud Leeds. And, the first--you remember the old grease mark, the first grease mark--I stood either one or two in the entire Fourth Battalion, that included the Seventh and Eighth Company by the stripers grade. Swanston dropped me to anchor man in the battalion, anchor man in the battalion. The grease mark in your Second and First Class year counted more than your whole Plebe year.

Q: That was just being vindictive?

Loughlin #1 -19-

Adm. L.: Yes, it was. And, I never forgave him. I certainly admit my culpability in not being smart enough to get rid of the damned table before I requested permission from my company officer to have it in my room. But, he was a very vindictive person.

Q: What was your relationship with the town?

Adm. L.: Very little. Very little. I don't remember ever having any relationship with any civilian during the time I was here. Of course, in those days you didn't get out. The Plebes didn't get out at all, so that's where you would make your initial contact. The only ones that I knew knew me. Even today, Jack, I walk down the street and, this has happened for years, someone says, "Hey, aren't you Elliot? I used to watch you play basketball." During depression days this was the only entertainment. The only free entertainment for the PG school. They just came in droves to the basketball games and tennis games because they were busy studying up there and that's all the recreation they had the same as the townspeople. Pip Moyer, he was just a young guy I guess at the time, but he used to come to the basketball games. I can't answer why we didn't. There was no effort made to my knowledge to have community relationships between the Academy and the townspeople. I don't think there was any effort made whatsoever.

Q: Very often the enticement of some attractive gal that a midshipman knew in town?

Adm. L.: Kitty Hopkins lived right here. Of course, Tommy, was out of 1932, so I really didn't consider that a civilian family. Professor Crosley, Henrietta they still lived down on Prince George Street. We had some contact, but it was because of people at the Naval Academy that we knew rather than a civilian contact per se.

Q: Did you participate in all the hops and the social life of the Academy?

Adm. L.: Yes, yes. Carvel Hall used to be the focal point on Sunday afternoon.

Q: I guess it was.

Adm. L.: I used to thoroughly enjoy that. I dragged a girl for the first three years. A very pleasant relationship. Yes we went to all--don't forget, well with such a pay scale in those days, two dollars as a Plebe, four as a Youngster, seven as a Second Classman, and ten as a First Classman, as I recall. I had no spending money. My mother couldn't afford to send me anything. So, whatever you did you did without the benefit of money. That's the reason, I think, that Carvel Hall was so popular and the hops were so popular.

Q: What did you do when you went on the summer cruises? Especially on the one when you went abroad. You had no supplementary income.

Adm. L.: Tennis was the open door thing.

Loughlin #1 -21-

Q: To be entertained?

Adm. L.: Yes, I mean, Edinburgh all these knights and nobles, not nobles, but wealthy people would find out who the tennis players were and invite you out to spend the weekend there. All you had to do was bus there or even they would pick us up. The same way in France. We went to Cherbourg and, of course, everybody went to Paris. I think the three days I was in Paris I played tennis morning and afternoon the three days. They gave you an open door. I couldn't afford to go down to London from Edinburgh. Most of the midshipmen did go down. I stayed there and played tennis.

Q: Talking about demerits and that sort of thing you, just off tape, you told me that one source, I suppose, of potential demerits which you --

Adm. L.: Well, in those days, Jack, the Thompson Stadium stands abutted Prince George Street which at that time was the town.

Q: I remember.

Adm. L.: And if you could avoid the Jimmy Legs* and avoid having your bunk inspected at night, why, it was very easy to get onto the football field particularly from the Fourth Batt which is where the dental and dispensary and sick bay is now. That was the old Fourth Batt. You could go across the stadium and get up in the stands, and climb the stands and then drop down on Prince George Street. It was simple. Nothing to it.

*"Jimmy Legs" is a nickname applied to the Naval Academy campus policemen.

Q: How about getting back?

Adm. L.: Same way. It was a Ship offense, but I didn't see anything morally wrong with it.

Q: It was an achievement.

Adm. L.: I never got caught.

Q: What did you do with your leave once you got it?

Adm. L.: Well, oh, for instance, the William and Mary tennis team would come down and their number one player was an old friend of mine. We played in tournaments all the time. He also had money and a car. So, he'd take me out to Washington. We'd get back at two, or three, or four, or five in the morning. But, it was just a lark. Nothing malicious about it.

Q: Now, we come to graduation and the President was the speaker at your graduation.

Adm. L.: He was inaugurated on, what, the fourth of March. Can I go back to athletics for a minute?

Q: Surely, surely.

Adm. L.: As you know, there was a hiatus between Army and Navy then because of the eligibility rule. Army insisted on the four years. No matter how many years you'd had at college you could still play three years at West Point. So, as a result, I think we played two charity football games during my four years there.

The only regular scheduled competition between Army and Navy my entire four years was the Army and Navy basketball game the day that Roosevelt was inaugurated. Either March the third or the fourth.

Q: March the fourth.

Adm. L.: 1933 and again it sounds like bragging, but we beat Army 52 to 24 and I scored 25 points which is one more than the entire Army team scored. Anyway, I remember that because it was the day President Roosevelt was inaugurated.

The day of graduation he was here with Claude Swanson, then Secretary of the Navy. But, the thing I remember most of the entire graduation ceremony, which was held in Dahlgren Hall, was when Mrs. Roosevelt, Eleanor Roosevelt, walked into that hall. She was a very tall and a very impressive figure though not particularly handsome. She got a standing ovation. Everybody in that hall stood up when Eleanor Roosevelt walked in there. That really is my most memorable recall of the entire graduation.

Q: She had already made quite an impact on the nation before he became President?

Adm. L.: But, it was a thrill to shake his hand, he shook everybody's hand. Four hundred and sixty some odd graduates. He shook everybody's hand.

Q: Standing?

Adm. L.: Standing.

Loughlin #1 -24-

Q: Well, with graduation you said you really didn't know what you wanted to do in the Navy, but you did want to stay in the Navy. You had determined that.

Adm. L.: Yes, sir. I don't know what the regulations were in those days. I don't think there was any obligation. There couldn't have been if they made half the class get out. I doubt if there was any obligation of service. I had been ordered to either the BB IDAHO or the BB MISSISSIPPI who were being renovated down in, modernized is a better word, down in Norfolk. The intercollegiates were being played, as always at the Merion Cricket Club. The BB NEW MEXICO was being modernized at Philadelphia. Thomas S. King, commander in those days, had been on duty here at the Naval Academy. I got in touch with him and he was instrumental in getting my orders changed from one of those two ships, which ever it was to the BB NEW MEXICO so I could play in the intercollegiate tournament after I had graduated.

Q: A very sensible arrangement.

Adm. L.: That's what I thought.

Q: Apparently he did too.

Adm. L.: Shall we go on to the BB NEW MEXICO?

Q: Yes.

Adm. L.: I was there four years. I was there four and a half years actually. One of the big influences on my life was, I call him Mr. Rickover because at that time he was a Lieutenant and was called Mr. Rickover. He was the Assistant Chief Engineer and

I worked for him for two and a half years. We, meaning the Engineering Department, and we put three white "E's" on the ship. There are many feelings about Admiral Rickover. My feeling is that he is not a genius. He's intelligent, but he's not a genius. In my opinion he is the hardest working Naval Officer I have ever worked for in my life or I've ever known. Contrary to popular belief, if you work for him and he likes you, he is one of the most loyal Naval officers I've ever worked for. I could do no wrong with Admiral Rickover. At that time Lieutenant Rickover. Even though he was only the Assistant Chief Engineer the Chief Engineer was smart enough to let him run the whole darn show.

Q: He obviously has the ability to focus on what he is doing.

Adm. L.: That's right. He didn't like Warrant Officers and he still doesn't. He told me once, "I'd rather have four hard working Ensigns as my division officer than the best Lieutenants in the Navy." I hope you don't think this is bragging again, but at one time on the BB NEW MEXICO, the four division officers at that one time all made flag rank. Ed Batcheller, Charlie Curtze, Bill Brockett and myself. Brockett and Curtze ended up as the head of BUSHIPS and Deputy BUSHIPS. Batcheller had many major commands and I had quite a few. At one time those four were his division officers, all as Ensigns or had just made JG. I give him most of the credit for my maturing and growing up. I think I was doing it gradually anyway the year and a half before he came there or a year anyway. He made a tremendous difference. My attitude toward him---

Loughlin #1 -26-

Q: That's very interesting, can you say more about him because it would be useful for some future historian.

Adm. L.: Well, for instance, we couldn't get married for two years. We were the first class again affected by this rule. We couldn't get married for two years. So, one Sunday, and they had a regulation that you shouldn't play on athletic teams, on ships' teams. So, there was nothing to do except work. I didn't have any money. So, one Sunday I was in the Log Room looking up some material and an officer comes in and introduces himself as Lieutenant Rickover. He was relieving Allen Hobbs as Assistant Chief Engineer. So, he was going through some work. I had the A Division at the time. He was going through some work on his desk and he said, "What do you know about the gasoline system here?"

I said, "Well, it's in my division and I know that it starts in the peak tank forward and it runs through the ship. I traced it out once but not as thorough as I should have."

He said, "Well, that's not good enough. Let's take a look at it."

So, for two hours on that Sunday afternoon we traced that damned gasoline system out right from the stem to stern. I found out right there that if you have a job and if you are responsible for it then you'd better know where every darned thing there is to know. That was the very first time I ever saw him was that Sunday afternoon. He and I got into dungarees and for two hours we traced that system.

Q: He gave you at that point the secret of his success.

Adm. L.: I think he did. He was very unpopular on the ship because he wanted to be the most efficient engineering outfit in the fleet. Two or three typical examples, perhaps not typical, but two or three examples of how he worked.

I got married in 1935. Incidentally, Bill Dawson who lives out here in town and Bill Brockett who I mentioned before were my bridesmaid and best man. We went to Mexico to get married because we couldn't afford the three day wait in California.

Q: Is this a romance that was developing during---

Adm. L.: No, I had known this girl in high school. Rickover still had his transportation check from crossing the country, so he must have reported to the ship in the spring of 1935. He said, "Do you need any money?"

I said, "No, I've got ninety dollars in the bank."

He said, "Here is my transportation money." He said, "I really don't need it, you take it."

I said, "No. I don't know when I can repay it and I don't need it anyway."

"No." he said, "you go ahead and take it anyway."

I said, "Thank you Sir, but no."

Well, we went to Mexico and got married. Bill Dawson loaned me his car. I didn't even drive in those days so my new wife drove back to Long Beach. I had three days leave and the ship was leaving San Diego where it was at the time. It was to come back to Long Beach.

I got undressed that night and taking off my coat in the side pocket was Rickover's check, endorsed which I didn't cash, incidentally.

But, that's one side of his character which no one has any idea of. But, some of the unique things he did was during that three day period Dusty Dornin, whom I'm sure you've heard of, Dusty was my JO, and the damned evaps flooded. So, I came back to the ship, I was called back, as a matter of fact, and Rickover wanted to know how it happened.

I said, "Mr. Rickover, I wasn't even here on board."

He kind of laughed. They never did find out how it happened. The next day I went to town, Long Beach, and got time clocks for every engineering space on the ship. Not only my A division, but every engineering-space.

Q: This was your own initiative?

Adm. L.: No, no, no, he told me to do it. They were installed and I was given the responsibility of checking the inspection schedule to which people had to punch the clock. In other words, people had to punch the clock as when they inspected all dead engineering spaces every single night of the world. We never had another flooding of the evaps or any other accident there. There the record was, the inspection was made on such and such time during the midwatch, eight to twelve, or four to eight watch.

Q: That bears out his attitude toward nuclear submarines so there won't be any accidents?

Adm. L.: That's right. Showers, he plugged about three quarters of the holes in the shower heads to keep from wasting water. In port he could close off half of the radiators in the ward room to keep from wasting the auxiliary steam.

We went out to Pearl on a fleet cruise, a fleet maneuver and we tied up to one of the moles there where they all were in Pearl Harbor. During the midwatch Rickover and I and a few enlisted men rigged some hoses to the water supply at Ford Island and filled up all of our tanks with fresh water so we wouldn't have to use the evaps. He got the commanding officer to sign an order directing the officer of the deck, mind you, to get permission from the Engineering Officer of the watch in port to light off another generator whenever we were having battle station drills. He cut down so many things. Most ships had all four generators on for battle stations. We did it with one. They couldn't even hoist a boat up during gunnery drills in port. They couldn't even use a crane unless they got the Engineering Officer's permission. They didn't get it very often because it meant lighting off those generators. You were right on the upper edge of the curve with one generator. Everybody else was firing four for four. But, I mean this is just typical of his approach to all engineering problems.

Q: Does that carry through to his later career, the caring for expenditures and waste?

Adm. L.: I think so. When I got the submarine flotilla down in Charleston in 1964 and specifically called him up and I walked into his office in the old Navy complex on Constitution Avenue and he had the most ramshackle desk and carpet you've ever seen. Well it really was a matter of show in my opinion. I mean it wasn't fit for a dog and that's where he held court. But, in this particular case it was for effect I think.

Q: What about his personal life? I mean is he also as meticulous and sparing as--

Adm. L.: Well, it's hard to say. I was one of his few close friends. One of his few friends, not close. We were up at Bremerton and he and his wife, who died two or three years ago, they owned an apartment in the same complex there. He didn't entertain. But from a personal point of view, both professional and outside the ship he just, he couldn't have been nicer to me. But, there was no social life at all. I don't think he ever entertained anyone ever. You know his wife was even more brilliant than he was. She was a talented novelist and lecturer. A real brain.

When I was relieved as Commander Submarine Flotilla Six, Admiral Lowrance, Rebel Lowrance was COMSUBLANT and with his permission I got an FBM, Fleet Ballistic Submarine in Charleston. They had the change of command ceremony on there which was the first time it had ever happened. I wrote Admiral Rickover a note and invited him to come down to the change of command since it was going to be on an FBM submarine and because of our prior relationship. He picked up the phone. He said, "Elliott," he didn't even thank me. He said, "You know I don't have time to do anything foolish like that. How can I take time to come down to see a stupid change of command?"

I said, "Well, Admiral I just wanted you to know that you

were welcome."

Then he said, "Well, thank you very much."

Then you know, or perhaps you don't know, but in those days and probably right now he always sent his testimony before the Joint Committee on Atomic Power and---

Q: Yes, the House and Senate.

Adm. L.: To show the FBM and nuclear power skeptics. Of course, I had all the FBM's and quite a few SSN's down in Charleston, so somebody would always bring them down to read. It wasn't sent to me. So, he said, "Did you read my latest testimony?"

I said, "Yes Sir, I did."

He said, "What did you think of it?"

I said, "Well, you were thorough and direct as always, but you made one mistake."

You won't believe this, but this is a true story.

"What do you mean I made a mistake!"

I said, "Admiral Rickover, you continually stress the Naval Academy curriculum and its deficiencies. You're always harping on the Naval Academy curriculum. I have never seen any testimony from you in which you'll admit that over seventy-five percent of the career Naval officers come from the Naval Academy, not from OCS, not from ROTC, but from the Naval Academy." Dead silence.

His remark was, "Elliott, Jesus Christ made a mistake, can't I make one?"

I raise my right hand, this is the honest truth.

Loughlin #1 -32-

Q: Tell me more about the tour of duty on the BB NEW MEXICO.

Adm. L.: Well, we had a very fine Executive Officer. I went through four Skippers. There were four different commanding officers when I was there and I just missed Admiral Randall Jacobs who was in BUPERS. I was detached the day he was boarded aboard. But, we had a very fine Executive Officer who was interested in junior officers and insisted we rotate in jobs. I had to request a change once. For instance, I started off in the five inch AA gun division and I went to communications, and I went to engineering, and I went back to the five inch fifty-one caliber.

Q: That was the usual thing for an Ensign?

Adm. L.: It was except that, I think Commander Greig was even more interested in having somebody get a well rounded education.*
So, the two five inch batteries was a junior division officer and I had the division for two and a half years. I think that four and a half years really benefited me as far as being a career Navy officer is concerned. I got everything, communications, gunnery, and engineering. I was a plankowner on the ship when I was detached. I was riding the bus back to the ship one day and Tommy Peters, a classmate of mine, had been ordered to submarine school.

He said, "Why don't you put in for submarine school?"

I said, "I don't know anything about submarines, Tommy."

He said, "Well, I don't either. But six months ashore and you'll probably get your choice of where you want to go for duty after that."

*Commander Stuart O. Greig, USN

Loughlin #1 -33-

So, even though the deadline had passed I submitted my request to the commanding officer. He sent a dispatch in and they accepted me to sub school.

Q: And that was your first thought of going into submarines?

Adm. L.: Tommy just happened to mention it to me. I had never thought about it.

Q: Had you ever discussed your future career with Rickover?

Adm. L.: No. No, he had been detached by that time. I outranked him on time on this ship, so I just figured I'd just keep going. Probably go to destroyers and then to cruisers. The ironic part of this is I was down in Panama in 1942 to 1944, 1942 and 1943, and, I think the S-26, Captain Peters was the Skipper, was rammed by a YP patrol craft. And Peters, not Peters but Earle Hawk was Skipper. Bob Ward who died just in the last couple of months, and a quartermaster on the bridge, they got out. The ship sank immediately. Those three were the only survivors. Tommy was the Exec and he was caught down below in several hundred feet of water and probably lived for two or three days and they had no way of salvage. The nearest one was Key West and they could never get it there because it was on the other side of Panama. But, Tommy was the guy who talked me into going to the submarine force. I'm sorry he was lost.

Q: Well, it's very fortunate to have some able officers as inspiration. Who else?

Adm. L.: Well, Captain "Savvy" Soule, I'm sure that name rings a bell, "Savvy" was one of my commanding officers. He's one of the fairest but toughest officers you'll ever run into. His fitness reports, about 3.4, was as high as you could get.

There was lieutenant on there named Rat Conlon who was passed over for Lieutenant. He came up to remonstrate with the Skipper. Everyone thought the world of Lieutenant Conlon. Captain Sole said, "I thought I gave you the highest fitness report I've ever given a Lieutenant in the Navy." Three four. But, that was his standard and that's how he worked.

Frank Jack Fletcher was one of my Skippers. He was my Skipper when my brother was killed. He couldn't have been more solicitous and nicer to me when this happened. He was a fine officer. I understand some remarks have been made about his conduct in the Battle of Coral Sea. But, I'm not that much of a student of history, but I thought he was a very, very fine Naval officer.

Q: The BB NEW MEXICO was largely in the Pacific was she?

Adm. L.: Yes. We shook down in the Caribbean in the spring of 1934.

Q: Is this a fleet exercise?

Adm. L.: No, it was just a shake down cruise.

Q: Oh, I see.

Adm. L.: And the fleet came from the West Coast in the spring of 1934. Then we had a big fleet parade off New York about the first of June. We stayed on the East Coast, visited Newport and places like that. Then back to Norfolk in December and then we went back to the West Coast, I guess, in January 1935.

Q: What are your memories of that fleet review for the President and the reasons for it?

Adm. L.: The biggest memory I have is, I don't know where I was in the fleet review itself, I can't recall and therefore it didn't make much of an impression on me, but the most vivid memory I have were the flying moors the battleships had in the Hudson River. What were there, twelve or fourteen battleships there in a column. Each one made a flying mooring. That wasn't too bad. I had midwatch the first night and when that six knot current swung you, your ship just moved sideways. I knew that we were going to drag anchor and go ahsore and we would all pile up in the Hudson River there. I'll tell you it is a heck of a thrill to see that ship swing to a flying mooring in a four, five, or six knot current. But, I don't remember much about the fleet review. I think the President was on the INDIANAPOLIS which was the ship my brother was on at that time.

Q: I'm quite sure it was, yes. It was in a sense a message to the rest of the world, wasn't it? I mean, that we had quite a fleet?

Adm. L.: Well, being young and not very smart in those days I couldn't make that comment. I wouldn't know that. Certainly we were still in the midst of the depression. Even though he gave everybody a fifteen percent pay cut, he made us take it I mean, he certainly--

Loughlin #1 -36-

Q: I think circumstances forced that?

Adm. L.: He certainly was a friend of the Navy. There is no quest about that. We were just caught in the bind like everybody else.

Q: In retrospect it looked like Roosevelt, one of his efforts to build up the Navy and the importance of the Navy in the eyes of the people---

Adm. L.: I think so.

Q: Were there any interesting fleet exercises you engaged in while on the BB NEW MEXICO?

Adm. L.: There were two in particular which bring back rather strong memories. I think Jack Fletcher was the Skipper on one of them. We were up in the Aleutians and a williwaw came up. We got out of it all right. We held --

Q: It was your first introduction to that?

Adm. L.: It was the first time I had ever been in the Aleutians and the first time I had ever seen a williwaw. I was on deck when I saw this thing approach in the flat calm sea there. All of a sudden you could just see these waves building and come right toward you. It must have gone from zero to sixty-five or seventy knots in nothing flat.

A destroyer went aground there. It was still aground when we left. I had the midwatch, about the third night out headed toward Pearl and this destroyer rejoined the formation. We exchang calls and I knocked on Captain Fletcher's door and said that umpty-ump had exchanged signals and had joined the formation. I turned in at four or five am and at eight o'clock in the morning or at seven thirty I got a call, "The Captain wants to see you on the bridge right away! Immediately!"

So, without shaving or anything I threw my clothes on and went up. He asked, "Why wasn't I informed that umpty-ump had rejoined the formation?"

I said, "Captain, I knocked on your sea cabin and so informed you at two forty-five."

He gave me a very piercing look and said, "Loughlin, you don't know how glad I am that I remember that."

The only other incident, which is rather ludicrous on the face of it, we were on a fleet exercise. I never had been across the equator and this, I know exactly because my daughter was born on Memorial Day 1936, so this was early May of 1936. The BB MISSISSIPPI and the BB NEW MEXICO had identical turbine trouble. As a matter of fact, I had the watch and Rickover had called for me to come up to his cabin. He said to turn it over to a guy by the name of Clark. I was up in his cabin when this happened. What happened was one of the turbine throttles had a long, as you open or close it, had a long bar. I guess you would call it a bar it ran on and the vibration had knocked off the bar and it stripped the turbine and the BB MISSISSIPPI had the identical casualty within a half an hour. We were only a few miles from the equator. So, we turned around and went back home, all the way to Long Beach. And, Rickover had the ship's Boatswain and they lifted that turbine, which I don't think had ever been done before out of a Navy yard to inspect it. We didn't know what the damage was or what had caused it. Then we had to go up to Bremerton to get the thing fixed. That was a real feat of seamanship to lift the turbine.

Q: Was it determined what caused it?

Adm. L.: It was obvious as soon as they looked at it what had stripped it. And, the BB MISSISSIPPI had done the same thing. But, they found out after they got to the yard.

Adm. L.: What about athletics in the fleet in those days?

Adm. L.: Very, very strong for enlisted men. Do you remember the TENNESSEE? Admiral Harry Hill I think was Exec on the TENNESSEE and they had a basketball team that was undefeated for some four or five years. The basketball competition was really terrific. I happen to remember this very vividly as we were up in Bremerton, probably at the same time that this casualty took place to the turbine. A bunch of officers on the BB NEW MEXICO, Mush Dornin, who was Dusty's brother, Dusty, and I and some other people challenged the TENNESSEE to a basketball game. Here this was a team that had been undefeated for five years in the fleet.

Q: They were a little complacent, maybe, at that point?

Adm. L.: I guess they were because the game, we were one point behind and I happened to get the ball and got off a shot just as the buzzer rang and it went in and we beat them by one point. The TENNESSEE never got over it, a bunch of pickup officers beating this bunch of pros. They were good. They really had a good team.

But, there was good competition in football. There was good competition in basketball. Primarily those two.

Q: Wrestling too?

Adm. L.: I don't remember too much about wrestling. It could have been, Jack, I just don't remember.

George Rasmusson used to be the care taker over at the Trona field in San Pedro. So, all the football games were played there and then the basketball coaches, also from San Pedro. So that really was the only two sports that I remember about.

Q: What about your tennis, were you able--

Adm. L.: I frankly gave it up.

Q: You couldn't do anything with that. Was golf a possibility in the fleet?

Adm. L.: Not to my knowledge. I never played golf. I don't remember. Selby Santmyers, who was a classmate of mine, was a very active golfer as a midshipman. I'm sure he must have played. I don't remember much enthusiasm.

Q: Your family life, how did you accomplish that in those days?

Adm. L.: Well, I had two children the first two years. We were married in early June, the fourth or fifth of June, and our daughter was born on the thirty-first of May. Our second daughter a year from that July.

Q: The family lived where?

Adm. L.: They lived in Long Beach.

Then I went to sub school. We all came back to New London for six months. Then I went out to Pearl and we all went out there. My family life wasn't disrupted except for exercises, which is normal operations in and out of Long Beach.

Q: You didn't get to experience then the kind of wardroom life that the bachelor--

Adm. L.: The first two years I did, the J.O. Mess because we couldn't get married and we had J. O. Mess. I think we had twenty officers out of my class in the BB NEW MEXICO. So, we played poker and bridge and things like that. As I said, nobody had any money, Jack.

Q: So, that was your home?

Adm. L.: Yes. We went up to L. A. quite often. But, most of us really just stayed aboard ship.

Q: I was talking with Frank Uhlig the other day about the present arrangement of the wardroom on some of the new destroyers, the SPRUANCE class destroyers, where they mess with the sailors.

Adm. L.: I think all battleships had a J. O. Mess inboard midship and the officers' mess was aft. I guess you stayed there as an Ensign. I guess when you made JG you moved.

Q: Charlie Duncan, one of your classmates, talked about the J.O. Mess at some length and what it meant to him as a bachelor. It was a learning process.

Adm. L.: The whole four and a half years on the BB NEW MEXICO was a learning process as far as I'm concerned.

Q: Now, that's something that the old battleship contributed to, the development of a whole Naval officer.

Adm. L.: Definitely.

Q: And something that can't be duplicated on a smaller ship.

Adm. L.: That's right. I don't want to get into anything that's controversial but I really think that the Air Force has done the Navy a great disservice in forcing the Navy to do away with the shipboard qualification of officers before they go to Pensacola. I've operated with carriers in a task force, I've been aboard carriers and I just don't see how anyone who's gone directly to Pensacola from the Naval Academy goes through flight training and goes aboard a carrier, I don't know how he is ever going to qualify as Officer of the Deck or even an Engineering Watch Officer.

Q: Doesn't he have to?

Adm. L.: I don't see how he can do it with the tempo of operations. I don't know what the aviators say. But, gee, when I was out in the Seventh Fleet working on the USS ST. PAUL or USS OKLAHOMA CITY and visit Tommy Booth on the USS CORAL SEA quite often for days at a time, boy, the tempo of operations was such that I don't see how these kids that are flying have strength to do the flying and then go up and stand a four hour watch, being

Loughlin #1 -42-

Officer of the Watch, or Officer of the Deck. Maybe they can, but I think we're much better off as far as career service is concerned if we make them join the fleet for two years and make them qualify before they go to Pensacola.

Q: Why was that eliminated? Was it simply expedient to train them as aviators?

Adm. L.: I think the Air Force cornered the market on these kids, the Air Force Academy. I think that people knowing that they had to serve two years in the fleet before they--half the people who come in here, I had one the other day, half these young men who come in here they --some want to be nuclear submariners, but by far the majority want to fly. Now, that's the reason they are coming to the Naval Academy. They want to fly when they graduate.

"Well," you say, "You're going to have to put in two years on destroyers, or a battleship, or a cruiser, something like that before you go to Pensacola." Then they're not coming to the Naval Academy in my opinion.

Q: That was, in effect, an apprenticeship for the Naval officer.

Adm. L.: It gave them some basic qualifications which you're not going to get active as aviators.

Q: But, you see that across the board in civilian life, the neglect of the apprenticeship training that used to be to achieve the objective that they had set out to achieve.

You said you won engineering "E's" on the BB NEW MEXICO, tell me about the competition of the units of the fleet.

Adm. L.: Well, it was by class. We won the white "E" from all battleships in the fleet. At that time, I think, we had fourteen. The white "E" was symbolic of having the highest engineering score for that particular year.

Q: You used planes as spotters did you?

Adm. L.: Planes?

Q: Yes, did you have spotters?

Adm. L: No, the spotting was done from the various Directors.

Q: Did the BB NEW MEXICO have some observation planes?

Adm. L.: Yes, we had one or two I think. Two I think. Oh, yes, Eddie Ewen was a famous aviator on there.

Q: Oh, he was?

Adm. L.: He was on there, yes. I had the fifth division which is the five inch fifty-one caliber. Let's see, what was it, the cast and the dog method I think. One was you picked him up from the stern on the stern hook and the other while they taxi up the starboard side, and lowered the hook down and picked him up here and you are in the life boat waving the signal flag to tell him which way to go.

Q: Did you catapult off at any time?

Adm. L.: No, I never did. I wasn't an aviator and there wasn't any reason for it really.

Q: We're about to leave the BB NEW MEXICO in December of 1937 and you told me a little bit earlier about what caused you to turn your eyes toward submarine training, so will you pick up the story at that point and tell me about the impact New London made upon you.

Adm. L.: The submarine school was entirely different environment and atmosphere than the battleship Navy that I had been on for four and a half years.

Q: It was almost from one extreme to another wasn't it?

Adm. L.: Yes, it was. Yes, sir. In the first place most of the instructors knew me personally from the Naval Academy, not that I got any special favors, but it was kind of a personal relationship. The class only consisted of about twenty-eight or twenty-nine. You really got personal instruction. If you ran into trouble I'm talking about in the classroom now, they were always willing to help you, night or day. If you had any questions or any problem why, you could go to them. If you worked hard, which most of us did, why, it was a pleasure. After exams on Friday we had the weekends off. My family was living in Philadelphia, so I'd go over on Friday night and back on Sunday.

Q: You drove down?

Adm. L.: Yes. We had our operational operations on little R boats based up there. I thoroughly enjoyed submarine school. As I said, it was very strange to me.

Loughlin #1 -45-

Q: Who was the Skipper of the school?

Adm. L.: Tony Ziroli was the Skipper and Dickie Edwards was Commanding Officer of the submarine base.

Q: Dickie Edwards became Admiral King's deputy?

Adm. L.: But, Tony Ziroli was the Officer in Charge, a real fine officer. We had an outstanding group in this particular sub class. In fact, you'll remember some of these names, Dick O'Kane, Slade Cutter, Dusty Dornin, Bub Ward. All two, three, or four Navy Crosses. I didn't do too badly.

Q: Indeed you didn't!

Adm. L.: There are others that were good, but didn't have the opportunity--I'm the first to admit that when we get to the submarine part of my career, I'm the first to admit, it's not how good you are or how skillful you are in making an attack, it's how lucky you are.

Q: This was one of Tommy Hart's themes that luck was a great element in a Naval career.

Adm. L.: You could have--well, we don't have to get into that now, but there was really an outstanding group of officers in that sub class. There were five, six, or seven who were really tops or among the top in the business.

Q: Now, your experience in the BB NEW MEXICO and especially under Rickover in engineering must have been a tremendous help to you?

Adm. L.: It was. I was one of the--my class having been four and a half years on the BB NEW MEXICO I was the senior, in the senior class, in other words, the class consisted of people out of 1933, 1934, and 1935. I don't think anybody from 1936 was there. So, we were the senior ones who had been out for four and a half. And yes, I think my experience on the BB NEW MEXICO was valuable assistance to me. I stood pretty high in the class. I stood five in the class. It was something like that.

Q: Had you acquired that meticulous approach to things. too?

Adm. L.: I think thanks to Rickover I did and the gunnery department. You have to be awfully careful in the gunnery department. I think I was more mature than a lot of the people up there. For instance, I believe I was the only one in the whole class who had Government, Naval Mutual Aid, and a New York Life insurance policy. The only reason I bring it up is I think it's a sign of maturity. The others let things go and don't bother about it.

Q: And you look at it from another angle it was also underscoring the dangers of that particular branch of the service.

Adm. L.: Well, I had gotten this before I ever went to submarine school. I had it all when I was on the BB NEW MEXICO, so you can't really draw that parallel.

Q: But, the fact that they had a seminar at submarine school in this subject.

Adm. L.: I think so because, you may not know this and I doubt if you know, but until sometime in World War II or after World

War II the reason the submariners got the extra twenty five percent in pay was not hazardous, it was the extra arduousness. That's how the law read. The aviators got it for hazardous. The submariners didn't, they got it for extra arduousness.

Q: Arduous duty.

Adm. L. That's right.

Q: Well, the enlisted men on board the submarines got extra bonus for every dive didn't they?

Adm. L.: Not to my knowledge, no sir. Not as early as 1938. It may have been in the years before that.

Q: It was earlier than that, yes. They were very anxious to dive because they got extra pay for it.

Adm. L.: I didn't know that.

Q: Well, talk a little about the training itself at the submarine school. You used the R boats and you went where?

Adm. L.: In Narragansett Bay there along Block Island, Block Island Sound. It was a daily operation. I don't think we ever went out overnight. We'd just go out in the morning and come back in the afternoon.

Q: Did you exercise with destroyers?

Adm. L.: No, no. No tactics, it was just basic submarine training. The classroom work really took precedence, I mean there was much more classroom than there was underway training. The current was so strong there and still is there was no chance to develop seamanship. In other words, the Skipper or the Exec always made the landings there.

Q: What was the depth of your dives, your practice diving?

Adm. L.: Oh, I don't think Block Island was probably more than eighty or ninety feet. We very rarely went below periscope depth with dives or for drills. We had a lot of drills out there incidentally. We would lose all power and the lights would go off. Things like that. Lose power for the stern planes. Have to shift to hand. It was well run. There is no question about it, they were a bunch of pros and they probably still are, which I'm sure they are down in Pensacola also. You have to be in this modern Navy.

Q: Without having pros you certainly can't. Well, this school training convinced you that you had chosen the right branch of the Navy?

Adm. L.: I liked it. Yes, Sir, I had no fear of submarines in diving or being below or cooped up in a small place.

Q: Did you wife have any reaction to this?

Adm. L.: No. I will make this comment. This is probably not the appropriate time to do it, but the submarine is a young man's game. Someone told me once that he thought he had reached the peak of his efficiency when he was thirty-one or thirty-two years old. I was, what twenty-eight I guess, when I went to sub school. But, I know that the things I did in World War II I could not do now if I were the commanding officer of a ship. I know that as well as I'm sitting here.

Q: Illustrate. Just what do you mean?

Adm. L.: Well, make an attack. Not taking chances. Holding my attack on an escorted convoy. All you're worried about is not depth charges or getting sunk. All you're worried about is getting into position so you can fire your torpedoes and sink the ship. Whereas the older you get the more cautious you get and I think you would take into consideration what could happen to you if you were detected.

Q: And your obligations and all that sort of thing?

Adm. L.: Yes. I don't mean that you get to be a coward as you grow older. I think you just get to be more cautious.

Q: The same thing applies in aviation?

Adm. L.: I expect. I would assume so. I'm talking abour war time experiences. I'm not talking about peace time exercises.

Q: Well, that school was of short duration.

Adm. L.: It was about six months, yes.

Q: Was that adequate in your opinion?

Adm. L.: It gave you enough background. I was very fortunate when I went to the S-35 which was my first submarine. One, I had an outstanding Skipper. I'm sure you've heard of the Silent Service, the old TV thing having to do with World War II. Well, Tommy Dykers was the originator of the Silent Service. In fact, he did all the narration. He was the first Skipper. I think you always have an affinity for your first Skipper, be he good or bad. And, Tommy was outstanding.

And, I was fortunate when I joined the boat, Ed Stephan who later made Admiral was the Exec. He got his own boat. I was number four when I joined, because I had a classmate, Joe Enright who was senior to me. But, Ed Stephan got his own boat shortly thereafter. Joe Enright transferred to another S boat that was going to go back from Pearl to New London. We got two replacements both junior to me, so I ended up being number two in a matter of, oh, a couple of months after I'd got there. I grew up with Tommy Dykers. I mean, he had to take me in as number two. It was just a marvelous opportunity for me to get responsibility that fast.

Q: That never would have happened on a battleship?

Adm. L.: No.

Q: It took much longer to mature.

Adm. L.: That's right. And, it took a year to qualify in those days. You couldn't qualify in less than a year. That was a big thrill to wear your regular submarine pin.

Q: It was a milestone.

Adm. L.: Yes, it was. You notice that Admiral Nimitz always wore a submarine pin, always. I mean, in all of his pictures.

Q: And, most of the submariners I know have done the same thing.

Interview No. 2 with Rear Admiral Charles Elliott Loughlin, U.S. Na

(Retired)

Place: Annapolis, Maryland

Date: Thursday, 28 August 1980

Subject: Biography

By: John T. Mason, Jr.

Q: Well, my friend, last time you concluded your remarks about your training period at the submarine school in New London, Connecticut that was completed in June 1938, and you got your pin as a submarir

Adm. L.: I have to correct you on that. You don't get the pin unti you qualify in submarines.

Q: Oh, I see. All right. You got designation.

Adm. L.: Well, designation as having attended submarine school. That's correct.

Q: O-kay, do you want to take up the story at that point?

Adm. L.: I asked for and got an S-boat. We only had, really, two types, three types of boats in those days. The R-boats which were the training boats up in New London and the S-boats which were both at Pearl and on the East Coast. Then we had what we called the fleet boats. I wanted to go to an S boat for the reasor there were only four officers on an S boat.

So, I went out to Pearl and joined the S-35. I think I mentioned before that Tommy Dykers was my first Skipper. He was the one who was responsible for the production of the Silent Service series following World War II. He was an outstanding peace time commanding officer and he had an outstanding war record. He had the USS JACK during World War II and did an absolutely splendid job.

Q: You want to give me a verbal acount of the submarine base at Pearl in those days?

Adm. L.: We had a senior Captain who was the submarine base commander and we had, I guess, three divisions of boats, submarines there, three different squadron commanders. As a matter of fact, Admiral Dyer was out there at the time, right here from Annapolis.

Q: Yes, I recall it.

Adm. L.: We had peace time operations, going out and firing torpedo practices. The men were quartered in barracks. The enlisted men were quartered in barracks right off the base there. There was an officers' club there, so the bachelor officers, the few there had quarters right at the officers' club. Most of us were married and lived in town. From 1938 to 1940 you could get a fully furnished apartment for forty-five to fifty-five dollars a month. Can you imagine that?

Q: You can't even get a garage now.

Adm. L.: It was run in a very, very exemplary manner in my opinion Captain Scanland happened to be the Base Commander when I was there and his son Worth Scanland out of 1934 was also a submariner. As I said, it was mostly peace time operations although once a year we had what we called a modified war patrol that lasted for ten days. We had to make our own water and own provisions. An S boat could make very little water.

We had training exercises where planes would be sent out to try to find you and you would have to avoid them. You'd end up by firing an exercise torpedo run. Very interesting and it pretty well simulated war time conditions.

Q: How far out did you go?

Adm. L.: Oh, golly, not too far on a simulated war patrol. But, we did make extended cruises around the islands. We went to French Frigate Shoals as a division as a training exercise. We'd go down to the big island, Maui, and operate off Hilo and off the Western side there.

Q: You didn't get to Midway or way out?

Adm. L.: No. I think French Frigate Shoals was the farthest I went to in the two and a half years I was there.

Q: Was there anything on French Frigate Shoals?

Adm. L.: No.

Loughlin #2 -55-

Q: Just a shoal?

Adm. L.: Just a navigational training exercise to get you at sea.

Q: And your potential enemy was always Japan?

Adm. L.: It's a long time ago, but I presume so, yes. I don't think we thought too much of war at the beginning. However, when they sent, you recall, the Hawaiian Detachment that was sent out there when they shifted heavy cruisers and battleships, a big part of the fleet was out there as early as, well, 1939 or 1940.

Q: That was under Richardson?

Adm. L.: Yes, it was. Then, of course I left in October 1940 and later on, I might add this one comment, I had never seen the fleet in such a state of readiness as in October 1940. It was superb. And what happened between then and December 1941 I just think they kept them at sea all the time and just trained the living be-Jesus out of them. Of course, it was common practice to be in port on Sunday, as you well know. It was just an act of God that the carriers weren't there. They happened to be out on an exercise. That's the reason they didn't get the carriers, but all the battleships.

Q: Yes. I was reading a report the other day that there was some sort of a very special alert just prior to the seventh and the alert ended on the fifth, so there was a general relaxation after that. Before that there were double watches and that sort of thing.

Well, it was just training.

Loughlin #2 -56-

Adm. L.: Just training.

Q: Did it meet your requirements? I mean, this S boat in that you were trying to get special training because of the smaller number of men.

Adm. L.: I was very fortunate. I may have mentioned in the previous interview, I was able to fleet up to be--well, you have to have more than four officers to be called Exec. You follow me?

Q: Yes.

Adm. L.: The normal complement was four officers. Say you were number two, unless you had a fifth officer, then you became Exec. I reported aboard as number four. Then within a short period of time I was able to go up to number two.

I qualified in the minimum time which was one year of operating experience and that's when you wear your submarine pin, your dolphins.

I was very close with Tommy Dykers, who at that time was a Lieutenant. He was, as I say, a marvelous man. I learned a great deal from him. He certainly was one of the peace time Skippers that did well in war time. A lot of the peace time Skippers didn't, but Tommy was one that did extremely well during the war.

Q: How did you do with your torpedoes, your practice torpedoes?

Adm. L.: We got our share of misses, I guess, but Tommy was an excellent man on the periscope. He did most of the firing. We did not stand one in the division. We were probably midway through the division of six submarines.

Q: That was a relatively short period of time you were there.

Adm. L.: Two and a half years. Then we came back to Philadelphia and I have to use the word I, I with twelve men put the S-14 into commission because the Skipper who had been ordered there was still out in the Philippines, Dick Lake.

Q: You have to use the word I very frequently in this story and that's the purpose of it, it is your story.

Adm. L.: But, I was the only officer onboard and I have twelve enlisted men and I commissioned the S-14.

Q: Were there any problems?

Adm. L.: Oh, all kinds of problems.

Q: What?

Adm. L.: They were decommissioned originally because of structural defects. They had had what we called a main drain that ran underneath the hull and the hull, itself, between the bottom of the hull and the top of the main drain they almost touched. There was all this corrosion and they had to take the main drain out and repair the whole length of the hull in order to make it structurally good enough to dive.

Q: How old a boat was it?

Adm. L.: I don't know when the S-14 boat was built. Probably in the early twenties or before that. They had the German MAN engines which had all metric measurements. Spare parts were a complete headache. We had nothing but operational trouble the whole time I was on it.

Q: That seems to have been pretty general when they were used.

Adm. L.: The German MAN engines were not reliable mainly because of the difficulty in getting spare parts.

Q: That gave you some added experience too, getting a ship ready for--

Adm. L.: It did and we, after our shakedown, deep dive, and a few other things, we were deployed with the other boats in the division obstensibly for Panama, but we went to St. Thomas. On route there, which would be in September of 1941, we ran into the darndest hurricane I've ever been in. I'm frankly surprised that we survived but we did and got to St. Thomas. Then they called us off with the S-15 and we stayed in St. Thomas. The other boats went on down to Panama. We were to go to Panama to relieve a bunch of R boats who were down in Panama for training and send them back to New London.

Q: Back to the hurricane, can't you dive when you're in the presence of a storm?

Adm. L.: I never wanted to dive, Jack. A lot of people who are not submariners don't understand this, but when you surface in a hurricane in real heavy sea you have practically no freeboard what-so-ever. You can't blow enough water out of your tank. You have to pump it out. So, when you surface you are very, very low in the water. In a hurricane, no matter which, with turbulent seas and no pattern to the seas you take an awful chance of flooding your conning tower and if you didn't lose your boat you'd lose all your fire control equipment or you might even lose your boat. So, I much prefer, even in a fleet submarine in World War II we had two typhoons, and I much prefer to ride them out on the surface.

Q: Just ride them out.

Adm. L.: Just ride it out on the surface. Yes, sir. None of us dived on this particular trip. We all rode it out on the surface.

Q: Was this left to the discretion of the Skipper? I mean, there were no regulations covering it?

Adm. L.: No. Well, we had a division commander who was riding the tender. I think the USS DIXIE was the tender. I don't think anybody --but this was a terrible storm. I certainly wouldn't have done anything in this storm.

Q: What was the purpose of going to St. Thomas?

Adm. L.: Somebody with foresight had seen this coming and they had built a very, very good submarine base in St. Thomas. We got there in October 1941. It was a fully operational submarine base with a machine shop and a BOQ for officers and quarters for enlisted men. You almost had to have places for the enlisted men. It was just impossible for the whole crew to sleep aboard an S boat night after night, day after day.

Q: Especially in warm waters.

Adm. L.: That's right. There was a very efficient operational submarine base by the time we got there and had been for some months before. As I said, somebody really had some foresight because they knew that if we ever did go to war the Caribbean was going to be a happy hunting ground for the German submarines and we know that turned out to be.

Q: Well, it was a haven at that time, wasn't it?

Adm. L.: Yes, sir.

Q: Weren't they operating at that time quite extensively?

Adm. L.: Well, not, I don't think, in October they weren't. I never saw one until right after Pearl Harbor. We were there when Pearl Harbor took place on the Seventh of December.

Q: Was John Hoover in command then in the Caribbean?

Adm. L.: He was in command of Com 10 in San Juan.

Q: At that time?

Adm. L.: Yes, sir. As a matter of fact, he's the one, we had an operation order that called for us to go to Panama on the eighth ninth or tenth of December that had been put out several weeks before. When we heard of the holocaust out in Pearl, we said, "Gee, what do we do? Do we follow the operation order?"

Genial John said, "Follow your operational order."

So, I think it was the tenth of December we set sail for Panama. Again we didn't see anything. But I think the German boats had not had time to get over there at that time.

Loughlin #2 -61-

Q: They didn't waste much time getting over there.

Adm. L.: No. We finally got to Coco Solo and I walked in the Operations Office and Willy Hoffheins was the Operations Officer and had been in charge of putting the S-14 into commission back in the Philadelphia Navy Shipyard.

He said, "What are you doing here? You're supposed to be in St. Thomas."

The wives had been stopped from coming down and they were evacuating the wives, so they let us stay over Christmas and then we turned around and went back to St. Thomas again for two months. We made what were called defensive patrols.

Q: Now, what was that? Looking for German submarines?

Adm. L.: Oh, yes. At that time they were all over the Caribbean. There was a detachment of light aircraft there at Bourne Field, it is now Truman Field, but Bourne Field in St. Thomas, and they had, I think fifty caliber or thirty caliber machine guns. When they were out and a German submarine was on the surface they would just wave to the planes. They didn't even dive for them.

Q: Now, tell me, how does a submarine battle another submarine?

Adm. L.: You just have to be submerged and try to catch them on the surface. That's about the only way. We had no radar, and no sonar equipment, nothing. You just had to be lucky and catch one of the surface while you were submerged. That's about the only way you could get one.

Loughlin #2 -62-

Q: That was his tactic too?

Adm. L.: Well, except that they thought that they were pretty well immune in the Caribbean area. They were very, very arrogant in their actions. They were just sitting ducks. There was no escort, no convoy, no nothing right after Pearl Harbor. The carnage was terrific in the Caribbean in January, February, and March and from then on. They operated with impunity there for several months until we got the convoy system going.

Q: What can you say about Hoover's operations down there?

Adm. L.: I had very little to do with it, with Admiral Hoover. He was, as I say, Com 10, the Commandant of the Naval District, but he was not our operational commander. We still operated from COMSUBLANT and his chain of command. He was technically our boss because we were in his command area. He had nothing to do with our operation orders and our operations.

Q: Did you have anything to do with Ben Custer?

Adm. L.: No.

Q: Ben seemed to be all over the place. Did you have any interesting experiences during that second deployment at St. Thomas?

Adm. L.: The most horrifying experience I ever had in the submarine force was on the S-14.

Q: Tell me about it.

Adm. L.: You held you breath frankly. The boat was really

unreliable. The stern planes were out half the time. The bow planes wouldn't work half the time. We were going on this trip down to Coco Solo, when we left either the tenth or eleventh of December. We saw a plane and in those days you dived for a plane. I don't know why because it was probably one of our own commercial planes. How could it be a German plane?

Q: But it was a question of identification.

Adm. L.: So, we tried to dive and we couldn't dive. The boat just settled by the stern. I was the Exec and the Diving Officer. I shifted some ballast and Dick Lake the Skipper said, "Come on, we have to do something." So, he started pumping water all over the damned ship. Well, I knew the trim had been good and we finally got down. We'd go down about a thirty degree angle and then put full rise on the planes and come back to the surface. Then we would do it again all over again and then come back to the surface.

Q: You thought you were a porpoise.

Adm. L.: I'll tell you it was as harrowing an experience as I've ever had in a submarine.

Well, after about an hour we found out that the connecting rod leading to the stern planes had broken aft of where the indicators came off. In other words, the indicators in the control room would indicate a full dive or a full rise, but the shaft had been broken after that and the stern planes were jammed on full rise. Well, you can't dive a submarine with the stern planes on full rise.

Q: I guess you can't. It was never intended to.

Adm. L.: So, I tell you after about three or four times of this porpoiseing thing we went down almost to test depth before we'd get the bow planes under control and you would just pop to the surface.

Q: What about confidence of the crew?

Adm. L.: We were all scared; there is no question about that. We were scared to death. I was! I'm sure everybody else was because we didn't know what was wrong. We knew that something was wrong, but we didn't know what was wrong. The submarine had never acted that way. We shifted all this ballast from aft forward so we were horribly out of trim.

Q: Even after the fact you must have had not much confidence in that ship?

Adm. L.: We never did have any confidence in the ship. We never had any confidence.

Q: It was reported, this incident was reported I take it?

Adm. L.: I doubt it. I don't think it was. We couldn't fix it. We had to stay on the surface the rest of the way to Coco Solo and there we got it fixed. So, we were not able to dive from wherever this happened on the transit, I can't remember, probably about half way there.

Then we were in Colo Solo from, right after we got there I--oh, first we came back to St. Thomas.

Q: Two months you said.

Adm. L.: For two months and then made some patrols Pointe-a-Pitre in Guadeloupe. The French fleet, the Free French fleet were at Pointe-a-Pitre in Guadeloupe. JEAN BART, and I forget who else was there. So, they sent us out there.

Q: The BEARNE was there, I think.

Adm. L.: I don't remember. The JEAN BART is the only one I remember.

Q: Was Admiral Robert there?

Adm. L.: Well, we never got there. All we did was patrol off the entrance there to be sure that they did not make a dash in order to get back to join the German fleet. So, we did that for two months around that area. But, we had mechanical breakdowns and all kinds of trouble.

Q: What were your intentions in case they did make a dash?

Adm. L.: Just report it. That's all.

Q: But not to attack?

Adm. L.: Then they sent us back to Panama in March. When we got there Dick Lake was detached and went to command the fleet submarine up in Portsmouth and I became the commanding officer. So, I became the commanding officer the first week in March.

Probably was the first officer in my class to get command of a submarine.

Q: In March of 1942?

Adm. L.: In March of 1942 and I stayed on board until August of 1943 and continued making what we called defensive patrols. Most people still thought that the Japanese might send a task force down and hit the Canal. So, they kept several of us out on the West in the Pacific there just to patrol the area and keep a watch to see if anyone was going to attack or not.

Q: Were the other submarines also old?

Adm. L.: Well, there was a divison of B boats down there. The USS BASS, the USS BARRACUDA and as a matter of fact I was on patrol within fifty miles or so of, I guess it was the USS BASS,* when she had that horrible fire and lost thirty-five, forty people. They had a battery fire. Pretty sad thing.

Q: Did you have further trouble with the S boat?

Adm. L.: Just the normal mechanical trouble. They were just not operational. You couldn't depend on them. They were all in the same category, everyone.

Q: So, at that stage they were all assigned to areas that weren't crucial?

Adm. L.: No combat areas.

---

*Battery fire on board the USS BASS occurred 17 August 1942, while she was on patrol off Panama.

Q: Did you have anything to do with the Galapagos Islands? Any thought of fortifying them?

Adm. L.: Not on board a submarine. Much later on in the late 1940's when I was the Exec on the USS ORION we made a trip to the Galapagos Islands on the way down to Peru.

Brooks Harral on the S-17 made a patrol down that way. So we did have folks that went there, but I didn't go there.

Q: I know that FDR was interested in the possibility of fortifying the islands and sent Paul Foster down there as his special emissary to see if something should be done.

Adm. L.: I think as the weeks went on it was obvious, as we began to take the offensive that the Pacific was, obviously, the Japs were not going to make a feint down toward the Canal Zone. At least I thought it was obvious. I don't know if anybody else did or not. They never did to my knowledge. They never made any attempt.

Q: I suppose the mere fact that it was the Canal and it was such an important artery for us.

Adm. L.: Yes, sir.

Q: What about the prospect of sabotage in that area? What precautions did you take?

Adm. L.: A lot of people were more afraid of the German submarine coming through the entrance there in the breakwater and firing a torpedo. As a matter of fact, we had some exercises to--

Q: At the locks?

Adm. L.: At the locks. We had a mine field on the Atlantic side. You had to penetrate the mine field. Then you had a breakwater with a fairly wide entrace. It was a straight shot from that breakwater right into the first set of locks. A straight shot. We debated many times if a German submarine could follow a merchant ship through the mine field. There was enough water to remain submerged and then get a torpedo shot off at the first set of locks. Why school would have been out.

Q: What kind of mines did we have? Moored mines?

Adm. L.: They were moored mines. I don't believe they were contact I believe they had to be activated from a control station on the beach. We did have merchant ships sunk in the mine field.

Q: Did that cause submariners any special worry?

Adm. L.: No because we knew where the mines were. The channel was well marked to us so we knew how to get through the mine field. So, it didn't cause any particular worry.

We didn't operate too much on the Atlantic side once we got there. Almost all of our operations were such that we made the transit to the Pacific and made our area patrol.

Q: Is there any particular problem in making the transit of the Canal in a submarine?

Adm. L.: No. It's just hot.

Loughlin #2 -69-

Q: It was that all right.

Adm. L.: I learned a lesson in seamanship on one of those transits through. One of the lines leading, I think they call them the mules. You know the mules that towed you through the locks. Just as we were about to cast off, the bow line couldn't be cast off. We were going ahead two-thirds and the current running with us. The bow was being pulled right into the locks. Well, my instinct, and incidentally under FDR to my knowledge the Panama Canal was the only place in the world and still may be where the pilot has the authority and responsibility for the ship. Not the commanding officer.

Q: Yes, he's relieved of that.

Adm. L.: It's very unusual. Well my instinct is that if the bow is going this way we'd give right rudder to keep from hitting it. This guy said "Left full rudder," and got just enough slack to get that bow line off and then he said "Right full rudder," and he came within that much of hitting the side of the wall there. But he was smarter than I was.

Q: He had more experience?

Adm. L.: Naturally, he wanted to get some slack, see, and it worked.

Q: Why was that provision made?

Adm. L.: I don't know, I don't know except that, perhaps just because of this reason it really took someone with experience to get the big ships, the carriers and big ships like that through the locks without damaging the locks. If the locks had been damaged, school would have been out. I think that is probably the reason for it.

Q: Who were these pilots? Were they U.S. citizens?

Adm. L.: They were all U.S. citizens that worked in the Canal Zone. They worked for the government down there. They were all good too. I took the boat away once. When I deployed in the USS QUEENFISH we were making a night landing on the Balboa side and none of the pilots really had much experience in landings of submarines. They could get them through the locks all right. I could see in his approach that he really didn't know what he was doing, so I just said, "I relieve you, Sir."

Q: He didn't object to it?

Adm. L: No. Technically, I guess he still had the responsibility. We were through the last set of locks and going into the submarine base there at Rodman. So, there would have been a question, I guess, whether he had the authority or not. But he didn't object. He didn't want to make the landing either. I think he was kind of happy that I took over.

Q: You had achieved a certain rung fairly high on the ladder when you got to be Skipper of an S boat.

Adm. L.: As a Lieutenant, then with the acceleration in promotions, golly, this was March, 1942 and my classmates made Lieutenant Commander in June, I think, of 1942. I was a Lieutenant Commander

Loughlin #2 -71-

from then on until I made Commander in August 1944. So, I went from a Lieutenant to Commander in two and a half years.

Q: Were you itching a bit though? You were the Skipper of a submarine, but you were in the Canal Zone. Were you itching to get out in--

Adm. L.: Oh, yes. I wanted to get back to new construction. As a matter of fact, I came very close to getting this done. The USS POGY came through with George Wales and George got pneumonia and had to be relieved. Not detached, but relieved. He just couldn't make the trip from the Canal Zone out to Pearl. Ralph Metcalf who was thirty-five, two years my junior, was the Exec on there. I think there was some question whether I'd be detached and get command of the USS POGY and take it out to Pearl. But, they let Ralph take it over there. So, I had to wait my turn to get to new construction. This didn't take place until August 1943.

Q: Who was running submarine matters in Washington at that point? Who was in command?

Adm. L.: Well SUBLANT was really--

Q: Who was it?

Adm. L.: Let's see now, Charles Styer, I guess, was COMSUBLANT when I put the USS QUEENFISH into commission.

Q: You were down there and watched the development of the German activity in the Gulf of Mexico along the coast and their attacks on all these tankers and their tremendous success, did this involve you and the other submariners very much?

Adm. L.: Not on the Atlantic side. The Key West boats probably were involved to some extent. We had some R boats down there. We just weren't equipped with no sonar and no radar. We just weren't equipped to engage in anti-submarine warfare.

Q: Hardly any submarines had radar at that point.

Adm. L.: No, that's right, but the fleet boats at least had sonar where you could detect the submarine when you were submerged. But, we didn't even have that. We had a piece of equipment that you wore earphones. I forget what the name of it was.

Q: Asdic I suppose.

Adm. L.: No, it wasn't that. But, you'd be very fortunate to hear anything within a few hundred yards of you.

I can't think of anything of real import that happened down there. As I said, everyone got the feeling that after a few months the Japanese were not going to attack the Canal Zone and they didn't. So it was just routine going to sea on area patrols and coming back in and going back to sea again.

Q: Clay Blair in talking about your time in the Canal Zone used the word trapped. You were trapped in an S boat down there. Is that really the way you felt?

Adm. L.: Well, see, I became a commanding officer so early when Dick Lake was detached and I guess they figured it out that I ought to stay there for a couple of years, which I did.

Q: Settle into command.

Adm. L.: So, when I became senior enough, I guess, then they gave me new construction orders.

Q: That was a big day, wasn't it? Tell me about that.

Adm. L.: Well, the strange part of it was the S-14 was, had orders to depart the Canal Zone and go back to New London. This was in mid-August of 1943. My relief had been ordered for weeks and hadn't shown up. He didn't show up, didn't show up, didn't show up. Jesse Hull was my Division Commander at the time. Let's say that we were going to leave on a Wednesday morning and Monday night he called me in and said, "All right, if he doesn't come tomorrow you're going to have to take the boat back," even though I had orders for PCO school.

Q: What was going to happen to the S boat? Was she going to be overhauled or decommissioned?

Adm. L.: No. She was just going to do submarine training at the submarine school just like the R boats used to.

Well, sure enough this guy came in Tuesday morning. He had been delayed. He couldn't get a plane down or something. So we had a change of command on Tuesday afternoon and, then at eight o'clock on Wednesday morning he took off for New London in the S-14. I flew back to the States and went to PCO school.

Q: Where was your family during that time?

Adm. L.: The day of Pearl Harbor my wife, who subsequently died, and two children were onboard a passenger ship in New York City sailing the next morning for the Canal Zone. But, they stopped the sailing after Pearl Harbor. So, they were in North Wales, Pennsylvania for the duration. In fact, subsequently they evacuate all the wives down there except for those who worked for the government in the Canal Zone. There were two or three wives, if my memory serves me right. Don Weiss's wife worked for Pan American and she stayed and there were a couple of others who stayed. But everybody else was evacuated, both from St. Thomas and the Canal Zone.

Q: I guess Bill Irvin was down there about that time?

Adm. L.: No. No, he wasn't there when I was there.

Q: You went back by way of Pennsylvania, I take it?

Adm. L.: Yes. I had a week or so leave and then I went to PCO school.

Q: Tell me about that. At that state that was fairly new.

Adm. L.: Well actually, it had started at the beginning of the war or right after the beginning of the war. Of course, this was August, September 1943. But, Captain Patterson, you may know him here in Annapolis. He was the officer in charge of the PCO school. I think he had his doubts about me for only one reason, I had never been on a fleet boat. I had been on nothing but S boats. I had depended entirely on periscope operations. I didn't even know what a TDC, a Torpedo Data Computer was. We did most of our night work on the USS MARLIN and the USS MACKEREL. These were small replicas of Fleet boats, really. They were too small to make patrols, so they used them in the submarine school.

Q: You weren't unusual in that lack of knowledge were you?

Adm. L.: No. But, he seemed to think that I depended too much on my periscope operation and not enough on the TDC.

Q: Even that is understandable.

Adm. L.: He was just trying to be helpful, that's all.

Q: How long a period did you have training as a prospective--

Adm. L.: I don't remember exactly, but it was probably about a month. I think they had a class about every four or five weeks. Eight, or ten, or twelve in a class. We really got personalized instruction.

Q: It really was just mastering the ordnance?

Adm. L.: Learning the lessons of the boats. In other words, they had all the war patrols up there and we would analyze the war patrols reports. They would try to teach you what to do and what not to do depending on the experience of the boats that had just gone through this..

Q: And largely the boats of the Pacific.

Adm. L.: Oh, yes.

Q: What were some of the surprises that came to you as a student at that time?

Adm. L.: I really didn't have any. We hadn't made any night periscope attacks in the S boats and we did make night periscope attacks there which was an unusual experience if you'd never done it before.

I think we just read the war patrol reports and listened to these people who had been out in the war.

Q: Oh, they brought some of the men back?

Adm. L.: Oh, yes sir. Joe Willingham was an instructor up there. Karl Hensel was up there. So, we had people who in the early part of the war had made three, four, or five runs. Most people didn't make more than four or five patrols and they would either bring them back to the staff at Pearl or to one of the bases at Guam or bring them back to sub school to help in submarine training.

Q: What was the basis for that? I've noticed that, four patrols was a maximum.

Adm. L.: Well, it's pretty nerve-racking if you saw a lot of action. Some people got lousy areas and could go a whole war patrol and not even see an enemy ship.

Q: Even then, I suppose, it was nerve-racking?

Adm. L.: Yes, and frustrating. For instance, Red Ramage when he got his Congressional Medal of Honor, the next run he went out and after eight-six days he didn't sink a ship. He said he thought everybody ought to have to go through that experience. Thanks, but no thanks.

I came back from my first run, I graduated, I guess I weighed around a hundred and fifty-five pounds which is what I weigh right today. But, I was down around a hundred and thirty-two or thirty-three pounds. But, I don't eat very much. It wasn't that I was nervous or scared. It was just I was on my feet all the time, around the boat all the time and I just lost a lot of weight. Nothing organically wrong. I think that after four or five runs you were ready for a rest. We did get the three weeks in rest there.

Q: Was that fairly general in the Navy as a whole at that time, outside the submarine, that same kind of compassion was it demonstrated elsewhere?

Adm. L.: I think it was for what you might call successful runs. In other words, you sank, you had combat, successful combat runs where you sank one or more ships. Certainly we won't go into nanes, but there are many Skippers who really didn't do too well. Either lack of aggression or lack of opportunity or any number of things, they might have been relieved after one run or two runs. I know one Skipper that made five runs on a ship and I don't think he sank anything. He was just in areas where he never had the opportunity. So, as I pointed out once before, you have to be lucky in this business.

Loughlin #2 78-

Q: You have to be lucky. Also this brings up a question about war time efficiency contrasted with efficiency in peace time. Not every man can make that transition.

Adm. L.: Jack, you're absolutely right. The best friend I have in the Navy did not do well or didn't do much on his first run or two and he was relieved and he never made Admiral because of that. There are many peace time Skippers who just did not do well in the war.

Q: How do you account for that? What qualities are lacking?

Adm. L.: I wouldn't know because I didn't serve with them. I think I was fortunate in the very first run I was in convoy college and made many contacts the first run and was successful in my very first attack.

Q: Yes, you were a rip snorter once you got out in the Pacific.

Adm. L.: I think that gave me and certainly the crew confidence. See, I had never been on a fleet boat but I never detected any lack of confidence in either my officers or my crew, but I'm sure they were just as tight as I was when we made our first contact and our first periscope attack and sank our first ship. The first ship we fired at. You could just feel the confidence spread throug out the ship.

Q: He's got it!

Adm. L.: Well. I still get calls from many of my enlisted crew. They are in town or over on the Eastern Shore, down in Tennessee or someplace. They tell me how much they enjoyed serving on the USS QUEENFISH with me. It certainly builds up my ego.

Q: You went up for the completion of the USS QUEENFISH. This was in Portsmouth, New Hampshire. You went there in 1943?

Adm. L.: I would say October, 1943 and she was just starting to be built. So, I went through almost a complete building period. We weren't commissioned until March of 1944.

Q: That was an educational period too, wasn't it?

Adm. L.: Oh, absolutely. I was able to learn an awful lot about a fleet boat, never having been on one. Not only that, Lew Parks was up there and he ran a kind of a training school for the new Skippers. Tactics and strategy and again just like PCO school, the lessons we'd learned and the lessons other people had learned. Practically all of the Skippers up there, except me, had already made war patrols and had been sent back for new construction after these three, four or five runs. They had given leave period and then sent them back and gave them six months new construction period, take the next boat out. So, we had a wealth of experience up there. You could talk to them.

Q: That was great.

Adm. L.: Yes, sir.

Q: That was more than luck wasn't it? I mean that assignment?

Adm. L.: And, then the fact that I could see the equipment going in and the fact that it was a government yard as new equipment was developed or something was found to be out of place you didn't have to have a change order. Andy McKee, who was the commanding officer up there, he would just see that it was changed. Whereas in the EB company, or the other private shipyards you were on a contract basis and--

Q: They had to go to Washington for--

Adm. L.: No, but you had to get change orders. It was much easier a government shipyard to get things done. It was much easier. I know Tommy Withers was in charge of the Naval Base and he was just absolutely magnificent. Everything you wanted you got from the Portsmouth Naval Shipyard, from all the officers right on.

Q: Say something more about the Portsmouth Naval Shipyard at that time, in war time conditions, how were they functioning?

Adm. L.: Well, they had, they reached a peak--I don't know what it was, but under Admiral Withers they, the peak of building was just about that time in 1943, 1944. I can't recall what the number was they were turning out, but they just turned them out so quickly and they were all deep diving boats. They were all the four hundred foot boats. Whereas, EB company was still in the two hundred and fifty foot boats because of this contract. So, all of these ships and, I guess, any one time six or eight boats would be operating at the same time and as soon as you finished your shakedown why, down you'd go to Newport for your torpedo training, and then to New London, and then deployed. It was a very efficient yard and top officers. I think Andy McKee was recognized as the best submarine designer in the world. I don't think there is any question about that. When he retired, he went to work for EB company in the design section. He died several years ago. But, the Production Officers, the Planning Officers, Admiral Withers, the boss, the Commissary Officer. You know we had the old points up there for meat. This guy, Harold Rigby, I think was his name, you'd go to the commissary store. He'd say, "You keep that. You may need these points for a weekend." We'd get lamb-chops and steaks and anything we wanted and no points. No stamps required. That was the type of cooperation I meant.

Q: Now, that was a Naval Shipyard functioning in war time. Was it quite as efficient; do you have any observations of the Naval Shipyard in peace time? The contrast.

Adm. L.: I know they tried to close the shipyard; I think that was more of an economical reason because of the lack of skilled personnel. Periodically they review what Naval Districts should be closed and what shipyards should be closed.

Q: Then it depends upon the local politician, whether he's influential enough to keep it open.

Adm. L.: I think Portsmouth is still open.

Q: What about the new ordnance that went into the USS QUEENFISH? This was at the time when all sorts of new things were coming on-stream?

Adm. L.: Well, of course, everything was new to me. One of the biggest changes was the Mark XXIII torpedo which was a very short torpedo. I don't know what the size of it was, but it was launched just like a torpedo and then it attacked ASW vessels. It didn't have too much of a warhead. I'm not digressing, I'm progressing a little bit, but when I deployed, finally, we stopped off at Key West to relieve another boat to make practice shots of this Mark XXIII at patrol vessels. Then I took the first load of Mark XXIII's out to the Pacific. Then I spent two or three weeks out there demonstrating XXIII to the SUBPAC staff.

Q: You were a rep out there were you?

Adm. L.: Well, they had never seen one before. Then, of course, the Mark XVIII torpedo had just come in. That was an electric torpedo. I never fired a steam torpedo on any of my four patrols. I fired Mark XVIII electric torpedoes. This was a big benefit because if you were undetected at the time you fired then you're undetected from then on because it left no wake. The Japanese then never knew what hit them.

Q: So you never got involved in that torpedo hassle?

Adm. L.: No, sir. We had no magnetic exploders.

Q: You were lucky in that sense. Now, what else? What about the sonar that was installed on the USS QUEENFISH?

Adm. L.: We had both active and passive. Far superior, of course, to anything we'd had before. It didn't even exist on the S boat. But, I can't remember the names, the designations on them.

The active was particularly helpful to me, and I know many other officers, because the tactic had been evolving that when you didn't have sufficient periscope observations making a periscope approach to really get the course and speed down and know exactly how far, what we called, off the track you were, you would check that by, what we called, a single ping range. You'd press this thing and a single ping would go out and come back and you'd just read the range off the range dial there. So, I used that several times in successful attacks.

Of course, the passive sonar was particularly helpful in detecting heavy ships. I mean, you could tell if it was a destroyer, or whether it was a merchant ship, or a big ship or a small ship.

Radars, we had the SJ radar which was a surface search radar and the SD radar which was an aircraft detection. It gave no bearing. The SJ did. But, the SD would just give you a wavy line so you would know there was an airplane in the vicinity. But, we had no idea where it was.

I had an expert radar technician on there by the name of Moore. He developed a technique which was used extensively. I think he developed it. You could transmit by the SJ radar to another submarine instead of using radio communication. You could actually send Morse code and transmit from one SJ radar to another quite a distance away.

Q: How interesting.

Adm. L.: We did that.

Q: Was that a technique that was passed on to others?

Adm. L.: Yes, sir. As a matter of fact, Moore was so good that, I forget which run, maybe after the second or third one, he got hauled off and put on COMSUBPAC Staff.

Q: You lost him. What about the training of the crew in preparation for--?

Adm. L.: I was fortunate Jack, I had an Exec that had made several runs. I had, well I can't say number three and four because Jack Bennett, I think, was technically number three. He had been on the SAN FRANCISCO when it had been mortally damaged with C. Young and you know Bruce McCandless, the one here on duty at the Naval Academy who got the Medal of Honor for bringing it back. He died. He had multiple sclerosis or something. But, he brought the ship back. Bennett had been wounded the day before. He would have been the Officer of the Deck, but he was not available.

Jack went from the SAN FRANCISCO right to submarine school and then came to the USS QUEENFISH. So, he had not made any war patrols. He had just come from sub school. All of my other officer every one of them had made three, four, five war patrols. So, I really had an expert wardroom.

Q: Then, what about the enlisted crew?

Adm. L.: The enlisted crew basically had war patrol experience. See, what happened after every run, particularly during the early part of the war and up to the midpart of the war almost a third or a fourth of your crew were transferred to go back to new construction. The rate of construction was so great that they had to get a nucleus of trained personnel in order to--

Q: Yes, you were like a cell.

Adm. L.: I was able to get around six or eight of my S-14 sailors. I got them ordered to the USS QUEENFISH where we had served for three and a half years. But, the nucleus was there. They all had war patrol experience. Training was not a problem.

Q: Now, this being very important for submarines, what about damage control and training for that?

Adm. L.: I guess we had too much confidence for that. I really didn't put to much trust in that sort of thing because, Jack, if anything happens to a submarine when you're submerged you're probably going to lose your ship anyway. If you get a bomb, or damage that punctures the hull, I don't think you're going to save the damned ship.

The lights never went off the whole time I had the boat. We had one dive of all the hundreds of dives we made that was not an absolutely perfect one hundred percent normal dive. Up in Portsmouth in a cold weather spring we cleared the bridge one day and one of the lookouts dropped a glove and they closed the hatch and the light went on the control that there was enough contact to make the green light go on. There was enough aperture there where the water came in the conning tower. Not a huge slug of it, but a leak. So, we went down and leveled off and came right back again. But, that was the only other than normal dive we ever had all the time. We must have had what, five, six, or seven hundred dives. It was the only one that was not absolutely

Loughlin #2 -86-

as we say in torpedoes, hot, straight and normal.

Q: What a record!

Adm. L.: I'm very proud of that crew.

Q: Were you informed about ULTRA at that point?

Adm. L.: Yes.

Q: Tell me about that because it was so closely guarded?

Adm. L.: We had gotten many ULTRA dispatches. But, only once in my first attack did it ever pay off for me. The very first attack I made. I was with the USS BARB and Ed Swinburne was the wolf pack commander. We got this ULTRA and I happened to be nearest to him and made contact first. Actually we saw the smoke, it was night, and even before we made radar contact we saw the smoke on the horizon. I got in and made an attack and it was based on the ULTRA. I think that we were in such position that we would have made contact a few hours later anyway.

Q: But, I was interested in when you were informed about the existence of this knowledge of code breaking.

Adm. L.: Well, I don't know whether we were informed or not. But, I guess you could put two and two together. But, the message would come from ComSubPac and it would tell you that convoy umpty-ump was reported to be umpty-ump and its course and speed. There was nothing in the dispatch that indicated that they had broken the Japanese code.

Q: So, they didn't really disclose that knowledge?

Adm. L.: We knew it, but it was never disclosed by contents in the messages themselves.

Q: Yes, submariners of all people would know that because of the frequency of the messages.

Then came the great day for the commissioning of the USS QUEENFISH.

Adm. L.: Bobby Theobald, whom you might know. He lives here in Annapolis. His mother was the sponsor of the ship. I think his father was on duty at the Naval District in Boston. She sponsored the ship. It was a normal commissioning ceremony. Nothing spectacular about it. We started operating immediately.

Q: No shakedown?

Adm. L.: Well, we operated shakedown going out and making training dives and torpedo approaches and things like that.

Q: But, very short period for this?

Adm. L.: Most of the training was done in the New London area. They wanted to get you out of the shipyard as soon as they could. Get the torpedo trials at Newport, and then go to New London for training exercises and wolf pack exercises, and more torpedo training.

I did have one unique accident. I guess it was the second or third day that we operated. We were down about a hundred and twenty feet and I heard a sound. Incidentally there was a heavy fog. All my trouble seemed to happen in the fog. There was a heavy fog and I heard this sound. I could tell that we had hit something. So, I ordered the ship to surface and to bring her up on an even keel. Normally you blow and put the bow planes on rise and you come up this way, but we came up this way and found that we had wiped off the sound head. Well, as soon as we hit the surface I had the Exec take a radar range and the return from it at a fairly close point, a prominent point so we knew exactly where we were. The water was supposed to be seventy-five or a hundred feet deeper than the depth we were. Weary Wilkins was my Division Commander and I said, "Captain Wilkins, here is our track and I don't know what we hit. But, I'll bet my life it wasn't the bottom."

He said, "Write up a full report."

He didn't think much of it. I don't know if he believed me or not.

There are two aftermaths to this story; one, when I got down to New London two or three weeks later, I don't know if you know Steve Barchet or not, but Steve was one of my Division Commanders later. He died. He had this report in front of him and I walked in his office to pay my respects.

He said, "What do you want me to do with this?"

"Captain Barchet," I said, "If I were you I'd put it in the circular file."

He said, "That's exactly what I'm going to do."

He threw it in the trash basket.

Well, the second aspect was after the war they found a merchan derelict in the precise position that we had plotted our position and we had hit part of that sunken ship.

Loughlin #2 -89-

Q: You mean they didn't know it was there?

Adm. L.: That's a true story. I knew that I couldn't have hit the bottom with the thing. But, they found this hulk.

Q: You said you had some training in wolf pack. Tell me about that. Was it copied from the Germans?

Adm. L.: No, I think this was our own idea. Not mine, but the submarine force. What they did, they had a big war game board out in Pearl. I think I made a mistake. We really didn't have any wolf pack training in New London Sound, it wasn't big enough. But, they had a big war game board up in Pearl when you got out there. Normally the wolf pack consisted of three submarines. There was a wolf pack commander and they stressed area coverage and communications primarily. I was in a wolf pack on all four of my runs. We each had certain areas and if any of us made a contact, the first thing you did was get a contact report off telling where it is.

Q: So it was really cooperation.

Adm. L.: It just expanded the area covered. As long as the Skippers did their job and as long as the communication system worked it paid dividends.

Q: Was that any different than the Germans in the Atlantic?

Adm. L.: You know, Jack, you would know so much more about this. I thought most of the German submarine warfare was more or less on an independent basis.

Q: Oh, no.

Adm. L.: Well, certainly at the beginning of the war.

Q: Yes, at the beginning, yes. But, they developed the wolf pack technique when they would shadow a convoy.

Adm. L.: What it does is get a concentration of submarines in one place. That's the object of the exercise.

Q: Yes. I would think it would build up confidence in the Skipper of the individual submarine also, to know that he had some confrere right near.

Adm. L.: That, and also they were covering areas that you couldn't cover.

Q: Yes. Did you find everything in working order when the USS QUEENFISH started out on her trial runs?

Adm. L.: It's amazing. We had no trouble whatsoever. No mechanical breakdowns. No machinery breakdowns. We had the Fairbanks-Morse engines. The most reliable engines ever built I guess.

Q: Spare parts available?

Adm. L.: Yes.

Q: Did you take spare parts with you or did you rely on--?

Adm. L.: We had quite a bit, but, of course, during the refit period where ever it might be at Pearl or Guam, anything that went wrong that you couldn't repair onboard was taken care of during the refit period. But, I can't recall any major casualty or defect the whole time we had the USS QUEENFISH.

Q: You're on operational duty the minute these trial runs are over and you're en route to the Pacific.

Adm. L.: Except we stopped by Key West and fired these Mark XXIII's for eight or ten days before we deployed.

Q: Did you sight any Germans en route?

Adm. L.: I think we were more worried about our own aircraft than we were about the Germans. A classmate of mine, "Penrod" Schneider, was sunk on his way down to the Canal Zone.*

Q: What special communications did you have to identify yourself?

Adm. L.: This was one of the weaknesses during the whole war. you just couldn't talk with the airplanes. Whether it was their fault or our fault I don't know.

Q: Or whether it was trigger happy.

Adm. L.: Well, it was in this case. But, even if you tried to. For instance, we were in air-sea rescue operations covering the B-29 raids over Japan and when the fighter planes finally got up near Formosa and the B-24's would fly over us I never could raise them on the radio. I don't know whether it was our fault or if it was their fault. We never were bombed by anybody of our own planes.

Q: Did you encounter any blimps off the coast?

---

*Lieutenant Commander Earle Caffrey Schneider, USN, was commanding officer of the USS Dorado (SS-248) which departed New London, Connecticut 6 October 1943, bound for the Canal Zone.

Loughlin #2 -92-

Adm. L.: No. Jimmy Fife was quite a believer in the blimps, you know.

Q: Yes, I know.

Adm. L.: I made him mad by saying, "Admiral you can see that blimp for thirty miles way up there in the sky. You aren't going anywhere near him. You'll change course and get the hell out of there."

He said, "Ah, you don't know what you're talking about."

Q: So there was no incidents on your way out to Pearl. Charles Lockwood was in Pearl at that time?

Adm. L.: Yes, sir. Dick Voge was the Operations Officer.

Q: That was quite a team wasn't it?

Adm. L.: Yes. Bill Irvin was the Communications Officer.

Q: So, when did you arrive out at Pearl?

Adm. L.: The Fourth of July, I believe. Around the Fourth.

Q: And you didn't go on your first mission until?

Adm. L.: Not until August because I had to spend about three weeks firing, taking the staff out and demonstrating this Mark XXIII torpedo. I think we left in August for the first run. This was late in the war, but it was also the apex of the submarine sinkings August, September.

Q: Yes, there was good pickings at that point, weren't there?

Adm. L.: There certainly was.

Q: And, why was that? I mean, the Japanese didn't have enough escort vessels?

Adm. L.: Well, I never ran across anybody that was not escorted. Every attack I ever made there were escorts all around.

Q: Adequate escorts?

Adm. L.: Well, they weren't adequate because, one, I always have claimed the Japanese were blind. Their night vision I mean. A lot of them didn't have radar and the radar they did have was not efficient. They had good sonar; once they detected you, they were pretty good at keeping contact.

Q: But they weren't efficient in radar?

Adm. L.: I made most of my attacks on the surface at night. To the best of my knowledge I was never detected by radar during night surface attacks.

Q: Tell me about your first tour in the wolf pack out to Luzon Strait.

Adm. L.: The first or second day there George Pierce who had the USS TUNNY got caught in the late afternoon by a plane coming out of the sun. It bombed him. Gene Fluckey saw the attack. I didn't. I was looking in another direction, too far away. Apparently he dived, the the bomb did damage to a vent uptake within the boat and then he couldn't dive, or if he dived he couldn't stay down. He had to go all the way back to Mare Island. So, he had one day on patrol. That left Fluckey in the USS BARB and Swinburne was riding the USS BARB, and the USS QUEENFISH, that left us there as a modified wolf pack.

For a first run it was very exciting. Many stories to tell. I guess the first attack was the most exciting that we had. We sank the ship the first--

Q: Because it was a first attack.

Adm. L.: And, also you sank a ship too. But, I think there were two incidents in particular that come to mind, perhaps three. One of them is that we made a second attack on that same convoy the next night.

Q: That was a very large convoy, wasn't it?

Adm. L.: Yes. It was. Then a couple of days later in a flat calm sea in midafternoon we detected a convoy by spotting smoke. We were submerged. I was pretty far off the track. I probably could have gotten in if I used all my batteries, but I said, "The heck with it." So, we just watched and let them go by. They were way out of torpedo range. I surfaced as soon as I could and then started what we called making an end around.

Q: You obviously weren't trigger happy at that point, were you?

Adm. L.: I just thought the odds, we were way out in the open sea and I had complete confidence that we could make an end around and get in position and make a submerged attack at night.

They had a plane that was patrolling. He made us dive two or three times. We would pick him up on the SJ radar, not the SD radar, but the SJ radar. Once the range was forty-three hundred and closing and we dived. As soon as we started to dive the range began to open, so we came right back up again.

But, the particular thing I had in mind was the Exec wanted me to bore in. When we got abeam of them to go ahead and make the attack.

I said, "No, no. I'm going to get up ahead of them."

We were gaining ground on them all the time. I wanted to get up ahead of them some more and make the attack from ahead. We had quite a little discussion about it. There was no anger or anything, it was just a frank discussion. I guess you know who won.

Q: The Skipper did, naturally.

Adm. L.: We got ahead and we made the dive. We passed immediately under the convoy escort and then sank two ships. From then on-

Q: There was no arguing about the technique.

Adm. L.: I'm talking about the crew. From then on this spread among the crew. They said, "Well, the Exec wanted to do this and the Cap wanted to do this and we sank two ships."

I think that instilled more confidence in them, the officers and the crew than anything else.

Q: And, one of those two ships was a tanker wasn't it?

Adm. L.: No, that was in the first attack. We got a big transport on that other attack. I say a big one, I think it was eight or nine thousand tons.

Then there were two other incidents noteworthy. You're familiar with the USS PAMPANITO and her sinking the Japanese transport with the British and Australian prisoners of war.

Q: Yes, yes.

Adm. L.: We were just about to make a submerged patrol in the Luzon Strait when, just before we dived actually,---

Q: That was in September wasn't it?

Adm. L.: We got this dispatch from ComSubPac which said, proceed umpty-ump to pick up prisoner of war survivors. The umpty-ump was about four or five hundred miles away. I only had four torpedo left. So, I immediately got a dispatch off and said, "Am complying with ComSubPac umpty-ump." In the meantime with four engines on the line we're heading due west and a few minutes later they answered and voice radio came back and said, "What is ComSubPac umpty-ump?"

Well, the point of the story is had Gene dived before he got my dispatch, he wouldn't have gotten that until the next transmission which would have been from two to four hours. So, he wouldn't have gotten this dispatch which I had gotten.

The sequel of it is that night I ran smack into a tremendous convoy and didn't attack until I passed the word on to Gene and got him in position. We made a night surface attack and fired our last four torpedoes and got one hit on a huge ship. We thought it was a carrier. He got away and we went around and trailed from the stern. My Exec said, "The blips disappeared. I think we sank the ship."

I said, "I don't know how we'd do it with one hit."

Just about that time, wham, I saw this huge tanker go up in flames. Gene had gotten it.

Well, later on I found out that he didn't know what he was firing at either. He fired one salvo and he sank a twenty-two thousand ton aircraft carrier and a twelve thousand ton tanker. Thirty-six thousand tons in one salvo.

The point of the story is had he dived he might never have gotten in on the convoy if he hadn't gotten the dispatch we had sent him.

Q: Tell me about picking up the survivors?

Adm. L.: After that I had no torpedoes left so we beat it on out there and I happened to get there about a half an hour ahead of Gene. We picked up, I think, sixteen survivors. At that time a typhoon was approaching. It wasn't that rough, but all the signs were there. I think Gene picked up around twelve or thirteen.

Q: How many survivors could you carry?

Adm. L.: Well, the USS SEALION and the USS PAMPANITO, I think the USS SEALION picked up around seventy. They must have just put them in droves and stacked them.

The only trouble we had was three, or two of ours died and we had to bury them at sea.

Q: What was the state of the survivors?

Adm. L.: They had been in the water five nights and four days. Just driftwood. No life raft, no nothing, no food, no water. The most horrible human beings you've ever seen in your life. We had to send swimmers out.

Q: They weren't even rational were they?

Adm. L.: One of them was. A guy named Bancroft, an Australian. He was helped aboard by a swimmer to the bow plane, to the deck. He staggered toward me, I was on the bridge, shook his fist and said, "I knew you bloody Yankees would pick us up."

He slept for twenty-four hours and then from then on he was up and around the ship for the rest of the patrol.

Q: He was a toughie wasn't he?

Adm. L.: He's still alive too. But, two of ours died and we had to bury them at sea. The typhoon did come up that night. If we hadn't gotten them, the ones that were left they would have certainly have been drowned.

Q: Did you stay on the surface for that typhoon?

Adm. L.: Oh, yes, yes. Then I was running short of fuel and had to go back to Saipan. So, we set sail for Saipan and got there without incident.

Q: What happened if you did run out of fuel?

Adm. L.: Well, you're not supposed to run out.

Q: But sometimes, in certain circumstances I would think it would happen. Didn't it happen on occasion?

Adm. L.: I don't know of any. Well, what you would do, Jack, you'd just slow to one engine and just make five, six or seven knots. Your fuel consumption would be just a fraction of what it would be if you had two engines or four engines on line.

I understand that the first indication that the State Department knew, you know these survivors had been from the HMAS PERTH. Was it the HOUSTON, the two cruisers that were sunk under the Dutch right after in the spring of 1942?

Q: The PERTH and the USS HOUSTON.

Adm. L.: The USS HOUSTON, Yes. I understand that until they got our dispatches identifying these prisoners of war, that this was the first knowledge that the State Department knew there were survivors of the sinking of those two cruisers. This had happened, what, two and half years before?

Q: Yes. Quite some time before this. Where had they been?

Adm. L.: In a prison camp near Singapore. They were transporting them back from Singapore to Japan.

Q: I see. They were going back as laborers I understand.

Interview No. 3 with Rear Admiral Charles Elliott Loughlin, U.S. Na
(Retired)

Place: Annapolis, Maryland

Date: Friday, 5 September 1980

Subject: Biopgraphy

By: John T. Mason, Jr.

Q: Last time, as we concluded, you had run out of torpedoes, you were running out of fuel, you were going back to resupply.

Adm. L.: For what we call a refit.

Q: Were you going back to Pearl?

Adm. L.: No, to Majuro.

Q: Do you want to take up the story at that point? How long did the refit take?

Adm. L.: We got back to Saipan and discharged the poor souls who were in fairly good shape. I guess it took us three, four, or five days to get back.

Q: You lost two enroute you said.

Adm. L.: Yes, they died and we had to bury them at sea.

Q: Did you read the service?

Adm. L.: No, Commander Bennett did. He was the number three officer. He was really more, he was in charge of the rescue operation on deck. So, I thought it was appropriate for him to do it. He knew these people and was with them every day and almost every minute for the whole time we were on the way back.

Well, we got to Majuro without any undue problems and refit and then went back on our second patrol after two weeks.

Q: And, on the second patrol in November we find you at it again.

Adm. L.: We were very fortunate. We were given two most productive areas for the first two runs.

Q: This was in Luzon Straits still?

Adm. L.: No, this was up in, we made passage through south of Kyushu and were in the Yellow Sea right off the Western Coast of Japan.

Q: That was an even more dangerous area for operating wasn't it?

Adm. L.: It was very shallow. That's what made it dangerous.

Q: Shallow to what extent? How deep could you dive?

Adm. L.: A couple of bad depth charge attacks we had we were very fortunate to be in fairly deep water, four or five hundred feet, but most of the area in which we operated was around a hundred and fifty, a hundred and sixty, or a hundred and seventy feet. Just like the Taiwan Strait between China and Taiwan where I made my last two, my third and fourth runs.

Q: So, that meant that you couldn't in that kind of water you could only dive about a hundred feet?

Adm. L.: Or a hundred and twenty or thirty, something like that.

Q: Then what about the depth charges if they went down lower and exploded did they?

Adm. L.: Well, really, the only two bad depth charge attacks we received were in deep enough water so that we could go down as deep as we wanted to. In the first one we attacked a convoy which was the only persistent depth charge attack the USS QUEENFISH received in all four runs. He just stayed with us for five, six, or seven hours. I remember it distinctly. It was an Armistice Day, November the Eleventh.

Q: Would a submarine be in danger even though submerged and not hit by a depth charge and not damaged from one dropped from above, but if it, in shallow water, went down below and exploded?

Adm. L.: Well, they all explode, to my knowledge, on depth. That is the pressure. So, if they are set deeper than the depth of the water they wouldn't explode, Jack. They would just hit in the mud and just stay there. As a matter of fact, we had a very unusual occurrence there, I didn't but Captain Foley, I think he was in the USS GATO, I'm not sure, but he had the surprise of his life when he surfaced after a depth charge attack and found a depth charge sitting on the stern of his submarine. In other words, at the depth that it hit was above the depth it was set to go off. So, had he gone any deeper he would, of course, have lost his boat. When he came to the surface, here was a depth charge sitting on the stern of his submarine.

Q: So, it was removed without any great fear?

Adm. L.: Just push it off. A very hairy experience I would think.

Q: On this patrol on November Eighth you were credited with a couple of successful sinkings.

Adm. L.: I forget how many we sank. I think it was three and damaged two or three. We had one very fine periscope attack in day light. Again, it was not too deep, but we picked up this convoy while we were submerged. You remember I spoke of this act of pinging the active sonar. You can hear that from your passive sonar for miles. We made initial contact of this convoy by hearing the pinging, the ping sounds from the destroyers. We headed toward the general bearing. I stayed at periscope depth without exposing my periscope and passed under the convoy which we'd done the first run at night. Then I was able to stick the scope up and we saw this aircraft carrier. We call it an aircraft carrier. It had a flight deck full of planes. We got four torpedoes off and got two hits. The three destroyers were practically looking down our throat.

Just sheer luck, I guess, or blind luck, I fired stern tubes and then turned toward the ship that we had fired at and made a complete circle, if you follow me.

Q: Yes, I do.

Adm. L.: The destroyers were only a thousand yards away. Three of them were just barreling down on us because they saw my scope.

We fired electric torpedoes so they didn't see the wake, but they saw the periscope. What happened we found out later was we sank this ship and by turning towards the ship we passed so close that they didn't drop any depth charges on us because these people were all in the water.

Q: You talked about lady luck and she was there then, wasn't she?

Adm. L.: We just made a complete three hundred and sixty degree turn and just snuck away and never had a depth charge dropped on us.

Q: In the attack on November eight/nine you were credited with three freighters. Now, these were small freighters which were being escorted from the mainland of China to Japan?

Adm. L.: We were fairly close to the Western shore of Kyushu. There were escorts, but it was a night surface attack and we didn't get any counter measures at all except at the very end. We didn't know if a ship had blown up or what, but there was a terrible explosion which sounded like it was directly above us. We submerge of course, after the attack. We fired our torpedoes. To this day I don't know if it was just somebody just lying there trying to catch us asleep or whether it was one of the ships blowing up. It was a terrific explosion. It sounded like it was directly above us.

Q: With these successful sinkings and so many, actually the morale on board must have been extremely high.

Adm. L.: Yes, sir, it was. I think everyone had confidence in me as Commanding Officer, which I think is the main thing. Then, of course, as I said, we had a real expert ward room crew and a real expert crew. So, we had everything going for us, plus luck.

Q: The submarine that seemed to always be accompanying you was that Gene Fluckey's -BARB?

Adm. L.: Gene Fluckey and the USS BARB.

Q: Tell me about Gene Fluckey.

Adm. L.: One of the finest Naval officers and one of the finest submarine officers I've ever known. Absolutely superb man and a superb submarine Skipper, and a superb Naval Officer. One of my best friends.

Q: Then on the fifteenth of November we have that big Japanese convoy taking the twenty-third Japanese Infantry contingent from Manchuria to the Philippines. You got in on that action. That's when you sank, you thought she was a carrier, but it turned out to be --

Adm. L.: It's in the Submarine Operations of World War II. With all due respect I only had about three looks at her through the periscope and she had a flight deck and it was full of planes, so it was an error which certainly could be excused.

Q: I would think so too.

Adm. L.: As a matter of fact, in the Submarine Operations of World War II they devoted several paragraphs to this ship because she had been mistaken as a carrier many times and survived numerous torpedo attacks. We finally got her. I think it was called the AKITSU MARU.

Q: She was a fairly sizeable ship too. Almost ten thousand tons..

Adm. L.: But, anytime you see a flight deck loaded with planes, why with a brief glimpse through a periscope you're going to call it a carrier. She was a plane carrier, but she was not an aircraft carrier.

Q: Tell me some detail about your attack on her.

Adm. L.: As I said, we passed underneath the convoy at periscope depth. In other words, sixty-five, sixty-seven feet. As soon as I could tell that the escorts had passed by me, we were on an opposite course, of course. We were heading toward the convoy and the convoy had passed over me. We were already at periscope depth so all I had to do was raise periscope and the first target I saw was this carrier. So, we got a very quick set up on it and took what we called single ping range. I believe the range was around twelve or thirteen hundred yards which is a very decent attack. I only had stern tubes left, so we fired four stern tubes shots and we got two hits. We then took the evasive action which I've already mentioned. We were very fortunate to get away complete scot-free. It was a flat calm sea.

Q: And very vigilant escorts for a valuable convoy like that.

Adm. L.: Yes, sir. As a matter of fact, that night, this happened sometime in the afternoon, not too late in the afternoon, it was early afternoon when we finally got away and surfaced at night. Everything was nice and calm and all of a sudden the diving alarm went. I was in the control room and couldn't see anything of course, until we got down and Jack Bennett who was the officer of the deck, "What happened?"

He said, "Well, we saw this flashing light real close aboard and I didn't know what it was, so I thought the best thing to do was to dive."

In retrospect we found out it was the survivors from this ship in life rafts or life boats. We were just a few miles away from them.

The reason we knew we had sunk the ship was because all I did, really, was claim damage at the time for a few hours. But ComSubPac with their intercepted messages sent us a message of congratulations saying that if you look at longtitude and latitude umpty-ump, umpty-ump you will see many, many Nips in the water. So, that's how we knew we'd sunk the darned ship.

Q: Will you talk a little about sending in reports on what damage you had accomplished in an attack? How careful were you?

Adm. L.: Well, we never found, our experience was the Japs never intercepted our dispatches. The format at the time was to give a pretty complete report if you could get it off. In other words, you gave the latitude and the longtitude and type of ship and all kinds of information which really wasn't necessary until you wrote your patrol report. Apparently ComSubPac wanted this type of information. The only trouble we ever had was getting somebody to come up and receive the message. You could spend a half an hour or an hour or more trying to raise some station. We had stations in Australia that we were able to raise and who received our messages and transmitted them on to Guam or back to Pearl. As I say, we never had any trouble with radio interception. So, if you were clear and on the surface and could transmit, why we never had any fear that anybody would--

Q: That the information would do damage to you?

Adm. L.: That's right, or they would intercept our transmission and be able to pinpont us which, of course, we could do. The U.S. Navy could, but the Japanese Navy could not do.

Q: You say that Lockwood wanted this information sent in by dispatc almost immediately. What were they doing, releasing this to the press?

Adm. L.: Oh, no.

Q: I thought PR business--

Adm. L.: No, sir. Not to my knowledge.

Q: It was still the silent service.

Adm. L.: I was at sea. I don't know what they did. But, I serious doubt that they used any public relations in giving any details of any damage the ship had done.

Q: Well, certainly the Japanese did all the time with Tokyo Rose.

Adm. L.: Of course, they exaggerated an awful lot.

I'm sure that on a real outstanding patrol, like a Medal of Honor. Like Red Ramage and Gene Fluckey and George Street, the three that come to mind they would give some details as the number of ships that were sunk, but I don't think they would ever give the area where--

Q: Oh, no, I'm sure of that, but making claims of what was done- this was good for the morale of the nation.

Adm. L.: Yes, but I think the morale of the submariners was more important. In other words, they would put out a dispatch every night giving the success of various submarines that had occurred that particular day or night. So, you knew what the rest of the sub force was doing. In other words, they would say the USS BARB had sunk three ships or the USS BATFISH had sunk two submarines or somebody had sunk this, or somebody had sunk that. This was just a general information dispatch which went to all submarines.

Q: During these patrols did you ever come across any Japanese submarines. They were using them extensively I think for varying purposes.

Adm. L.: I never saw one except the midget submarine which tried to sink us twice on the first run. But, Jake Fyfe on the USS BATFISH operating around the Philippines was able to detect, I think he sank two, either two or three on one patrol.

Q: They were supplying their own bases, their own men on outlying islands.

Adm. L.: They had spasmodic, I would call it, success. I mean the INDIANAPOLIS at the end of the war was sunk by a Japanese submarine. I'm sure we lost at least one or two submarines because the Japanese caught them on the surface. A very fortuitous, lucky situation. Normally they used them for supply. They did not use their Japanese submarines in any kind of an offensive way in terms in which the US and Germany did. They were, more or less, used to supply the isolated island stations, like Wake and other islands where they had men.

Q: It certainly was a necessity on their part.

Adm. L.: Yes, it was.

Q: They also early on they brought supplies from Germany.

Adm. L.: They had German submarines operating in the Pacific?

Q: The Japanese would get supplies from Germany and bring them back.

Adm. L.: I didn't realize that. I did know there were German submarines, we received intelligence, that were operating in the Pacific. What their function was, I don't know, whether it was a supply function or not.

Q: After the attack on this large convoy, was this the end of this patrol?

Adm. L.: Yes, I think so. I think it was the last attack we made. I'm not sure whether we had any torpedoes left or not. But, we were sent back.

Q: The next reference to you is December-January. This was in

November.

Adm. L.: We went back to Guam. We were one of the first submarines to refit in Guam.

Q: Lockwood was there then?

Adm. L.: Yes, sir. He was there.

Q: And Nimitz was there also?

Adm. L.: Yes sir. That was a rather unusual experience. When we went out to the rest camp after we arrived at Guam, Eli Reich had just come in with the USS SEALION. He had sunk this battleship, in this famous torpedo attack. I guess the only battleship sunk in World War II. So, Eli and I guess it was the Squadron Commander, whom I can't remember who it was, went out in a jeep to the rest camp which was, oh, some fifteen or twenty miles away. On the way back Japanese snipers attacked the jeep.

Q: There were plenty of them on the island.

Adm. L.: Still alive. We got to the rest camp without any strain, but on the way back Eli was enroute to Pearl. He'd just come into Guam to be debriefed by ComSubPac. So, he just went out to visit the rest camp and then came back the same day with the Squadron Commander and the Japanese snipers tried to get him. But, they didn't do any damage.

Q: You needed a convoy when you were going to the rest camp.

Adm. L.: That's right.

Q: What sort of rest facilities did they provide?

Adm. L.: Well, they were all quonset huts. Both for enlisted and the officers. We had liquor and beer, softball, The USO did a magnificent job during the war as far as I'm concerned. I remember Frank Leahy (Notre Dame) offered to come down and brief the USS QUEENFISH crew just by himself on football. Everyone was interested in sports of course. And, who was the famous banjo player? I never thought I'd forget his name, but they would have these organized USO tours that would come in there and put on magic shows and musicals, Really, USO I think--

Q: How many days would you have?

Adm. L.: Two weeks, I think.

Q: That's great for unwinding.

Adm. L.: Yes, sir. And we did unwind. We had what we called a refit crew from the tender that actually took over the submarine and the whole crew, officers and men, abandoned ship.

Q: You pay no more attention to it.

Adm. L.:No, not quite. But, we'd leave the job orders of what had to be done. Then we would have an officer come in everyday to check on the work to be sure it was done.

Q: Very sensible precaution.

Adm. L.: He didn't spend the night as I recall. But he would come in everyday and go over the work orders and go over the work

Loughlin #3 -113-

and keep an eye on things. Then he would come back and give us a report. So, it was not a hardship for anyone. Everybody got their two weeks rest.

Q: They got adequate spare parts?

Adm. L.: Oh, yes, sir. But, again, luck comes into it. We had no major casualties the whole time I had the submarine. We never had that problem, never.

Q: You were by that time one of Admiral Lockwood's fair-haired boys. Did you see him in Guam?

Adm. L.: Yes, sir. He would have us in for dinner one night when we first came in. He would stop by and talk to the staff and get briefed for the next patrol run. Dick Voge was just a magnificent person. He was his Operations Officer during the whole war. There is no finer person, really, in the submarine service than Dick Voge. He was universally respected and admired. He ran the show for Admiral Lockwood. There is no question about it.

Q: Lockwood himself was very close to Nimitz. That's one reason he moved there in Guam.

Adm. L.: He was close to him and so close that Admiral Nimitz refused to let him go on war patrol. He did ride a boat from Pearl to Midway once in a while. But, he would not permit him to go on war patrol. Whereas Jimmy Fife could and did.

I told you this story didn't I about after the war when he had all the four star admirals, three star admirals here at a parade?

Loughlin #3 -114-

Q: No.

Adm. L.: Well, this broke my heart really. I have nothing but respect for Admiral Fife. I mean I served with him as Operations Officer after the war. I know he did a wonderful job down in the southwest Pacific, but--

Q: But, as an active officer he wasn't that loveable was he?

Adm. L.: Well, there is a difference between love and respect. I think everybody respected Admiral Fife. But, all of these four and three star admirals, Halsey, and King, and I think Admiral Nimitz was there.

Q: Was that the Operation REMEMBER?

Adm. L.: No, it was a dress parade right here at the Naval Academy. And, lo and behold Admiral Fife shows up as a full admiral because he had made a war patrol and had gotten a decoration. He got an automatic advance from three stars to four stars and Admiral Lockwo who was not permitted to make a war patrol was there as a three star admiral.

Q: One of those distinctions. One of those fine distinctions. Well, there was another Operation REMEMBER in New York after the war and they all paraded.

Adm. L.: It probably was in the same series--

Q: It was a tour they were making.

Adm. L.: But, this was a dress parade they were making right here at the Naval Academy. I was here.

There is an interesting thing happened as we left on this third patrol--Kenny Nauman who had the USS SALMON was forced to surface from a depth charge attack and had a running surface battle with a destroyer. He couldn't dive and he was able to get away. It was a tremendous exhibition of courage and will to get out.

That got a lot of publicity within the submarine force. That happened just before we left to go on this third patrol run, again with the USS BARB. That was three straight I made with the USS BARB and the USS PICUDA.

Q: And, this was a slightly different locale. Wasn't it the Formosa strait?

Adm. L.: This was the Formosa strait, yes sir. We had to go all the way north. We transited into the islands the same transit we made on the second run because of this huge mine field that ostensibly existed from the tip of Formosa which ran Northeast all the way up to the Western side of Okinawa. You couldn't get through. You had to go all the way up and then down.

Q: We knew the extent of that mine field.

Adm. L.: Yes, sir. Apparently they had gotten some documents or interrogation or something, but there was intelligence. Roughly they knew the location. But, it meant a real long way Northwest and then due South for two or three hundred miles in order to get down into the Formosa strait between Formosa and mainland China.

Q: Perhaps you should be diverted for a moment to talk about the value of intelligence of that sort in operational warfare.

Adm. L.: I think I mentioned this before that we knew about ULTRA. But, the only attack that I made in four war patrols based on ULTRA was the very first one. The very first one. Now, we'd get ULTRA messages, but I was never able to take advantage of them. Either the Japanese would change course or change rendezvous or change locations. But, this was the only one I was able to get in. The mine fields were, I think, particularly important although we did lose submarines in mine fields. I'm sure Moke Millican in the USS ESCOLAR was lost in a minefield. I know there was another one lost in a mine field. So, it certainly wasn't a hundred percent intelligence. But, at least it gave you the general location to steer clear of. But, undoubtedly, there are two submarines that I'm convinced we lost to mines and maybe more to Japanese mines.

Q: After that little diversion, go back to the patrol that made you not so happy.

Adm. L.: Well, I think I ought to preface this by saying that an incident happened on the second patrol which enabled us to get in position for this unsuccessful attack. During the second patrol Gene Fluckey had contact on a carrier and had fired either four or six torpedoes and had gotten either one or two hits and had damaged it. He reported it to us on the wolf pack frequency. He didn't give us the course and speed. So, I waited and waited and waited as I knew he was busy and might have even been submerged by that time. I finally sent him INT, (interrogatory course and speed), which he had failed to give. By the time we got it we headed over toward the general direction and we picked the carrier up on radar, but we could not get in firing position. It kind of irritated me considerably because it was just a bust on his Communication Officer or somebody on the USS BARB not passing the word down to the other members of the wolf pack.

So, on this third run we got this contact report from Fluckey on the convoy which was proceeding from mainland China over to Taiwan. Knowing what had happened on the previous run Gene stayed on the surface and trailed him and kept giving us contact report until both the USS PICUDA and the USS QUEENFISH were able to make radar contact. This was a night attack. When we acknowledged to Gene that we had contact I sent the USS PICUDA one place, I took one place and I knew where Gene was. He wreaked havoc on that convoy. I have never seen so many ships go up in smoke. Ammunition still kicking, the sea exploding and we got right in the middle of this thing and fired all of our torpedoes at decent ranges; decent, well, everything was perfect. Never got detected. This was all on the surface. And, we didn't get a single hit. We had over fifty percent hits the first two runs with the same fire control party.

Q: How do you account for it?

Adm. L.: I account for it in this manner; when we came back from that run the sub base went over our fire control system with a fine tooth comb and could find nothing wrong. We had the same fire control officers and enlisted men. The same ones we had had before, two consecutive runs. This is the third run. The same TDC operator. Everyone the same. The tender that had been in Guam, this was the first load of Mark XVIII torpedoes that they had gotten ready. The very first load. I never used this as an alibi, but I just can't help from thinking that those torpedo were not made ready in the proper fashion. I was on the bridge and it was incredible to fire and see the ships. It was at night, but hell, I could see the ships. Our bearings were perfect on the thing and to have these submarine torpedoes go out and nothing happen. So, I really believe it was the fault of the tender in making ready the torpedoes.

Q: And, that was true of all of the torpedoes you carried on that tour?

Adm. L.: The last four we fired was at an escorted ship.

Q: It was a tanker?

Adm. L.: A tanker. I did a very foolhardy thing. I was so damned mad. We went in on a straight shot towards his beam. In other words, this ship was, say, proceeding on a due south course and we were on a due east course. A destroyer was on a due south course on our side of this one ship. I kept boring in until I got within firing distance and fired my torpedoes, fired four torpedoes and at that time this destroyer was only eight hundred yards from me. I was giving him a ninety degree aspect. He was headed right for my beam. He never saw me. We got two hits on this tanker. The destroyer veered off to the left over towards where the tanker was and we got out of there and never had to dive. But, it was really a foolhardy thing to do. All this guy had to do, if he saw me--

Q: Just laid yourself open.

Adm. L.: Laid ourselves wide open. So, Gene said, I queried him later on the wolf pack frequency. He said the ship sunk. But, I notice in the war patrol that three of us were given credit. In other words, there were so many ships sunk. The USS PICUDA sank two. I think Gene sank four or five on this one. So it was all in the same action. I don't think they could really separate the pieces. I think three of us, if you look in the <u>World War II Operations</u>, I think all three of us were given credit for sinking this one ship.

Q: Blair gives you credit for having two hits.

Adm. L.: I saw the two hits.

Q: But, that doesn't say you sank it.

Adm. L.: Well, Gene said we did and he was on the surface in that area.

Q: He was master minding that whole attack.

Adm. L.: So, I turned around and got the heck out of there because here this destroyer was only eight hundred yards from me.

No, we know we got two hits. We know that.

Then the last four torpedoes I had, it was the only time in my life that I fired on an unescorted ship. There was a ship plowing up the coast there and we got in perfect position with a very small range and fired four torpedoes and zero hits. Then we came on home, back to Pearl. So, we got two hits out of twenty-four torpedoes after getting over fifty percent on the previous two runs.

Q: That sort of deflated your balloon didn't it. Gosh.

Adm. L.: It was a grievous disappointment.

Q: But, that's when you had the careful inspection.

Adm. L.: Yes, sir. When we got back to Pearl. It was so incredible really. All you had to do was read the war patrol or talk to me or talk to the other officers. It was just a situation which you just couldn't explain. So, the experts went over our whole fire control system and couldn't find anything wrong with it.

Q: The next torpedoes you took aboard were the Mark XVIII's also.

Adm. L.: Yes. I never fired anything but Mark XVIII's. That's all I fired.

Q: Now you begin your fourth patrol. After two weeks of rest?

Adm. L.: Yes, sir. We went out and stopped at Saipan for a briefing. This is the second step and I certainly won't go through all of the laborious steps which led to the sinking of the AWA MARU.

Loughlin #3 -121-

Q: You know, even though it's been written about I'd like for you to tell me the whole story.

Adm. L.: The first thing was that--well, I have to digress a second. On the way in to Saipan--Saipan, you know, was where we had a submarine tender. We were three thousand miles or more from Pearl and we're interecepting wolf pack frequencies that boats operating out of Pearl were using. This is unheard of. They were supposed to be good for only thirty or forty miles. The atmospheric conditions. Here we could listen plain as talking to you. Twenty-five hundred, three thousand miles away. Well, what had happened was ComSubPac had sent out a plain language dispatch and I must say this and I'll be the first to admit it, no one paid any attention to plain language dispatches during World War II. Anything that was important was classified.
Well, this plain language dispatch is the first dispatch which was sent out which gave the route of the AWA MARU. Because of the atmospheric conditions we could not get the complete transmission of it. We just didn't receive it. It caused no one, including me, any concern. One, it was plain language and two, we knew we would get it when we got to the tender in Saipan. O-kay?

Q: Yes. Did you have any background on this ship?

Adm. L.: No. No, not at that time. The second thing was, and this sounds again like bragging, but it isn't, I think I was one of the few submarines that instituted a procedure whereas the officer coming off watch had to break every dispatch that had been received during his four hours on watch. He could not turn in until he got to the code machine and broke every classified dispatch. Again, it caused us no concern because we knew we would get a copy when we got to Saipan.

We got to Saipan and we were briefed by an Operations Officer on the ComSubPac staff. No word was ever made of the AWA MARU in this briefing. It was missing. It should have been one of the main purposes of the briefing. In other words, they briefed you on the area, what ASW measures you could expect, the nearest airfields, the depth of water, minefields, and all that kind of information. Not a word was said about the AWA MARU.

So, we went on patrol. After we got on station I was working with Bill Post and the USS SPOT and Roy Klinker in the USS SEAFOX.

Well, Bill ran into a convoy and, again, didn't send out the contact report to the members of the wolf pack. He fired most of his torpedoes and then he was hauled off and either sent back home or given another area. I don't think he had many torpedoes left. This left the USS SEAFOX and the USS QUEENFISH alone.

They sent me back up to Shanghai on a, probably an ULTRA contact. I don't recall at the moment. But, on something that was supposed to be up there which wasn't there. When it didn't pan out we headed back toward our patrol area which was between Formosa and mainland China.

As we were diving one afternoon we received this ULTRA and decoded it while we were submerged. As soon as we decoded it we surfaced and headed toward this spot. In the meantime Klinker did the same thing that Bill Post did. He made contact on the convoy and did not send a contact report.

Loughlin #3 -123-

Q: How is that explained? Just the excitement of--

Adm. L.: No, I asked him about it. I don't know what Bill Post did, maybe Bill Post sent it out and we didn't receive it. But, Klinker admitted that he didn't send it out because he said, "I thought you were up at Shanghai." And, I said, "Gee, Roy, that's beside the point where you thought I was, the doctrine is any time you make a contact you send out a contact report to the wolf pack."

He admitted he was wrong. But, the point is had we gotten that, or had he sent us a contact report we very easy could have been a hundred miles away from where we actually did pick up the AWA MARU the next night. Maybe it was even that night. I'm not sure. It was probably the next night. This was on the fourth patrol. This was in April. The first of April.

Well, a couple of nights before we picked up the AWA MARU and saw this big light and didn't know whether it was the moon rising or not, but actually it was a hospital ship. It was clear and we could see the cross and lights and everything. So, we just got out of the way and let it go. I only mention this to indicate that this deliberate firing at AWA MARU was not deliberate. I mean anyone who saw a hospital ship let it go by.

Let it go, of course. So, we picked up this contact at night on the radar with a heavy fog. It was a heavy fog. You couldn't see, someone said two hundred yards. It wasn't anywhere near two hundred yards. You could barely see past the bow. We got into a range of seventeen-thousand yards, as I recall, which is just about the range that you would pick up a destroyer with the SJ radar. Just about that range. We tracked it and it was tracking at sixteen knots. A single ship, unescorted. We got into position to fire, and, oh, wait, I'm ahead of my story.

The night before we'd gotten the first dispatch that I saw. It was addressed to every submarine from Australia to the Aleutian Islands. Every submarine.

Q: Again, a clear dispatch?

Adm. L.: No, this was classified about the AWA MARU saying it was going to pass through, I can quote it today, "It will pass through your area. Let it pass clear." The white, I mean, the crosses and lighted and all this stuff. "It will pass through your area" and it was addressed to every submarine from Australia up to the Aleutian Islands.

I said to myself, "Gee, this is the most stupid dispatch I've ever seen in my life. Why, in God's name, don't they tell us what area he's going to be in. Here, he could be any place."

So, I did have that knowledge. I saw that dispatch. That was my first knowledge of the AWA MARU being anywhere in the Western Pacific.

So, when we made this contact we thought it was a destroyer because of the range, because of the speed. He wasn't zig-zagging. So, we made an attack. I brought the spread in to three hundred feet. That was the length of a destroyer and set the fish at three feet which is due for a destroyer. We fired four torpedoes and got four hits from the stern tubes. Again, I fired from the stern tube because I thought if the guy detected me and turned towards me, at least I was going away from him. I could dive and get clear of him.

By the time I turned around--we saw two flashes. I think it was about a thousand yards range. As the torpedoes exploded we would see through the fog a dim flash. We could not only hear the hits, but we did see the flashes. By the time I turned around and headed back the ship had sunk.

We got back into the area in a few minutes and there were, oh, twenty, twenty-five people visible around the bow as we stopped to lay-to and they would push the life-lines away, the life-rings they would just push them away. We were under orders to bring back survivors from sunken ships if we could. This one person yelled, I didn't see him at the time, he yelled and I headed over toward him and threw him a life-ring. He grabbed it and we hauled him up the side of the ship as we were lying-to. He banged his head on the hull as we were hauling him up aboard and knocked himself out. We couldn't pick up anybody else because they wouldn't be picked up. This was around eleven o'clock or eleven-thirty at night and at six o'clock in the morning, why, Jack Bennett, who was Exec then, Harry Hicks had been detached, said, "We sank the AWA MARU."

Q: How did he determine that?

Adm. L.: The prisoner had recovered. So, we got a dispatch off to ComSubPac and then all hell broke loose.

But the point is if we hadn't told ComSubPac that we had sunk the AWA MARU the Japanese to this day would never known what happened. If we hadn't picked up the survivor I would have gone to my death bed insisting that we sank a destroyer.

Loughlin #3 -126-

Q: You might as well tell me the balance of this story now.

Adm. L.: Well, we were--Admiral King, as you probably know in his book by Mr. Buell, Professor Buell, said, "Have him relieved and give him a general court martial." Period. No details at all.

Q: It sounds like a typical King--

Adm. L.: No details at all. He didn't get any details for two, three or four days after he had given this order. So, they brought us back in and on the way in we were sent a dispatch about a PB4Y down and conducted a search for her and rescued thirteen aviators who had been in the water for four or five days.

Q: What condition were they in?

Adm. L.: Oh, they were in a life raft. They were in good condition. No strain. Then the next day after that, I think, Mr. Roosevelt died. It was the thirteenth in our time. I think it was the twelfth back here. We got back to Guam with the thirteen survivors I think there were thirteen. Admiral Lockwood met us and asked, "What happened?"

I said, "Well, Admiral Lockwood I just feel that 'we ain't been done right.'" I said, "The only thing I knew about the AWA MARU was the message we got the night before which said, 'let it pass clear and it's going to pass through your area." And, I said to myself and my officers, what area? What are are you talking about? It ranged from Australia to the Aleutain Islands. Every submarine in the Western Pacific was given this dispatch."

Then Bill Irvin who was the (ComSubPac) Communications Officer went down and when we'd been alongside the tender and the briefing the plain language dispatch had been delivered to the ship and my Communications Officer had seen it! And, had filed it without showing it to anybody else on the ship.

Q: What was his reason for doing that?

Adm. L.: Plain language again. I'll tell you, Jack, the layman doesn't understand that we really didn't pay any attention to a plain language dispatch.

Q: But, a submarine officer should have understood it out there in Guam?

Adm. L.: He certainly should have understood it. He was derelict in his duty and as much as I liked him I had to give him an unsat fitness report for failing to bring to the attention of the proper authority a dispatch which he himself had seen.
So, I got the general court.

Q: How soon after?

Adm. L.: Oh, three days, I guess. Two or three days. Maybe four days. Admiral Lockwood went back. He saw Admiral Nimitz, obviously, and I think he went back to see Admiral King. I think that's in Buell's book. He either saw Admiral King or Admiral Nimitz. He is on record saying, "If any fault occurred that he was equally responsible." That's a matter of record. He really went to bat.

King would have no part of it. He said, "No, nothing doing."

Admiral Lockwood did get Chester Bruton and a Lieutenant Colonel named Hoffman, in the Marine Corps to be my counsel.

Q: Chester Bruton had quite a reputation.

Adm. L.: Yes, sir. He was one of the few, he and George Russell and Ed Stephan, oh, there are four or five line officers who went to GW Law School who were commanding officers of submarines and yet were lawyers.

Well, the only thing that happened in the court which I, in retrospect, am sorry, as you probably know I was charged on three counts of deliberate disobedience of orders. I forget the other one and negligence. I was convicted of negligence which, in retrospect, was correct.

Q: That was the minor charge?

Adm. L.: Well, I don't know if it was minor. I was convicted of it primarily because it was obvious we didn't have a track on the AWA MARU. No one ever thought to ask the witnesses whether I knew where the AWA MARU was or not. That's the reason we didn't have a track on it. Nobody knew the darned ship was there.

But, Chester convinced me that the burden of proof was on the opposition, so to speak. He didn't think that I should take the stand. I think now, and I thought then that this whole thing would have been clarified had I taken the stand. I think I would have still been convicted of negligence.

Loughlin #3 -129-

Q: You mean you had to sit there and listen to the testimony, but you couldn't--

Adm. L.: I did not testify. You are not required to, as you well know either in civil or criminal cases.

Q: But, that's probably a mistake not to---

Adm. L.: In retrospect I think it was.

Q: Who sat on the court?

Adm. L.: Well, Genial John was the President, and a very, very fair person.* Very fair. Lew Parks, and Babe Brown were the two submariners. A Vice Admiral who had the battleship command. Isn't that strange, I can't remember his name.

Q: Willis Lee?

Adm. L.: No. Not Willis Lee. I can't remember his name. There was an aviation admiral. It was the highest ranking court that has ever been in the history of the Naval Service. I've been told this. I think there were two Vice Admirals and three Rear Admirals and two Captains.

Q: This was in response to King's reaction?

Adm. L.: Oh, he said "Relieve him and give him a general court."

Q: What was the basis of King's violent reaction to this?

Adm. L.: Well, the State Department had given this ship safe conduct and it embarrassed the State Department. It embarrassed the United States.

*Vice Admiral John H. Hoover, USN.

Loughlin #3 -130-

Q: So, how long did this ordeal last?

Adm. L.: Two days. The reason I say Admiral Hoover was so fair, McCutcheon was the Judge Advocate and he and his helper, whose name escapes me, asked me a couple of, I thought, stupid questions or made some stupid assertions. Bruton immediately objected. In other words, because I had fired it was deliberate. That's what their claim was.

Q: Proof of guilt.

Adm. L.: And, Admiral Hoover said objection sustained. Then once there was some testimony about the current, what the set was and what the drift was, and one officer contradicted the other of my own ship. Admiral Hoover just looked at me and said, "All right, this is off the record. Loughlin, what was the set and drift? Clarify this discrepancy between the two, off the record."

This I did. But, he didn't have to do that.

So, I got the letter of admonition, Jack, as you probably know. The members of the court got a letter of reprimand which is a more severe punishment than mine by Admiral Nimitz.

Q: Why did Nimitz react this way?

Adm. L.: He was so damned mad that they had only given me a letter of admonition.

Q: He shared King's point of view.

Adm. L.: Apparently so.

Loughlin #3 -131-

Q: It sounds rather surprising for Nimitz to react that way. He being a submariner himself.

Adm. L.: I'm making the supposition. I don't know, Jack. It could have been that King got on the horn and said to crucify these people on the court martial for letting this guy get away with something. That was the apparent end of my submarine career. Admiral Lockwood said "What do you want to do?"

I said, "Well, I've been relieved and I've made four runs. I'd like to go back to new construction."

By that time we didn't know the war was going to be over in six months. So he said, "Fine."

Q: Well, King had also said you couldn't have a command?

Adm. L.: No, not at that time. So, I went back to Pearl and was in the training Command. Admiral Babe Brown had been on the court and I was under his command there for a month, I guess. By that time the word had filtered down that I couldn't have a command.

Q: This was, again, King's orders?

Adm. L.: To the best of my knowledge it was, yes. The way it was explained to me, the rationale was, that if anything ever happened to me and they found out that I was the guy that sunk the AWA MARU that would be curtains. Well, I don't know if that is true or not. Or if they were using that as an excuse or not.

Q: What was the Japanese reaction, by way of propaganda from Tokyo?

Adm. L.: Gee, I don't know, Jack because the war was over so shortly after that. This was April, May, June, July, and August, four months later. I think they had other things to worry about than the AWA MARU. Of course, they had lost their very, very valuable ship.

Q: There is one aspect of it that you haven't mentioned on tape and that was that the ship was actually doing something it was not supposed to do which was bringing back needed supplies.

Adm. L.: That's not true. That's not correct.

Q: It isn't?

Adm. L.: My understanding is that the State Department gave them carte blanche permission to bring back anything they wanted to as long as they took the Red Cross supplies down.

Q: Oh, I see, they were able to do that?

Adm. L.: Dick Voge brought that up. He testified in my behalf and through intelligence he told the court what contraband, or what this ship's cargo consisted of and what it consisted of going down there. They took planes down. They took ammunition down. They took all kinds of things down in addition to the Red Cross supplies.

The court's attitude was, "How is Loughlin supposed to know that? He didn't know that. You can't use that as a justification for sinking the ship." And the court was right.

Q: You had picked up some bales of rubber?

Loughlin #3 -133-

Adm. L.: Yes. Rubber and some manganese, I guess it was. This same Communication Officer was a geologist, but he couldn't determine what these little bags were. I think it was manganese.

Q: How many members of your crew were called to testify?

Adm. L.: Golly, I can't remember.

Q: The Communication Officer did.

Adm. L.: Yes, sir. See, we stipulated, I didn't bring this out either, we stipulated that the message had been received. Which it had been.

Q: In the open?

Adm. L.: In plain language. I think this is the reason that nobody in the court saw fit, or even thought about, well if the ship stipulates that they received this dispatch, then the Commanding Officer must have seen it. But, nobody thought to ask that. Chester Bruton said, "Look, the log shows that you got it and the Saipan log shows that you got it so there is no sense of trying to deny that you didn't get it." So, that's what you call a stipulation. We stipulated that the message had been received.

Q: Lockwood was not present at that time. He was back in Washington?

Adm. L.: No, he was gone. The timing is a little bit off. I know I had dinner with him the night I got in. Now, whether he was back in Washington or whether he'd left for Washington right after that or after the court I don't know. He must have left right after that because he's the one that said if there is, or what ever fault there is I'm equally responsible.

Q: Is it customary to hold a general court so quickly after an event? It seems to me they didn't take time to sift all the evidence or to gather the evidence.

Adm. L.: They only had one witness, who couldn't speak English. We admitted that we had sunk it. We'd sent the dispatch saying we had sunk it. So, on the face of it, it was so cut and dried that the court was held as soon as they could get the court together. And, I think there was an awful lot of pressure put on them by Admiral King. I don't think there is any question about that. I think the State Department put an awful lot of pressure on them. It was a serious embarrassment to them and the United States. There is no question about that at all.

Well, anyway, I stuck around Pearl for about a month and then went back to the East Coast where my wife and new baby were and went down to the Bureau and Frank Watkins, a fine gentleman, was in the bureau at the time as was Johnny Davidson. Frank Watkins came in and handed me my letter of admonition and said, "What do you want to do with it?"

Q: What do you do with a letter of admonition?

Adm. L.: I think he suggested I throw it away. He said, "What do you want to do? Where do you want to go for duty?"

I said, "Gee, Captain Watkins, I just don't know; this is a plain disaster to me after having done pretty well for three war patrols."

He said, "How would you like to go to the Operations Office at ComSubLant?"

I said, "Gee, that sounds magnificent."

He said, "Well, Dickie Edwards called up. He said, 'Frank see that the young man gets a good job.'"

Dickie Edwards was number two to Admiral King. So, I went off and relieved Jimmy Dempsey as Operations Officer.

Q: Do you think this reflected King's attitude at that point?

Adm. L.: I wouldn't make that surmise. I wouldn't know. It certainly reflected Admiral Edwards' attitude because Frank told me, he quoted him. He said, "See that the young man gets a good job."

Another interesting thing, it might have reflected on Admiral King's attitude because I got to know Admiral Ingram and his staff quite well as Operations Officer of ComSubLant. I worked with CinCLantFleet quite closely.

Q: Jonas?

Adm. L.: Jonas Ingram. And, Jonas came in with his flag ship at New London once--I guess it was on this flag ship and we had occasion to talk. He knew all about it. He knew all about the whole thing. So, as I recall he said, "Don't worry, this isn't going to hurt you. Don't worry about it." You know, he was a big rough guy and a darned sight smarter than a lot of people gave him credit for.

Q: Well, there are other people who've had this too. I think Admiral Nimitz had one once upon a time didn't he?

Adm. L.: I was told that I was the only one that was ever convicted at a general court martial that made flag rank. Now, other flag officers, or other Captains had had general court martials. Like Earle Hawk. You remember the S-26 down in Panama.

Q: Yes.

Adm. L.: You remember I told you about Tommy Peters who got me in the submarine force. Earle Hawk was, what's the expression, fully and honorably, I mean you can be acquitted or you can be fully and honorably acquitted. In other words, whatever the expres is it means there is absolutely no stigma, no fault whatsoever. Well, that's what Earle had when he had his general court martial. This patrol craft just made a turn without any signaling and rammed him broadside and sunk him. There was nothing Earle could do about it. They were all on a darkened ship.

I think "fully and honorably" is the expression. So, I know that there are many captains that had gotten a general court martial.

I don't know this for a fact, but I've been told that I was the only one who was ever convicted of an offense in a general court martial and subsequently made flag rank.

Q: Jonas Ingram was right. But, it must have been a depressing thing.

Adm. L.: It was.

Q: How old were you at that time?

Loughlin #3 -137-

Adm. L.: Well I was born in 1910 and this was 1945, so I was thirty-five. The only thing is I never had a guilty conscience, Jack, because based on the information, I've told Japanese interviewers this, I've been interviewed several times by people from Japan. I've told many people who have discussed it, I mean in depth like we're doing, that based upon the information that I had at the time I would do the same thing.

I have failed to point out one thing which is in my favor, Tom Gatch was the Judge Advocate General. You remember Admiral Gatch?

Q: Yes. I know about him, I never knew him.

Adm. L.: I saw on the cover sheet of the record of the general court martial in his own handwriting, he said, "Loughlin was in a very tough spot. Based on the information he had, had he not pressed the attack he would have been subject to a general court martial for failing to press home the attack."

This has been my attitude all along.

Q: You were damned if you do and damned if you don't.

Adm. L.: Damned if you do and damned if you don't. Now, he actually put that in his own handwriting after he reviewed the court martial. This has been my point all along. Based upon the information that I had I felt that I was justified in making the attack. Based upon the information that I had I would do the same thing over again.

Q: How did these Japanese who interviewed you post war react?

Adm. L.: Their whole thing was whether it was a deliberate attack or not. There are so many things that show it wasn't, I mean, it was a deliberate attack on a ship, but not a deliberate attack on the AWA MARU. There were so many things, the main thing being pulling the spread into three hundred feet and setting the depth at three feet for a twelve thousand ton ship, anyone who has made any war patrols or even an inexperienced Skipper would never do that, Jack. He would never do it.

Q: That is pretty weighty evidence.

Adm. L.: The ship was eight hundred feet long. You're not going to pull four torpedoes into three hundred feet.

Q: No, you've got much more space to shoot at.

Adm. L.: This, to anyone who's been in the war and been in submarines, this is absolute positive evidence that I was not shooting at a twelve thousand ton ship.

Q: What were these Japanese who came to interview you? Newspaper people?

Adm. L.: No. One was a person who I really became pretty good friends with. He was interested in salvaging this ship.

Q: Was she near enough to--

Adm. L.: Oh, yes. She was only twelve miles off the beach. Incidentally, mainland China, the mainland Chinese have located and salvaged it. They have taken bodies off the ship.

Q: They have?

Adm. L.: Yes, sir. That was his interest. The other was a Japanese TV crew that came over and interviewed me at my home here in Bill Russell's garden about a year ago.

The original Japanese who has been here several times saw it in Japan. He saw the TV thing. He said they didn't do badly. But, I told them the same thing I'm telling you.

Of course, as you probably know, the American government after the war was over and General MacArthur was ensconced in Japan, why there was an agreement signed where the Japanese government waived all claims for the AWA MARU. The U.S. had offered to replace the ship in kind before the war was over, which happened, as you know, in April and the war was over in August. But, they waived all claims after the war.

Q: Now, you came to the Atlantic. You were Operations Officer.

Adm. L.: I was Operations Officer for two years. This was a very interesting time.

Q: Well, tell me about it.

Adm. L.: Well, the very first thing was I relieved Jimmy Dempsey in July. Of course, the war was over in August. As a matter of fact, I was in Washington on a business trip when the bomb hit Hiroshima. So, it was just a matter of three, four, or five days, I guess, wasn't Nagasaki within three days?

Q: Yes.

Adm. L.; And, in another two or three days it was all over. So, it was an interesting time because we had all of these submarines. I guess we had almost two hundred operating submarines at that time in the Pacific. A great many of them had to be brought back to the East Coast. Admiral Styer was ComSubLant and I had to find a spot to put all these people, all of these boats. The Magic Carpet was in full force.

Q: It was in full operation already.

Adm. L.: What we did was start them through the Canal and put them in Galveston and I think Pensacola, and Key West, in Charlesto and New York, and Philadelphia, and New London.

Q: This was moth balling?

Adm. L.: No, this was just to get them back someplace. And then, gosh, with the Magic Carpet, why some of them lost so many officers and men they couldn't move after they got here. I remember Phil Beshany, who later made Vice Admiral and was on the S-14 with me, Phil had come back on a tender after the war was over and was dying to get a submarine, even though the war was over. We sent him right down to Galveston to take over a boat that had lost so many people it didn't even have a commandin officer.

Q: It wasn't only the submarines during that period.

Adm. L.: No, but that was my work. Then we had captured these Type 21 German submarines, you know. We had to get a crew together in New London and bring them back up to New London for all of the examination as to what they had. You know they were the first snorkel submarines.

Q: Now, the Navy was anxious to do that?

Adm. L.: Oh, we wanted--see we didn't have any ships with snorkels. We didn't know what a snorkel was until we captured the first Type 21.

Q: Now, this is in contrast to in the 1920's after World War I when Tommy Hart wanted to bring back some German submarines to see why they functioned so well and he met the worst kind of opposition from the top brass. They just didn't want to do it.

Adm. L.: Well, they wanted to do it at the end of World War II. They wanted to get these two Type 21's because that could have made a big difference in the war against us had we not sunk so many German submarines. Have a guy being able to go eight, ten, twelve knots snorkeling covering all that ground without being caught on the surface where radar could get him.

Q: But, it presented problems bringing them over?

Adm. L.: Well, we had to get the crews together, the commanding officers and the crews and we were having all kinds of Magic Carpet troubles with our own boats in New London, the local squadron being SubRon 2.

Q: Was the submarine command caught unawares of this Magic Carpet, the effect of it?

Adm. L.: Oh, I think everybody in the Navy was. We had nothing to do with the point system. Who ever made the determination of the points, you reached a certain number of points and if you wanted to go on out, you went. I don't think we were any worse off then anybody else.

Q: Well, there had been some preplanning before the war ended as to what the different aspects of the Navy would do.

Adm. L.: We had done that too. We had made up peace time plans of where the squadrons would be located and where the tenders would be located, what type of boats would be in this particular squadron. It was mainly by engines, like the Fairbanks-Morse or the Wintons, or HORs. They would all be in the same geographical locations because of the spare parts. We had that pretty well planned, but I don't think anyone realized the personnel losses that occurred off these submarines.

Then we ended up with too many Chief Petty Officers. You see the Chiefs didn't want to get out.

Q: No. They were career men.

Adm. L.: So, you could end up with a submarine that had all Chiefs and no Indians. It was a very interesting and challenging.

Q: How did you try to solve this problem? Recruitment?

Adm. L.: No, I think, we put a lot of boats out of commission. I know that. I think the personnel people just had to adjudicate and allocate sufficient personnel to keep the boats operating.

Q: Is there any different technique in moth balling a submarine from what there is for a destroyer or cruiser?

Adm. L.: It's mostly below deck. The took the guns off later on. We didn't have any topside thing. Just preservation of machinery. I didn't really get into this.

Q: Have some of them been used again or not?

Adm. L.: We did put some back again.

Q: You needed them for Korea.

Adm. L.: When we went to what they call guppyize them, you know streamlining the hull and the super structure. Then, of course we went to the snorkel after that. I can't answer your question. I know we did bring, for instance the USS PERCH, I'm pretty sure the USS PERCH was mothballed and then converted into a cargo ship with a big hangar on the after deck. Then we had a couple of guided missile submarines within two or three years of the war.

Q: But, your major problem was personnel?

Adm. L.: Personnel.

Q: What other problems did you have?

Adm L.: I won't mention names, but there was an awful lot of jealousy about Dick Voge. You see, Dick was the Operations Officer and he ran the staff. And, they had Planning Officers. They had Strategic Planning Officers. And, they had all of of these types of officers, some of whom were senior to Dick, but he ran the staff under Admiral Lockwood. So, one of the first things ComSubLant did, after they changed admirals up here, was to reorganize the entire staff and bring in a Planning Officer who was next to the Chief of Staff. In other words, they downgrade the Operations Office. Of course, I was a very junior person on the staff of the Operations Office. There were several months I ran the thing for Admiral Styer and for the Chief of Staff because this was the way it had been done in the whole war. Then they reorganized the staff and placed the Operations Officer under the Planning Officer. So, the Planning Officer became the chief operating officer. Then, again, shortage of personnel, they pooled all their yeoman help. I always had my Chief Yeoman there who was a whiz. He was so good. So, they took all of the Yeomen away for each individual office and put them in a central pool. This caused havoc. So, there were some growing headaches about the reorganization on the staff.

In the meantime John Wilkes had relieved Gin Styer and then Jimmy Fife had relieved John Wilkes and I served with all three of them.

Q: Somewhere along in there wasn't there a big submarine conferenc It was out on the West Coast. They had submariners from all over.

Qdm. L.: I wasn't there if it was. I was there from July 1945 to July 1947. I don't remember that.

Q: Fritz Harlfinger was there, I think.

Adm. L.: I know they had a Joint Assessment Committee that poured over the records for about two years, I guess, after the war trying to find out just who had sunk what.

I go back to Gene Fluckey again. Gene actually fired, I think his last run when he used the deck gun and sent a landing party ashore and blew up the darned railroad track in Northern Hokkaido, or Northern Japan. He actually sank a ship and saw it sink through the periscope and was not given credit for it. There is no record of it in the Japanese files. But I think the Joint Assessment Committee did a superb job. I think they were probably ninety-five; ninety-eight (percent) accurate. you, a ship you have claimed to be sunk at night, you know you got the torpedo hits, but unless you actually saw it sink or the pip disappeared completely, who knows if they might not have limped back into port?

Q: Yes, unless it's corroborated by the Japanese records.

Adm. L.: That's exactly correct. So, I would say the Joint Assessment Committee did a tremendous, accurate, good job. But, the Japanese records left something to be desired too.

Q: And, how many of those pertaining to submarine sinkings were retrieved after the war?

Adm. L.: I don't think they ever changed the Joint Assessment Committee. In other words when they came to their final assessment I think that is still the official record. At least it is on the submarine operations.

Q: Well, I was thinking of that special survey committee that went out to Japan just immediately after the war and got many of the Japanese records, the Naval records.

Adm. L.: Well, don't you think that was taken under consideration by the Joint Assessment Committee?

Q: Yes it must have been. I just wondered how extensive it was as it pertained to sinkings. I've never seen that.

Adm. L.: Well, my Exec died two or three years ago, Harry Higgs, but I was on the bridge and he was in the conning tower and right until he was detached he just swore that this big ship that we hit we never saw it. But, it was a huge pip when we hit it. Then we got out from under and trailed it, oh, not more than six, eight or ten thousand yards astern of the convoy waiting for Fluckey to make his attack. He insisted to the last day I ever saw him that that ship sank. I never claimed the sinking. I just claimed damage. He said, "Look at the pip," and the pip was gone. It had disappeared.

Q: While you're on that subject, I mean, you've got many, many citations as a result of your patrols, would you say something about that? They are very much a part of the record. They stood you quite in good stead too.

Adm. L.: Yes, yes. Well, for the first few runs I was given the Navy Cross, I guess for the first two runs. Then we got the Presidential Citation for the sinkings we accomplished after the first two runs. The third run is where I had the horrible torpedo performance. But, I still got a Silver Star out of it becaue I was the wolf pack commander. We did sink, I think we were given credit for that tanker even though the Joint Assessment Committee split it up among the three boats. Then, of course, the fourth run was the AWA MARU and I got a Bronze Star with a "V" for picking up the aviators on the way home, the thirteen aviators. Then a couple of Legion of Merits, postwar. One when I was ComSubFlot 6 in Charleston and one when I was Commandant of the Naval District, Washington. So, that's the extent of the decorations.

Q: Now, you've really got your share of decorations, I would say.

Adm. L.: Well, I am not unduly modest, or perhaps not modest at all, but I mentioned this at least three different times, you have to be in the right place at the right time. You've got to do your job and I really think that I did my job, but you've got to be in a position to do that job. A lot of people during the war were in a position to do their job and didn't do their job! So, that's where I do take what credit I do take.

Q: Where that happened, where a man didn't do his job properly was it just a normal human failure or---

Adm L.: Undue caution I think. Perhaps fear. I talked to one commanding officer whose name, obviously, will not be mentioned, but he picked up a convoy skirting the coast of Formosa. He made no attempt to attack. It was too close to the coast and the water was too shallow and he said, "To hell with it."

Loughlin #3 -148-

That never appeared in his patrol report. I might add.

Q: It was too great a risk and he was risking his crew.

Adm. L.: I don't know what his reasoning was.

Q: Well, Styer you served under in the Atlantic. Do you want to say something about him?

Adm. L.: I thought Admiral Styer was--I was only with him a very short time. He was there when I brought the USS QUEENFISH through New London. Do you want to hear a sea story about that? This is a good sea story. Turkey Neck Crawford was Freeland Daubin Chief of Staff. We came down from Newport, after torpedo test runs and landed at New London and I had heard about these inspection that they would pull on you right off the bat. So, I got on my horse and immediately proceeded to call on the Chief of Staff Crawford and Admiral Daubin. As I left Admiral Daubin's office, this was just a courtesy call, I don't know if it was eleven o'clock or eleven-fifteen, but Captain Crawford said, "We'll be down to inspect the USS QUEENFISH at eleven-thirty." Well, this is right in the middle of a noon hour. You know, the crew is eating and the ship's, not a mess, but people back and forth. So, I left his office and immediately got on the phone before I went back to the ship and said, "Get the crew out of the mess hall and get the ship cleaned up. It's going to be inspected in half an hour."

So, they got down there and we started in the forward torpedo room. We had a slot machine on board, on the USS QUEENFISH. So, we prevailed upon Admiral Daubin to play the slot machine about ten or fifteen minutes.

Q: That was not contrary to rules then I take it?

Adm. L.: No. By the time he finished that mess hall and battery room looked like a million bucks. They went all through the ship and it was like we had a shining dress inspection and Crawford looked at me. Every department he would turn around and look. As he left the ship he said, "How in the dickens did you get that ship cleaned up? This is the first time this has happened."

I said, "Oh, well, we're this way all the time."

Q: Tell me about some of Jimmy Fife's foibles.

Adm. L.: Well, Jimmy was dogmatic. I think I mentioned that word before.

Q: Yes. A very apt expression.

Adm. L.: I think he is one of the most gracious gentlemen socially I've ever seen. He didn't drink in those days you know. I don't know when he stopped drinking, but he didn't drink when he was ComSubLant.

Q: He didn't drink when I knew him.

Adm. L.: But, he would come to parties, cocktail parties, dinner parties, and absolutely charmed the living bee-jesus out of everybody. Well you know him. I guess you know him better than I do. I never had a bad word with Admiral Fife. I think he liked me and he obviously knew my story. Even when I went down to Panama as Exec of the ORION when I left the staff there he would make inspection trips down there and have dinner with my wife and me. He was an absolute wonderful gentleman.

One thing he did which was unlike his predecessor was that he liked to entertain at the Officers' Club, Quarters D in New London. And, even though you had the duty he'd always have the officer with the duty come up and have dinner with him. In other words, there were yeomen and other people there who could man the phones and we were only two minutes away from the office. But, that was very unlike his predecessor because once you had the duty at the end of working hours you stayed in that office until eight o'clock the next morning. You slept, but you had the plug-in phone right next to your bunk. He always had the duty officer come up and have dinner with him in Quarters D.

I use the word dogmatic because I think this is illustrative of his attitude. Tommy Dykers, you remember he was my first submarine Skipper on the S-35, Tommy became Planning Officer on the staff. One Saturday he called me up, or I guess I was still at work, he said "We've got to work today and tomorrow."

I said, "O-kay. What's the problem?"

He said, "Admiral Fife wants us to make a study as to where the tenders go. Which tender goes where."

It had to do with tenders because at that time we already had the Key West and Norfolk and New London set up as squadrons. Well, Tommy and I worked for two days on this thing and came out with what we thought was a logical conclusion but Jimmy had already made up his mind before he had ever asked for the study.

He said, "Well, you've made some good points, but the tenders are going to go here and not where you recommend."

He had already made up his mind. Two days' work on a weekend down the drain. He wasn't about to change his mind. He had already made up his mind.

But, I have nothing but kind words to say about Admiral Fife. Professionally I never served with him except on the staff. He was very good to me on the staff. And, as I say, socially he was just a perfect gentlemen.

Interview No. 4 with Rear Admiral Charles Elliott Loughlin, U.S. Na
(Retired)

Place: Annapolis, MD.

Date: September 11, 1980

Subject: Biography

By: John T. Mason, Jr.

Q: It is a beautiful fall day. I wonder if you would resume your story by telling me about your tour of duty on the USS ORION? You arrived there in July of 1947 to serve as Exec. Tell me first about the USS ORION. She was a very special kind of ship.

Adm. L.: She was one of the, I guess at that time there were only four or five submarines tenders that we had. I mean their designation was AS, Auxiliary Submarine. We had a squadron of submarines in Panama at the time. Freddy Laing was the commanding officer. Creed Burlingame was the Squadron Commander for this squadron. Creed was quite a well known submarine officer in the USS SILVERSIDES in World War II.

I had just come, as you know, from being an operations Officer on ComSubLant Staff. Admiral Fife, at that time when I was detached, was ComSubLant. So, I knew everybody in, you know, the division commanders, the squadron commanders, and the operations officers. So, we had quarters there in Rodman, of the Canal Zone. It was on the Pacific side. That's where the base had been changed during the war. Prior to the war and up until, I guess, the end of the war the submarine base had been at Coco Solo over on the Atlantic side. They changed the location to the Pacific side because the threat was Japan obviously until the war was over.

I would say it was a real pleasant tour of duty mainly because submarine tenders are not known for going to sea very often.

Q: She was a sizeable vessel too, wasn't she?

Adm. L.: Oh, yes, sir. I would say twelve or thirteen thousand tons.

Freddy Laing was a real fine commanding officer. I was fortunate to join the ship in refresher training in Guantanamo. So, I had some underway experience in Guantanamo. I hadn't been on a big ship since the USS NEW MEXICO days which was way back in 1938.

Freddy was instrumental in getting the USS ORION to sea many, many times. For instance, we--I'll give you another anecdote about the Class of 1930. Perhaps you don't remember, but the Class of 1930 made Captain in 1947. They all had to revert to Commander.

Q: After the war was over?

Adm. L.: I don't know what the budget process was in those days, what caused them to revert, but they made them all go back from Captain to Commander.

Loughlin #4 -154-

Q: Maybe Louis Johnson was in the background.

Adm. L.: Well, it could be. I guess the Korean War didn't start until about 1949 or 1950.

Q: 1950.

Adm. L.: But, the anecdote is that we made a trip down to Callao, Peru. I never could understand why Creed Burlingame, who is one of my good friends, had to put his three stripes on just before we left for Callao, Peru. No one down there had to know, so why didn't he keep his four stripes on during the visit.

So, we had a beautiful trip down to Callao and stayed there for a week.

Q: The Peruvians did well by you?

Adm. L.: Yes, sir. At that time we were very good friends. As a matter of fact the ABC, the Argentina, Brazil and Chile Naval Attachés, they call them the ABC trio. We had a very nice visit. It was very amicable. A few things went wrong. We didn't have a saluting battery. So, we used the old five inch gun for the saluting battery. I was the Exec. I forget who the senior officer was who came aboard to board us, but the battery stopped firing after about sixteen or seventeen guns and he was counting. So, that was embarrassing.

We were moored to a pier there where the swells from the sea had a straight shot in so at midnight one night I was on board as Exec and the old lines started to pop just like a slingshot. I was able to get the Skipper at midnight. He had his wife down there.

I said, "Hey, you'd better come back here. We're just about to lose all of our lines.

Q: About to go out to sea?

Adm. L.: Well, we wouldn't have done that. We would have ended up on the beach there. This was a midnight, so the pilot refused to move the ship.

So, Freddy dashed back from town which was fifteen, twenty, twenty-five miles.

He came aboard and we moved the ship between twelve and one o'clock in the morning to another pier which was away from the breakwater opening which was causing these heavy swells to make the ship surge.

Q: The current along that coast is very strong. Isn't it the Humboldt Current?

Adm. L.: It is. We were in the harbor proper. They had a breakwater there. The big trouble was we were moored stern toward the opening of the breakwater and the swells from the Pacific were making us surge back and forth and it just started popping lines like that. It was kind of a frightening feeling.

Anyway, Freddy came back and he moved the ship with no help from the pilot. We moved, oh, to the right for two or three piers down and got away from the swells. From then on it was all right. It was a delightful trip.

Q: Did you have time to see any interesting sights there?

Adm. L.: No, I--the Exec, I'm not bragging, but the Exec of a ship, in particular when the Skipper has his wife down there, why, he was kind of tied up.

Q: His nose is to the grindstone?

Adm. L.: Yes, his nose is to the grindstone. I had a classmate who was a Naval Attache there and I remember there was a Marine Officer who was a Marine Attache who was a Medal of Honor winner from World War II. A very very fine person, Lt. Col Austin Shafner.

The Ambassador was Admiral Duncan who had been ambassador in the Soviet Union, during World War II. He was the ambassador there at that time. So, the social life when I could get off the ship was very nice. The Peruvians couldn't have been nicer. They were really delightful people.

I'm just illustrating this to say that Freddy was instrumental in getting the ship to sea quite often.

For instance, we went all the way up to Norfolk to bring back some personnel. I guess the money was so darned tight. I don't know why it was so tight in 1947 and 1948, but it had to be because they sent us all the way up to Norfolk to bring back a whole troop load of troops.

Q: It was a post-war economy that had been inaugurated.

Adm. L.: So, there were two long trips that we made and, as I said, submarine tenders were notorious for really not going to sea.

Q: Well, that's not their work is it?

Adm. L.: That's not their work. They are supposed to be there to refit the submarines. So, it was a very enjoyable experience, my two years there. My second year I had a division. I was Exec the first year and then, as a matter of fact I relieved Johnny Davidson, Admiral Davidson who's here in Annapolis. I was Division Commander and then about the time the tour was over the squadron was disestablished and moved up to Norfolk. So, I rode a submarine as Division Commander with Rollo Miller, who, again, lives here in Annapolis. We went via St. Thomas. We had a delightful trip back to Norfolk via St. Thomas which I hadn't seen since 1943.

Q: What were the specific duties of a submarine divsion commander at the time?

Adm. L.: Just had fleet exercises and training exercises. You had either four or six submarines in your division. You just supervised the operation of the ships in the division.

Q: Did you have any problems personnel wise? I mean, getting a sufficient complement.

Adm. L.: No. Not in those days. The only problem we had in Panama was there was a Polio epidemic which hit down there. We lost one officer on one of my submarines who developed Polio and died. So, it really scared the living bee-jesus out of everybody because in those days I don't think there was any Salk vaccine.

There was quite a famous vacation spot in Panama called Santa Clara which, I think, is seventy-five miles up the coast on the Pacific side. A classmate of mine owned a home up there. So, two or three of us just sent our wives and children and we just evacuated them. Got them up to Santa Clara and that's where they stayed for, oh, I think a couple of months when the Polio thing was at its height.

But, we did lose one officer on a submarine from Polio.

The ORION transferred to Norfolk and became the tender in Norfolk in June of 1949 when I was detached and came here to the Naval Academy.

Our interesting thing that we worked on down in Panama is that we knew a little about it during the war is that you could get a certain gradient, temperature gradient in the water at a certain depth. You had a bathythermograph to tape. In other words, you could see what the depth was. You could sit on the top of that gradient and stop everything and do what we call hover. We would just sit there and change your trim a little bit back and forth and without using your motors you could just sit there for literally hours.

Q: Without much strain on the battery?

Adm. L.: No, no strain at all. It was a good way of staying on station without using any power whatsoever.

Q: That was quite a discovery, wasn't it?

Adm. L.: Well, we knew about it during the war because most of us used to make deep dives on our first, what we called trim dive during the war. And, the bathythermograph would show you where this gradient was. In other words you get a sharp change in temperature in the water and that is where the gradient is. Incidentally, this is what you do during a depth charge attack. If you'd made this deep dive you knew where this gradient was, if you got underneath this gradient where the line was, where the sharp line of demarcation was it was almost impossible for sonar to pick you up. But, I don't think many of us ever used the hovering technique during World War II. But, as I said, we worked on that quite a bit down in Panama. You could stay there for literally two or three hours without moving anything on the ship except adjusting your trim back and forth. It depended upon people moving back and forth.

Q: Now, did that gradient, was it nonexistent when there were particularly strong currents?

Adm. L.: Well, you didn't get currents that far. It was normally pretty deep. I mean, a hundred and fifty or two hundred, or two hundred and fifty feet so the currents really weren't--

Q: I suppose I was thinking in terms of the Gulf Stream and that sort of thing.

Adm. L.: I never tried it in the Gulf Stream. As a matter of fact, I'm not sure how deep the Gulf Stream is. It's a terrific current. I've been in the Gulf Stream many, many times. I don't know what the depth of the turbulence is of the Gulf Stream. But, certainly, I don't think it would go down to two hundred and fifty or three hundred feet. I don't think so. I could be wrong on that.

But, that was a technique that we worked on. It was very successful.

Q: Is it something that is standard with submarines?

Adm. L.: Not with the nuclear boats because you have the power there.

Q: You don't have to, but the diesels?

Adm. L.: The diesels would be--had we had another war or had we kept our diesels it certainly would have been effective, an effective technique to use I think on war patrol in order to conserve your battery.

Q: Isn't there some promise that we might go back to some diesel boats?

Adm. L.: Only from the cost point of view.

Q: It's been touted about.

Adm. L.: I mean, they are so limited in their operational ability compared to an SSN. I think you would have to weigh heavily the differential in the cost versus the operational ability. The SSN's and the FBM's are, they are just worlds and worlds apart from the Diesel boats, Jack. I mean there is just no comparison between the two. They have the mobility and all of the operational things you'd want and unlimited endurance and they can go forever, practically. So, I would say, particularly as long as Admiral Rickover is still alive, I would say there would be no possibility whatsoever that diesel boats would be built.

Q: That was a very pleasant two years which you spent down in that part of the world. Then you came back to the Annapolis area. How did that happen?

Adm. L.: That's a story in itself.

Q: Yes, I rather suspected that it was.

Adm. L.: Admiral Fife came down on one of his frequent inspection tours. Larry Freeman, Captain Freeman who had had the USS WILLIAMSBURG, the presidential yacht, had the S-34 when I was in the S-35 my first tour of submarines back in 1938. He and Tommy Dykers were classmates and I became good friends with him. We had quite a bit of personnel trouble down there and Larry was detached and ordered to the Naval Station from the USS WILLIAMSBURG. He wrote me and asked me if I would come and be his Executive Officer.

Q: Personnel problems here at the Academy?

Adm. L.: Here at the Academy.

Q: What was the nature of that.

Adm. L.: It was before I came here, I think it was just the change of personnel was still taking place, Jack, from 1945 although this was four years later in 1949 it was just an imbalance in personnel, apparently. I think there were some racial problems too. I think the racial problems were probably the root cause of it.

Anyway, Larry wrote and asked me, and, of course, I was finishing my division tour of duty and Admiral Fife came down and I broached the matter to him. We were never, you know, close friends, but I could go to him and talk with him. He was that type of person.

He said, "Sure, go there but don't stay more than one year."

So, I accepted and came here.

Q: It became almost a life time occupation.

Adm. L.: I accepted Larry's invitation and came here and relieved Don Thomas as Executive Officer and had a most pleasant year and a half, I guess as Executive Officer living over on the North Severn. Then all of a sudden General Eisenhower was ordered to set up SHAPE in Paris. Larry's daughter was being married, I think, the first week in January. This would be in 1951. He got orders to be detached within a week to go on Eisenhower's Staff.

Admiral Harry Hill had relieved Admiral Jimmy Holloway. Admiral Holloway was the Superintendent and as I said, we were still in a bind with personnel. I remember this distinctly because Tiny McCorkle was head of the Department of Seamanship and Navigation. Do you know Admiral McCorkle?

Q: Yes. Yes, indeed.

Adm. L.: And, Mike Flaherty, when Larry got his sudden orders, was ordered to come in and relieve Larry as Commanding Officer of the Naval Station. This was the time of Louis Johnson. This is 1949, 1950.

Harry Hill said, "Well, the heck with this. I can save a Captain's billet. We'll change Flaherty's orders."

You see McCorkle had made Admiral and was to be detached from the Department of Seamanship and Navigation.

So, he said, "We'll change Flaherty's orders and have him relieve McCorkle in Seamanship and Navigation and let Elliott fleet up to relieve Flaherty as Commanding Officer of the Naval Station as a Commander."

This is exactly what happened. So, I became a Commanding Officer when Larry was detached and moved aboard the USS REINA MERCEDES. I don't think I'd mentioned that. Admiral Halsey and I were the only two Commanders in the history of the Navy who commanded the USS REINA MERCEDES.

Q: Tell me about the Naval Station at that time. What was the scope of their duties?

Adm. L.: It was a very unique command arrangement. It was distasteful to the aviators. For instance, the Naval Air Facility was part of the Naval Station and was commanded by a Naval Aviation Captain. Macpherson B. Williams whose daughter married Billy Lawrence and who divorced him while he was a POW. I'll tell you it's a long story.

They had the Yellow Perils. You remember the N3N's. One of them is in Dahlgren Hall right now, I think,.

But, it was a very, very touchy command relationship because we had the Naval Air Facility which was part of the Naval Station. And, we had the Small Craft facility which, of course, had all of the, same as it is right now, the sailing craft. That had an officer in charge and he was a part of the Naval Station directly under the Commanding Officer.

I never did it, I guess I lost my courage, but when Larry was here he would have personnel inspection of the Naval Air Facility. That did not sit well, I had to copy him and I had a classmate who was the Exec of the Naval Air Facility. It was kind of a touchy command relationship. Then we had a Marine detachment which was part of the Naval Station. The C.O. graduated from Georgia Tech four years after I graduated from the Naval Academy and he was selected for Colonel six months before I was for Captain. So, for six months I had a full Colonel working for me as a Commander. A wonderful guy though. Sid Kelly, he subsequently died. Then we had all kinds of trouble with the Stewards. We had what we called the APL. I think it was the APL-31. It was a barracks ship for the black stewards. We had very few Filipinos except in the officers' quarters, I mean except for the superintendent of the PG school who was here at that time, and the Commandant and the USS REINA MERCEDES and the Superintendent's quarters.

We had a real, real bad set up. We had a homosexual scandal that developed.

Q: Among the Blacks?

Adm. L.: We called the ONI down and I think thirty-five or forty people were involved in this thing. They were all summarily discharged.

Q: So you had no cooking staff.

Adm. L.: Well, we replaced them on the APL. But, actually, the Chief Petty Officers on there were just superb people and I think one of them lives here in Annapolis now. I still see him. I had no trouble personnel wise with the Stewards. But, once this homosexual thing developed and we got rid of them from then on we had no trouble.

Q: Had that been longstanding?

Adm. L.: It had gone on for apparently six months or a year. The only trouble was we didn't have enough people to man the mess hall. I'll tell you, Jack, it almost made me sick because we had port and starboard watch, for instance, and half the time we'd have to have people standing watch every other day. And, half the time we had to pull fifteen or twenty or twenty-five people who were supposed to have liberty and bring them back in order to have enough people to serve the midshipmen. The personnel situation was really one of the sorest points, I think in those days. So, the job had its headaches and it had its advantages. Obviously the USS REINA MERCEDES with Stewards and everything. The personnel situation on the APL was pretty bad.

Q: What about living on the USS REINA MERCEDES? You had the midshipmen incarcerated too.

Adm. L.: Yes, yes.

Q: Was that separate from your area?

Adm. L.: Well, we had the confinement area there on the USS REINA MERCEDES. I had nothing to do with it. I mean, it was Bancroft Hall.

Q: Administrative.

Adm. L.: I think one of the interesting stories about the USS REINA MERCEDES is that when Larry Freeman was still here he wrote an official letter to Admiral Holloway that the designation of the USS REINA MERCEDES was in commission and in reserve. So, he wrote a letter to Admiral Holloway requesting that he be allowed to serve liquor onboard the USS REINA MERCEDES. And, Admiral Holloway wrote him back, I don't remember the letter, I think I saw it and he said, "Captain Freeman you have two choices. If you would like to do away with the stewards on the USS REINA MERCEDES and change the designation of the ship, so be it, but if you want to keep your stewards and keep the designation in commission and in reserve, no liquor."

Well, there was only one answer to that. We keep the stewards. So, Larry built a little shack right on the dock which is between The APL and the USS REINA MERCEDES and set up a little bar there where he could serve before his dinner party. When I took over I did away with that because--

Q: You removed the shack?

Adm. L.: No, we removed the liquor because all of these Black stewards many of whom I became very close to because I had to work so closely with them because of all the troubles we had

Loughlin #4 -167-

and I just didn't think it was right to have them see a bunch of people in evening clothes right on the same dock drinking liquor. I'm not criticizing Larry a darned bit on this thing. But, I found a better way of doing that. I had two or three friends on Porter Road and we would keep our liquor supply on Porter Road and then anytime we had a dinner party, why, wherever we had the drinks that particular couple would be asked to attend the dinner party.

Q: That sounds like a good arrangement. Were there any communications facilities under your command?

Adm. L.: No, no. We had the NSS. The same as today, the Fleet Broadcast over here at the Naval Communications Station. But, we had no communications on the USS REINA MERCEDES and on the Naval Station except short range between the boats and the small crafts.

Q: Was there any research going on in your command?

Adm. L.: Not under my command. Actually during that period of time the hydrofoil became a hot item. It was Doctor Teller, I think at MIT. He was here quite often running his hydrofoil back and forth. It was based at the Naval Station. We also had our, the details are fuzzy now but, we had an experimental sea plane that was fast as the dickens. That operated out of Annapolis. I can't remember much of the details about that. It was a real, real fast plane. It took miles to get off. I mean they would go out almost to Greenberry Point before they would be airborne. But, the hydrofoil was an active project during my three years here.

We had the Engineering Experiment Station. Small craft to serve the Naval facility. In those days it was the Severn River Naval Command.

Q: Did you have the farm and the dairy under your command?

Adm. L.: No, the dairy was not under me, the band was, strangely enough. The band was part of the Naval Station. I had to inspect them and they came under me for administrative control Not under the Commandant. They are under the Commandant now, I believe. I'm sure it is.

Q: But the dairy was--

Adm. L.: The dairy was under the Commandant of the Midshipmen. Yes, sir.

Q: That is sort of an appendage. Well, you were exposed, once again, to athletics at the Academy even though you were not in any command relationship.

Adm. L.: I was very fortunate. A person by the name of Jack Mansfield. I got here in July or June, I guess of 1949 and Jack Mansfield had been the officer representative of basketball for the previous year and he had another year to go. So, Howard Caldwell, who was the director of athletics, and rightly so, of course, kept him on as officer representative my first year here. But, then when Jack was detached I became the officer representative of the basketball team for one year. Then the

Loughlin #4 -169-

second year I was elected by the other officer representative as Commander of the Board of Control of the, what do you call it, the Executive Committee of the Athletic Association. The reason this is important is I think it was one of the main reasons I was subsequently selected to be Director of Athletics.

Q: It led into that?

Adm. L.: I had been officer representative for two years of basketball. I had been on the Executive Committee, now it's called the Board of Control. So, being on the Executive Committee you're able to make all of the football games. Admiral Hill would take us in his own plane down to Houston, that is if we played Rice or any place else. So, it gave me some good experience in seeing how the Athletic Department ran.

Q: Would you say something about Admiral Hill and his emphasis on athletics at the Academy?

Adm. L.: I would rather tell a story about Pirie, rather than Harry Hill. Bob was his Commandant and they had a lot of hassle together. But, we played Yale up in the Yale Bowl in 1951, I guess. The fall of 1951 and it was a seven, seven tie, I remember that. Bob was the Commandant. I was the officer representative of basketball. The war in Korea had started. The NCAA had just passed the regulation that freshmen could play varsity sports. Well, of course, I knew all of the personnel. We had, let's see, McCauley, Lang, Wigley and Ned Hogan. I think we had four freshmen that I knew were capable of playing varsity basketball.

So, coming back in the train from the Yale Bowl I broached this to Bob. This was in the fall, and the basketball season didn't start for a couple of months.

I said, "What do or how do you feel about going along with the NCAA rules on freshmen?"

He said, "Over my dead body will any Plebes play varsity sports here!"

So, I gulped and said, "Captain Pirie, do you want to have a winning basketball team this year?"

He said, "That's the most stupid question I've ever had asked of me. Of course, I want a winning basketball team."

I said, "If you don't let Plebes play, there are four Plebes that would be starting every game this year if you permit them to play. If you don't permit them to play we're going to have one disastrous season."

He said, "Do you know what you're talking about?"

I said, "Yes, sir. I know precisely what I'm talking about."

He said. "O-kay, Plebes can play."

Q: Changed his mind just like that?

Adm. L.: Just like that. I mean, that's the reason I admire that guy so much. If you know what you're talking about and convince him that you are right he's not inflexible. He will change just like that. Not waver, he'll just change.

And, sure enough we had four freshman who started every game that year. We had a heck of a good basketball season.

Q: Your star rose at that point didn't it?

Adm. L.: I guess it helped. That's probably one reason that Bob is still one of my best friends.

But, actually, Harry Hill was very enthusiastic. He was a battalion officer when I was a midshipman. I've known the Hill family ever since 1931, 1932, and 1933. I was very fond of Admiral Hill. I thought he was very fair. I think he and Bob had their problems, but I didn't enter into it.

The only incident I had with Admiral Hill which you might be interested in is very embarrassing. After I relieved Larry as Commanding Officer we had the President of France visit here. He went out to take the parade and as he was standing there uncovered it was raining like heck and we started a twenty-one gun salute and again like Lima the seventeenth gun, nothing happened.

Q: Demoted.

Adm. L.: Oh, boy, Admiral Hill had a reception later and he was livid with rage. He said, "What happened?"

Well, one of the things that I'm real ashamed of is I didn't have enough foresight to move those saluting batteries down where they are now. You know, on the sea wall. In those days they were right in front of the chapel. I don't know if you remember or not. We had one on the sea wall down by the marina for visiting ships. But, for the parade we had telephone conversations to a set of quarters up there to these saluting batteries which were right in front of the chapel, right in the middle.

We had three guns and what we had was either three hang fires or two hang fires. But, whatever it was the Warrant Officer who was in charge did right. It would have been dangerous to unload this thing and fire it. So, that's the reason it stopped at seventeen guns.

Q: Did the French President notice it?

Adm. L.: Oh, yes. Sure. He was so wet. It was raining like hell.

Q: He was glad to get it over with.

Adm. L.: And, I tried to explain to Admiral Hill and said, "Admiral I know it shouldn't have happened, but it did happen."

In the meantime I had checked on the saluting battery shells and found that they were damned near World War I vintage. I said, "I can't help the performance of the saluting battery shells.

He said, "Yes, you can. You get new ones right away."

I found out what year they were made in which was years and years ago. Well fortunately I had a classmate up in BUORD, Carter Bennett, and I got him on the phone and said, "Boy, I'm in trouble." I explained the situation to him and then he got on the phone to, I think, some ammunition depot out in Nevada. Within a week we had a brand new set of ammunition and it never happened again.

Q: Did Hill's anger cool down at that point?

Adm. L.: Oh, yes. He was embarrassed for the President and he was embarrassed for me and I was embarrassed. But, without any alibi it really wasn't my fault.

Loughlin #4 -173-

Q: He had a practice of being everywhere sports were going on.

Adm. L.: He was one of the most enthusiastic Superintendents I've ever seen in sports, as far as sports is concerned. Absolutely.

Q: He was so emphatic in his beliefs that team work was essential in the training of a Naval officer.

Adm. L.: No, I have nothing but respect for Admiral Hill and Mrs. Hill. I knew Betty their daughter very well as a midshipman. As I said, I became close to them because I dragged a good friend of Betty's when he was Battalion Commander way back in 1931, 1932. So, I'd known Admiral Hill for, what, sixteen, eighteen, nineteen years.

Q: At that point you must have acquired a real love of this community?

Adm. L.: Yes. My wife, is, perhaps, rather unique. I say perhaps because I'm sure there are others, but Marjorie is really a civilian. Every place we have ever lived she's made a conscientious effort to make friends in the civilian community. Not that we don't do this in the Navy community. She just likes to make friends within any civilian community we've ever lived. For instance, here at this town she's been with the Hammond-Harwood House. She's been closely associated with the Hammond-Harwood House ever since we've been here in the last twelve years. I think it's really paid dividends because it gives you a broader outlook upon life and---

Q: It's a real bridge between the Gown and the Town.

Adm. L.: Particularly when you retire, yes, sir. It certainly is.

Q: The Navy life is separate from the town. And the town has a great deal to offer.

Adm. L.: It does. But, I know a lot of Naval Officers who once they have retired are completely lost because they don't get invited to Porter Road, or they don't get invited to the Superintendent's, or they don't get invited to this or that. We've had it both ways. I mean, I've maintained my ties with the Naval Academy. So we still have that, but we also have many, many civilian friends in the community here. It's made life a lot more pleasant. I would advocate that approach to anyone, or any person on active duty because it's going to pay dividends when you retire.

Q: And especially when a Naval officer retires to a community that isn't strictly Navy. It's essential that he get down and mix with the civilians. It offers also simultaneously the opportunity to use his talents, his training in civilian activities

Adm. L.: Yes, look at Jack Taylor. He heads up the board at Anne Arundel Hospital, I think. He's a retired Major General in the Air Force and Jack certainly, he's been here less than I have, but he certainly is engaged in the activities of the community here in Annapolis.

Q: You then went to another staff job didn't you?

Adm. L.: Yes. After leaving here I went out to be Joe Grenfell's Chief of Staff in--

Q: Submarine Flotilla 1.

Adm. L.: SubFlot 1 in San Diego in Coronado. We lived in Coronado. I had a very fine year with--

Q: You'd known Grenfell of course?

Adm. L.: Yes. During the war and before the war he had been a good friend of ours. I think he had asked for me. He certainly was not reluctant to accept me as his Chief of Staff Officer.

It was a rather unique command relationship there because the flotilla consisted of two squadrons. Both squadron commanders had their own jobs to do with their own squadrons and yet they reported to Flortilla Commander. So, it put the Chief of Staff Officer who was junior to both squadron commanders in kind of-

Q: Well, you were used to that weren't you having been here in Annapolis?

Adm. L.: I know, but it didn't make it any easier. Thank goodness the two squadron commanders were of the class of 1930 and both were good friends of mine.

Q: I would think a situation like that would develop your diplomatic skills.

Adm. L.: I hope it did. They are still good friends of mine, so perhaps it did. But, anytime anything came down that I knew was going to be distasteful to the squadron commanders, why, of course, I had to do the dirty work and tell them. But, it worked out fine and I got a squadron the second year.

Q: Tell me about that year with Grenfell. He was a top flight submariner.

Adm. L.: He was, and had been on ComSubPac staff. He had the USS GUDGEON during the early part of the war. Then he went to ComSubPac staff. He was darned near killed in an aviation accident. He was flying back to the West Coast sometime during the war on a Pan American sea plane. It crashed and he was lucky to get out.

Joe desperately wanted to make Admiral as I guess everyone did or does. He participated in every conceivable activity out there both Navy, military wise and civilian wise. He was well known throughout the entire community, both San Diego and Coronado. He was really a marvelous man to work for. There is no question about it. He was very decisive and very reasonable, if you had a point to make and you made it and you were right, why, Joe, would say, "Fine, let's do it that way then."

So, it was an enjoyable year. As I said, I knew the two squadron commanders personally. One of them was a real, real good friend of mine, Jack Lee. The command relationship caused no trouble whatsoever.

Q: And, what went on in the flotilla at that time?

Adm. L.: Well, we just did normal really, peace time activities and exercises. Jack, we had some new sonar installation on three of the boats. The USS BASHAW, the USS BLUEGILL, and I forget the other one. Big SQS sonars on the bow. A huge array on the bow. There was a lot of experimental work going on at that time.

But, other than that it was just routine submarine exercises. Nothing special, nothing out of the ordinary. Just normal submarine operations.

Q: In that time were they having the annual pow-wow's of submariners. Submarine conference, I guess they were.

Adm. L.: I don't think they started until later. When I was out there Admiral Russell, Admiral Momsen first and then Admiral Russell was ComSubPac. Of course we operated under ComSubPac's domain. They made frequent inspections tours back to the San Diego area. I think they started later where ComSubLant, ComSubPac had their, more or less, annual conferences. I don't recall any out there and this was in 1952 to 1954. I had made Captain just before I was detached here. I had been selected in the fall of 1951 and didn't make it until March, I guess, 1952. I was detached in July 1952. I was a new Captain for two years I was in SubFlot 1.

My experience was limited to three months tour of duty in Japan. What had happened was we had a detachment of, I believe six submarines whose home port was Yokosuka. Their primary mission was to make surveillance patrols up, not in the Aleutians, but what is the chain off Siberia? North of Hokkaido there.

Q: Yes, the Kuriles.

Adm. L.: So, instead of having a permanent division or squadron commander out there they rotated the two squadron commanders from Pearl and the two squadron commanders from San Diego for a two or three months tour of duty. This was in 1951, 1952.

I was out there when I got my orders to come back here. So, Admiral Callaghan was out there and Admiral Briscoe was there as ComNavFe. Again, having fought the war against Japan I was a little reluctant to go back. Particularly having sunk the AWA MARU, but that never came up.

Q: You weren't identified.

Adm. L.: No, I was not identified. But, I got to know many of the senior Japanese Navy officers there.

Q: Did you change your attitude?

Adm. L.: I did. Very much so. I encountered nothing but friendship and hospitality from all the Japanese nationals I met. I've had three or four tours of duty there. Even my wife, who felt very strongly about the Japanese got to like them.

Q: It's very interesting that almost unanimously Naval officers have reacted that way.

Adm. L.: Well, the only one who, I think, is still adamant is Dick O'Kane and I think Dick has reason to be. You know Dick was sunk in the USS TANG and was a prisoner of war. Dick was the commanding officer of the tender, the USS SPERRY, when I had my squadron. So, during my three months tour of duty in Japan, Dick became the squadron commander, acting squadron commander. Of course, I was way out in Yokosuka.

Then, subsequently, either after I came back or during that summer that I was detached, Dick became squadron commander, but he was forced to go back to testify in the war crimes, and he

Loughlin #4 -179-

fought it. He fought it like all get-out. He didn't want any part of going back there. He didn't want any part of the Japanese. Dick was just vehement in his dislike for the Japanese. But, I think he had a much more legitimate reason than I did. I never saw the Japanese suffer. They never did anything to me. I've read stories and I know about some of the horror stories that they did and things they did. But, I think some of our submariners did some pretty bad things during World War II also.

Q: Did you have any problems in terms of Japanese ports, the mines still remaining in the area?

Adm. L.: No, because the boats in that detachment were pretty well delineated from the areas in which they worked on, if you follow me. Apparently there weren't any mines. They had not mined that particular area. It was primarily communication and surveillance of Vladivostok, I guess, in that particular area.

Q: I rather think that's connected with something Bill Irvin told me. He was on the staff in Pearl and he made a trip out to the Far East to see if submarines couldn't be utilized in some way in the Korean conflict. He felt the submariners should have a part in it.

Adm. L.: That was my only connection with the Korean conflict. It was right in the middle of it. I got there in February and was there until May 1952. But, that's the only submarine activity that I know of that took place.

Q: It was an accommodation for submariners to have some part in the operations because their use in terms of activities around the Korean peninsula were nil.

Adm. L.: There was no mission for them.

Q: You say there was some labor problems developed in the submarine base.

Adm. L.: No, out in Yokosuka, and of course, the Yokosuka Naval Base had been taken over entirely by the U.S. Government. There were mobs several times who didn't actually storm the naval base.

Q: You mean Japanese citizens?

Adm. L.: Yes. They made threats to do so. I don't know what the cause was except probably inherent. Anti-militarism against the United States. We still had the carriers that came in there, you know? Although we had an agreement with Japan, I guess not to have nuclear weapons.

Q: They hadn't arrived yet.

Adm. L.: No. Again, I'm sorry, I'm getting ahead of my story. This is when I went back as a flag officer.

But the uprisings were when I was a Captain. What caused the uprisings I don't know unless it was just antipathy against the U.S. military establishment. But, they never did storm the gates, they paraded and marched in town.

Q: It was a sizeable radical element?

Loughlin #4 -181-

Adm. L.: Yes, sir, it was.

Q: You remember when Eisenhower's trip had to be cancelled to Japan because of the battles later?

Adm. L.: Yes.

Q: Did you have any brush with the MacArthur command in Japan?

Adm. L.: No. I operated directly under Admiral Briscoe and Admiral Callaghan. We were ComNavFe and Otto Spahr, a classmate of mine, was the Operations Officer. The short time I was there all my official duties had to do with the ComNavFe staff. Admiral Briscoe was away from there. Admiral Callaghan was there. Did you ever interview Admiral Briscoe?

Q: I never did.

Adm. L.: Absolutely wonderful, wonderful man. I think his widow is still alive and lives down in Mississippi.

So, to answer your question, the answer is no. As I said all my, well I was just a very junior Captain at this point with the staff at ComNavFe.

Q: That all came to an end in 1954. Then you got a call back to Annapolis?

Adm. L.: Then I saw my orders. The first I had heard of it. My orders were published.

Q: You hadn't had anything to do with it?

Adm. L.: Yes, I had.

Loughlin #4 -182-

Q: All right.

Adm. L.: When I left here in 1952 Ian Eddy, who was a very close friend of mine, had relieved Howard Caldwell as Director of Athleti In my last year as Officer Representative, Ian Eddy was the Director of Athletics. Charlie Buchanan, with whom I had served on the USS NEW MEXICO way back in 1934 to 1937, or 1935 to 1937, was the Commandant. So, I let it be known to both Charlie and Ian that I would be very interested in being considered for the job. So, that was the extent of my involvement. They were both friends and I had no reluctance of saying, "Hey, I'm in the right seniority bracket." Ian was out of 1930 and this was three years later and I'm out of 1933. Howard Caldwell was out of 1927. So, I was in the right seniority bracket to get it.

I don't know if I've mentioned this before or not, but perhaps I did. Didn't I discuss Killer Kane, Bill Kane coming back to--I thought I did when we were talking about the Thompson Trophy and the athletic sword.

Q: No.

Adm. L.: Bill Kane was over in Europe on duty and while I was deployed during this time that the decision was being made, he made a special trip back here to be interviewed or to see Charlie Buchanan.

At that time Turner Joy was ill, but he was still Superintende And, Charlie told him, "Gee, Bill I know your service reputation and know you. I've never served with you. I've served with Elliott. Ian has served with Elliott. We were both on the staff up at ComSubLant. As far as I'm concerned he's the one I am going to recommend for the job."

So, that is just what happened. Apparently Admiral Holloway who was the Chief of Bureau of Personnel, with whom I'd served also. He was the Superintendent when I came back here--

Q: You certainly had the inner track.

Adm. L.: Well, at least I was known. I think that was the main thing. And I had had the experience here as Officers Representative and on the Board of Control. So, I think all of those things, and the fact also Marjorie, my wife, was very well liked by the upper hierarchy. As a matter of fact, Slade Cutter, I was just reading through some letters here a few weeks ago and I hadn't even realized that Slade had written them. Slade, who incidentally relieved me in 1957, he wrote me right after my orders were out and he said, "Congratulations." He was in the Office of Information in Washington, Chinfo. He said, "I don't know who was in the running, or how close anyone else is to it, but I do know that Marjorie made a terrific contribution to your getting the job." Now, he volunteered that information. Whether that was through the Eddy's or through the Buchanan's or Admiral Holloway, I haven't the slightest idea. I doubt if Admiral Holloway had anything to do with it. I think he just went along with the recommendation.

Q: You might say something about the wives and their importance in terms of selections, the Board of Selections.

Adm. L.: I don't think, it's kind of a hard thing to say. I don't think they are as important in your getting selected as they are in not getting selected.

Q: You mean, if there is a difficulty there?

Adm. L.: Right. They help. But, I think they hurt more than they help. In other words, I don't think you're going to be selected because of your wife, I know you're not going to be selected because of your wife.

Q: If she is not able to carry out her role.

Adm. L.: And, if she is an alcoholic. It works both ways, I'm sure. My wife was a definite asset to me in my whole career. I know she was. But, conversely had she been a different person then I would not have gone as far as I did. That's just my personal opinion.

Q: Well, so the recommendation went through.

Adm. L.: It went through and as I said, I hadn't gotten a letter from anyone. You know the orders for officers come out on the dispatch. One morning I was going through the board and it said, "Orders for Officers," and here it was, Director of Athletics at the U.S. Naval Academy.

Q: Well, tell me about those three years, those very significant years.

Adm. L.: Let me start off by making a generalization. I got awfully mad at some of my friends up in Washington. I had only had one tour of duty here but they called it then and they call it now the Country Club down here.

Q: The Academy is a country club?

Adm. L.: And, I can truthfully say, Jack, that I worked harder and put more time in the director of Athletics job than any job I've ever had in my life. But, I loved it. It was something I loved doing. But, you try to tell these bureaucrats up in Washington and they just laugh at you. But, this was a six day a week or seven day a week job from early in the morning until late at night. You know, you went to the practices and you went to the games. I would go to the office on Saturday morning to get caught up on the work. As I said, I honestly put more time in on this job in those three years than any other job I've ever had.

Q: So, it's hard work, but pleasant.

Adm. L.: I loved it, yes, sir. I, unfortunately fell into a situation not of my own making, and I think this should be recorded without mentioning all the names. Before I came here a regular on the football team had been accused of a Class A performance. It had to do with an honor violation.

This had to be Turner Joy's administration because Charlie Buchanan was a central figure in this. It went through the chain of command and went to the Secretary of the Navy and recommended discharge. Well, the story I got and I cannot vouch for this, but the story I got was that Eddie Erdelatz, who was a coach, went over the Superintendent's head and the Commandant's head directly to the Secretary of the Navy to make a plea to keep this kid in and he succeeded. The kid was not kicked out.

Q: Who was SecNav at that point?

Loughlin #4 -186-

Adm. L.: I don't know when it was. Of course, I wasn't here. Now, this part is hearsay. But, what isn't hearsay is when Charlie found out about it he and Eddie just became poles apart. I was told that for the few months before I got here to relieve Ian Eddy that they would not even speak to each other. And, Charlie was Commandant for at least three months after I arrived and to the best of my knowledge they never spoke to each other. So, I had a schism here. I say I had it, I was working for both the Superintendent and the Commandant and had to work with all the coaches and Erdelatz particularly. Yet, here you had the Commandant and the head football coach who were just out and out opponents.

Q: Think of all those years you had trained as a diplomat.

Adm. L.: Then Taylor Keith relieved Charlie two or three months after I arrived. In the meantime Turner Joy had been retired and Charlie was acting Commandant and Superintendent. I mean Commandant and acting Superintendent until Freddie Boone arrived. Then Taylor Keith relieved Charlie. It was a very, very unpleasant situation to be in. I think I ought to add a word of explanation. To my knowledge, Jack, I am the only non-football player that's ever been the Director of Athletics at the Naval Academy. To my knowledge.

Q: But, you were right next door, basketball.

Adm. L.: I might also add that the three year record we had, the three years I was Director of Athletics, is the best three year record we've ever had in football at the Naval Academy.

So, there is a lesson there someplace. I don't know what it is.

Q: It should be tried again.

Adm. L.: There is a lesson there. But, anyway, I got along very well with Eddie because Eddie knew I was not a football player although I was an athlete. I said, "Eddie, you're the coach and I'm the Director of Athletics. So, let's just work together on that basis." And we did.

Q: As you came into this job did you have any specific objectives that you hoped to accomplish?

Adm. L.: I didn't have the day I came in. But, in a very short time I developed two objectives. Both of which I really am quite proud of. I found out that there was a big distinction between major and minor sports. And I found out in a very peculiar way. And the end of my first year here anyone who had gotten three letters in the, so called, major sports which were lacrosse, basketball, football, wrestling, and maybe swimming. I can't remember. There were four, five or six. They would get a blanket with their name on it. Anyone who had three letters the, so called, minor sports didn't get anything. And, I said, "This is ridiculous." I said this to myself. I said, "Just because--why shouldn't a person who gets three letters in gymnastics, why should't a person who gets three letters in tennis, why shouldn't a person who gets three letters in any varsity sport as long as it's a varsity sport, why shouldn't he get the same as anyone else?"

So, I brought it up before the Board and there was absolutely no opposition. So, from then on and I think it still pertains right now if you get your three letters in any varsity sport. We did away with the major and minor sport definition. There is no such thing as a major and minor sport. They were varsity sports at the Naval Academy.

The other thing was, having been at the Naval Station I was, although I'm not a sailor, the year after I relieved Larry the ROYONA was the first Naval Academy boat that ever won the Bermuda Race and was ever first to cross, I mean the first to cross the line and also first in Class A. She didn't win the fleet because a Class C boat almost always, always wins the fleet. But, she beat everybody across and was first in Class A.

So, I worked on an arrangement to give varsity letters to the sailors providing they met certain criteria. It would only affect Second Classmen and First Classmen had to go through navigation and then you had to be in part of Bermuda Race or part of the Newport Race. In those days we had a good sailing program, but nowhere near the comprehensive program we have now. We had the dinghys, and the Class A's, and the yawls and all that. But, Lord, the sailing program today is so huge. But, we did--I was able to get that, again with no opposition at all. We made sailing, based upon a criteria that we established eligible for a varsity letter.

Q: It seems to me those were two very commonsense objectives.

Adm. L.: It just made sense to me, Jack, having been a tennis and a basketball player. One a so-called major and one so-called minor, it just didn't make sense to me. I mean if some guy goes out there and works his head off and--

Q: Has a particular aptitude in that area.

Adm. L.: For gym or fencing. What difference does it make? Rifle, pistol. I don't care. He's working just as many hours as anyone else. So, those two things I am proud of. I did accomplish both, I mean I initiated both. I didn't accomplish them because the Board had to approve them. But, there was absolutely no opposition to it whatsoever.

Q: I suppose that practice had to do with money in terms of income to the athletic program didn't it?

Adm. L.: No, I don't think so.

Q: The major sports like football, I think, is the largest in terms--

Adm. L.: I don't think so, Jack. I really have sympathy for Bo Coppedge and his problems today. I didn't have the problems that he has. The money rolled in. We didn't charge anything. We played Maryland here on Thompson Stadium with fifteen thousand people there and didn't charge a penny. We did it deliberately to see how much of a crowd we could have. It was one of the biggest lacrosse crowds, probably the biggest that has ever been in the history of lacrosse that day and they beat us.

We went to a bowl game that first year and the transportation was cheap. The food was cheap. The lodging was cheap. We were in the black ink. Salaries were not--I mean, I think Eddie Erdelatz got something like fifteen-thousand dollars a year which was one of the highest salaries in the country. But, you just can't imagine the difference between what it costs to run the program today as to what it cost to run it back in 1954 and 1955. So, money was really no object. Money was no object.

I just think it was a throwback, with all due respect, to the Jonas Ingram and Bill Ingram, all the football players here always ran the program here as Director of Athletics.

Q: It was The Sport.

Adm. L.: They were the only income producing team that we had. So, I just think no one had ever thought about it. So, I can't agree with you that any financial arrangement complicated this at all. I don't think that anyone ever thought about it.

I remember a gymnast who dated one of my daughters and said, "Captain Loughlin, this is the finest thing that's ever happened to the so-called, minor sports at the Naval Academy." He said, "You have delegated us up to now we feel we're equal to everyone."

Q: Well, what were some of your headaches as Director of Athletics?

Adm. L.: Eddie Erdelatz was the only one. Eddie was, and I hate to speak disrespectfully, but Eddie was one of the most disloyal people I've ever met. Eddie would cut your throat and--

Q: Disloyal to people or disloyal to the Naval Academy?

Adm. L.: Disloyal to the Naval Academy. Eddie wanted to have his own little harem, his bailiwick football team. In those days, Jack, we had sections. Do you remember the football sections?

Q: Yes.

Adm. L.: Fortunately he never, I don't know if he pushed for it or not, fortunately the kids still lived in Bancroft Hall with other roommates.

Q: They were still a part of the Academy were they?

Adm. L.: If Eddie had had his way it would have been like Bear Bryant down in Alabama. He had a separate dormitory for them. I could not reason with Eddie. He was a very, very unreasonable person. As I said, he had absolutely no sense of loyalty to me, or to the Commandant, or to the Superintendent, or even to the Naval Academy. The football team was the only thing, but I must say he was one heck of a football coach.

Q: And that's why he got by with his act. Well, talk about the problem of getting potential players here at the Academy.

Adm. L.: Rip Miller was the Assistant Director of Athletics and in those days we had what we called a "bird dog" system. Now, we had I don't know how many people, maybe twenty or thirty scattered throughout the country who were on the lookout for prospective football players.

Q: These were former Academy men?

Adm. L.: No, not necessarily. Many of them are civilians. Rip would locate these people and we had the Foundation program going then. In those days the Foundation existed solely to assist athletics to get into the Naval Academy. Solely. George Welsh and Ronnie Beagle, Roger Staubach, and Joe Bellino. You name them up until 1963, every decent football player that ever came to the Naval Academy except Ned Oldham, who was a walk on, came to the Naval Academy through the Foundation program. In those days, the competition really wasn't intense. You didn't have Oklahoma, Ohio State, and Alabama monopolizing the headlines and all the bowl games. In fact, we went to three bowl games I think in five years then. That helped a lot. That helped the recruiting tremendously on both athletes and to raise the whole caliber of the brigade of midshipmen.

Q: I suppose the Army-Navy game itself helped, didn't it?

Adm. L.: Yes, I think it did. It's on national TV every year and sell out crowds every year, and good games, too.

Q: It's a major sports event.

Adm. L.: Oh, yes. That's when Army still had their horses. It was a wonderful game.

The only other headache I had, and I hope Admiral Boone doesn't see this, but Freddie was a very, very difficult person for whom or with whom to work. There are two reasons in my opinion. One, he knew nothing about athletics. And, two, he and Polly had never had any children. I just think that Freddie was the worst case of detailing I've ever seen to be ordered down as Superintendent of the Naval Academy.

Q: He wanted the job though.

Adm. L.: Yes, he and Switzer and somebody else were in the running for it. He got it.

The first thing he tried to do after I got here was to do away with the Sports Publicity Director over at the Naval Academy and put them all under the PIO Officer at the Naval Academy.

I said, "Admiral Boone, this will never work. This guy has to go on trips. He's got to meet with the sports writers. He's got to go to luncheons. He has to put out publicity releases. It just will not work."

Well, thank the Lord I convinced him of that. He gave in on that.

Q: He didn't see the importance of this?

Adm. L.: But, that's about the only thing I won the whole three years I was here. Everything else I lost. He's gracious. He's always a gentleman. But, he was a very, very difficult person to work with. Very difficult.

I have an anecdote about the Sugar Bowl game.

Q: This was in what year?

Adm. L.: This was at the end of my first year. We played on one January of 1955 and I got here in July of 1954. But, Mr. Hebert, you remember Mr. Hebert?

Q: Oh, yes.

Adm. L.: Well, Hebert wrote me a personal letter and asked for something like seventy-five or a hundred or a hundred and fifty tickets for the Sugar Bowl game. Well, we had already made a decision that Congressmen would be given the same privilege for the Sugar Bowl game as the Army-Navy game. In other words, they would get either six or eight preferential seats and as many nonpreferential seats as they wanted.

Q: Mr. Hebert was "Mr. Louisiana."

Adm. L.: Absolutely. So, I wrote back and told him and, boy, did I get a blistering letter. He just called me everything under the sun. So, I sat down and wrote an answer and fortunately I had the foresight instead of sending it off I took it over to show to Admiral Boone. Gee, did he kill it. He said, "You will not send this letter!" So, I didn't send it. But the conclusion to the story was that spring Mr. Hebert was on a board of visitors and Mr. Hebert and I had lunch together at the Yacht Club during the board of visitors meeting. And I told Mr. Hebert the story.

He said, "Elliott, the Superintendent did not have any right to do that. You should have sent that letter to me. You had every right to send that letter to me."

This was his reaction when I told him about the letter. We became firm friends from then on until Mr. Hebert died. I loved the guy.

Q: He was back of the demand for all of the tickets?

Adm. L.: Sure he was. I don't blame him. Hell, Bourbon Street. God, he must have had requests for a thousand tickets down there. I don't blame him.

If you are interested going to the first bowl game since 1924 is a kind of a story in itself.

Q: Well, I certainly am interested.

Adm. L.: What had happened was that a guy named Felix McKnight who was the managing editor of I think the Dallas Morning News, or one of the big newspapers in Dallas was a graduate of, I think, A and M. I'm not sure. And, a guy named Bob Cullum who was the president of the Cotton Bowl Association and was a graduate of SMU. I could have the two schools turned, but those two came up to see me when it looked like we were going to have a season good enough to go to a bowl game, and made a pitch. We arranged a meeting with the Secretary of the Navy and Admiral Holloway. I represented the Superintendent up there with Cullum and McKnight. We decided that the Naval Academy would consider it. Well, of course the Executive Committee had not passed on it yet. So, we met to discuss this thing several times and spent literally hours on end and decided that if we beat Army, at that time we'd lost to Notre Dame by 6 to 0 score and to Pittsburgh by a 21 to 19 score. we had lost two games, but we'd beaten some pretty good teams. We could have won both of those games. But, we decided if we beat Army and because of the advantages in the recruitment and the money and everything else we would make an exception and go to a bowl game, but not make it as a customary event. This was a once, you know we do it this year--

Q: Was there a tentative rule against participation in bowl games?

Adm. L.: Well, we just had never considered it before. Well, we hadn't had really many good teams except during the war years.

So, we did beat Army. One of the most wonderful football games that I've ever seen in my life. I was on TV and radio. I'm digressing, but I think this is an interesting story. I left my seat with about two minutes to go in the first half and before I got up to the press box there had been three touchdowns scored in the last two minutes of the first half.

Q: But, you missed seeing them.

Adm. L.: No, I saw them because I'd stop and look. But, we did beat them. And, then I guess I don't know who made the decision, but we let the team decide where they wanted to go. And, here after all that Felix McKnight and Bob Cullum had done after all they had done the team voted to go to the Sugar Bowl instead of the Cotton Bowl. So, that's where we went.

Q: Had both options been presented to them?

Adm. L.: Oh, we were invited to all of them except the Rose Bowl. So, we went to the Sugar Bowl instead and beat a good Mississippi team. George Welsh, the present coach, was the quarterback.

I never will forget Eddie Erdelatz was never an optimist. I didn't go down. Skip Giffen, my Exec, went down and also represented them. He went down to be with them during the training period. We had two or three people hurt and Mississippi had this terrific write up. They were undefeated all year. No one had scored a touchdown against them rushing all year long. So, the first time I saw Eddie and I was kind of down and out. We had just gotten in the night before the game. He said, "What's the matter Captain? What's the matter with you?"

I said, "It's the first bowl game, Eddie, and it means so darned much. With the injuries you have I just don't feel confident."

He said, "Forget it. We're going to win this football game."

It was the first time he ever told me that.

Well, we took the opening kickoff and went one hundred yards. Right down the field, the first touchdown that had been scored against Mississippi rushing all year long. We finally ended up by beating them by 21 to 0. So, the bowl game was a great success financially and otherwise. The only part part of it was that, again, I have to criticize Admiral Boone on this. He didn't take me into his confidence. Apparently the Secretary of the Navy was under some pressure to have the revenue from this game go to Navy Relief or some charity. He discussed it with the Superintendent and eventually the conclusion was reached that it would not go to a charity. But, what the Secretary of the Navy, and I can't remember who it was at the time. Oh, it was Thomas, that's who it was. It was Thomas. Thomas said,

"All right. The Naval Academy can keep their share, but I want every single penny accounted for from this game it case it comes up why we didn't give it to charity."

All Admiral Boone had to do was tell me that, which he didn't do. So, after the game was over it's been customary before, it's been customary then, and it's customary now that you give the people on the team some kind of a present. I discussed it with Eddie and he said, "Gee, I think a nice sports jacket with the Naval Academy emblem would be a real wonderful thing."

I said, "That's a fine idea."

I went to Admiral Boone and he said, "Nothing doing. You cannot spend one penny."

I said, "Well, Admiral Boone this is unheard of. You've got a hundred and seventy five to two hundred thousand dollars out of this team. I've checked with other coaches. This is customary. It's done every year."

He said, "I don't care. You will not spend one penny on them."

Well, Taylor Keith went to bat for me. He said, "Admiral Boone, in case you don't realize it you have approved a budget which gives Elliott authority to spend twenty-five thousand dollars of the budget on any project which he sees fit." This was true.

Admiral Boone said, "I don't care. There will not be one penny spent on jackets for the football team."

So, I had to call a meeting of the footall team with Charlie Minter. And, Charlie and I explained this to them without being disloyal to Admiral Boone. It was the toughest decision, or really the toughest moment I've ever had. Thank God the kids were a fine bunch. A fine bunch.

So, what we actually did was to make a blanket with Navy 21, Mississippi 0 with the name of each player on it. We gave that to them. I don't think Admiral Boone ever knew about it.

Q: And the money came from other sources. Talk about the Army-Navy series and its importance.

Adm. L.: I think it was important primarily, even though I said we had no difficulty with money in those days, the fact still remains in the Notre Dame and the Army-Navy game were automatic sellouts. In those days we played Notre Dame in South Bend or we had a wonderful arrangement with the Park Board up in Baltimore. We only had to pay, I think, five thousand dollars rental fee. We would bus the kids up and back. Therefore the expenses were nothing for fifty-eight thousand crowd. We just made a tremendous amount of money. The same way with the Army-Navy. I think the rental fee was either five or ten thousand dollars. We got all the concessions. We still do as far as I know. We did in the old days of the JFK stadium. We got all the concessions. We got all the parking. We got all the police protection. The traffic control and everything and it cost peanuts.

Q: Think of the revenue to the city of Philadelphia?

Adm. L.: Right. That's the reason we got it you see. Same way with Baltimore. So, I'm pretty sure that those two games represented about eighty to eighty-five percent of our entire revenue for those three years in football. The programs, you'd be amazed just how much we got out of the Army-Navy game. You'd be amazed.

So, we were then and now, we're the strongest supporters of Army to get back in the athletic picture. If we lose the TV rights to this Army-Navy game we're in real deep trouble.

Q: Well, you almost did a year or so ago.

Adm. L.: That's right, that's right. So, Bo Coppedge is probably the strongest supporter of getting Army back on track. That's the reason we all recommended so strongly they get Carl Ullrich up there as athletic director which he is now. If he can't get them back on track, then nobody can because he's one of the finest men that I've ever associated with in athletics.

Q: Now isn't it true that the funds that come in from the football game go not only to support that program, but also all the other sports?

Adm. L.: All the other sports. Yes, sir. Every varsity sport is supported by the revenues primarily from football. Lacrosse brings in a little. Basketball brings in a little. Wrestling a little. You know everything used to be free except football. Now, they charge for indoor sports, lacrosse-

Q: You must have some comments on the merits of insisting that the athletic program be self-supporting.

Adm. L.: In my opinion I think the main reason is that we don't have congressional pressure to play schools throughout the country other than the ones we have to play. The three years I was here I had just one letter from a Senator who tried to get a game scheduled with Oregon State. I think if we were government subsidized; I think that it would be an intolerable situation.

Q: That's a new angle I hadn't known about. You'd be open.

Adm. L.: Absolutely. I think this is one of the main reasons why, I think, we should keep it the way it is. You would just have all kinds of pressure to play these schools.

Q: But, at the same time in lean years it puts an awful burden on the Athletic Department doesn't it? And, yet it's such an essential part of the whole program.

Adm. L.: Well, they have a pretty good reserve. I don't know whether they publicize it or not, Jack. But, I think I'm correct, at least it happened when I was there we always had enough money in reserve to take care of the season. For instance, the Army-Navy game was almost cancelled when Kennedy was assassinated, if you recall. It was delayed a week, but it was almost cancelled. Now, if we lost the TV rights, there is, what, two hundred or two hundred and fifty thousand dollars down the drain. So, they can take care of a bad year with a catastrophe. But, I doubt if they can take care of say, two or three successive years. I think they would have to cut back drastically in the sports program here.

Q: Has there ever been any agitation in the Congress to subsidize the athletic program?

Adm. L.: I don't know. Not to my knowledge there hasn't been any.

Q: Doesn't the Board of Visitors have a real appreciation of the value of the program?

Adm. L.: I think they do, but since it has run this way for so many years, why I don't know. I didn't sit in on the Board of Visitors even though I was a member of the Athletic Board. I never sat in on the Board of Visitors. But, it's been this way forever and it's been a success, so why change it? Lord knows the Federal Government subsidizes enough things in this country anyway. I certainly wouldn't be an advocate of it.

Q: Now you also had the Physical Training Department. Now, what did that entail?

Adm. L.: Not very much actually. We had people like Tony Rubino down there and my Exec who was really the Physical Education Office He ran the Department with Rubino. I spent very, very little time on that particular aspect. Very little time. You didn't have the time to do it frankly. So, I did not get mixed up in the intramural sports program too much. The Physical Education fitness program. I supervised it.

Q: You certainly had the authority to step in?

Adm. L.: Right. Well, for instance, the swimming coach, John Higgins, wanted to change the swimming qualifications. He said, "Survival is really what we are looking for in the Navy, not being able to swim across the pool with a breast stroke and back with a side stroke. So, we made a basic change in those days and changed the swimming qualification to have a certain number of minutes in the water for survival.

Q: Is that a result of World War II?

Adm. L.: I don't know why John recommended it. But, it made sense to me. So, we made the changes. Anything that came up that had to be changed I had the ultimate authority on the thing. I really didn't get into the nuts and bolts of the thing. I don't know any athletic director who does. I don't see how he has the time to do it.

Q: And in that time you didn't have the problem of female midshipmen.

Adm. L.: No, and incidentally that's a problem too. You're talking about the bad years, as we get more and more girls in and more and more teams in with this Title IX, or whatever you call it, trying to get equal financial help you know, to have the girls participate equally with men.

Q: It's going to make a drain?

Adm. L.: Oh, it's going to make a horrible problem.

Interview No. 5 with Rear Admiral Elliott Loughlin, U.S. Navy
(Retired)

Place: Annapolis, Maryland

Date: 18 September 1980

Subject: Biography

By: John T. Mason, jr.

Q: A question that occurred to me in regard to the athletics at the Naval Academy; when Eddie Erdelatz was the coach his assistant was a man named Ben Martin who was a Naval Academy Graduate. He understood the workings of the Academy in a way that Erdelatz didn't. Then it brings to mind George Welsh who is there currently and who understands. Do you want to talk a little about that; the fact that Naval Academy men have an understanding of the demands made upon the players and the coach too?

Adm. E.: Precisely correct and that's the reason Ben Martin left. Ben was the principal assistant to Eddie my first year here which would be the 1954-1955 season. As I said, I think I mentioned this before, I don't like to desecrate the dead, so to speak, but Ben having stood sixth in his class and wanting desperately to stay in the Navy, but he was given a medical discharge against his wishes. He could not stand the way that Eddie Erdelatz operated within the constraints of the Naval Academy.

Charlie Minter was my Exec at the time and he came up to Charlie and said, "I cannot work with this person anymore."

So, he left and I was instrumental in trying to locate a head coaching job for him because he was, just simply an outstanding man in every respect. I think his coaching record bore that observation out later at Virginia and at the Air Force Academy.

Q: Well, a man like that would understand that at the Naval Academy these football players along with all the others are training to be Naval officers, whereas in college football elsewhere they are athletes and heroes and get all the consideration.

Adm. L.: As I said, the difficult time the three years I was here with Eddie was the fact that Eddie did not want to conform to the restrictions at the Naval Academy which he well understood when he took the job. He wanted to keep the football squad as an entity really outside the brigade of midshipmen. That just does not work here.

You might recall, Jack, in those days we had the so-called football sections and I still think it is the right thing to do. With all the time they miss on road trips, I don't know how they make up the time in the regular session. I presume they do it when the football season is over which, I think, is a little unfair to them. I don't think the fact that they are in football sections gave them any undue advantage over the rest of the brigade of midshipmen. I think it just enabled them to have their work load set up so that if they left on a Friday for a game, why, the next week their study and work assignments could be spread out so they could make up the work. I saw nothing wrong with it then and I see nothing wrong with it now. But, somebody in their wisdom decreed against that. I don't know when that decision was made, but I don't think there have been any football sections for a good many years now.

Q: I wonder if you would talk about the problem of scheduling games? Especially football games and the influence which, inevitably is exerted by the media.

Adm. L.: Well, it's easy to talk about, but it's difficult to give you, I think, the proper rationale. The basic fundamental ground rule principle that we worked on was the Naval Academy as a national institution. Therefore, the Naval Academy, did not want to be associated with any conference where you are limited in scope. We wanted to travel in the various sections of the country, the West Coast, maybe every other year, the Midwest, the South, the Northeast. If you look at our schedule over a period of years that is precisely what we do. Strangely enough political pressure, at least the time I was here, did not come into play at all. I only had one time when a Senator tried to get us to schedule a game out on the West Coast. We were able to circumvent that request. Of course, the schedules were made out in those days five or six years in advance. Now, they are made about eight to ten years in advance.

Q: Actually when you came there as Director of Athletics you had it all mapped out for you, didn't you? So, you were mapping it out for your successor.

Adm. L.: I was mapping it out for my successor, that is correct. A situation rather particular to the Naval Academy is that all kinds of media pressure is put on to play Maryland. In those days the Air Force Academy was just getting started. We have the longest intersectional rivalry with Notre Dame of any school in the country. We just didn't feel with the emotional impact of the Army-Navy game, the Notre Dame game, and the soon to be Air Force game that we could stand another great emotional game which, of course, whenever Navy plays Maryland in anything is an emotional game. However, I did schedule Maryland for a two game series which we played. But, I think that's the last time we played Maryland.

Q: This problem of scheduling so many years in advance is a risky thing isn't it because you might have an awfully bad team?

Adm. L.: That's a gamble you see. You gamble. Then, of course, something like Penn State happens. If you recall a few years ago just before the season started for the next year, why, Penn State just cancelled the series. That left them in a terrible bind here at the Naval Academy. You do gamble. There is no question about it. Before Bear Bryant went to Alabama when he was at Texas A & M they had nothing and he brought them up. I think the year before he went to Alabama they went way down. You know what he's done since he went there. So, five, six or seven years if a team is down now, why, there is just no way of telling what they are going to be.

Q: No, no indeed there isn't.

Adm. L.: But, again if you go by that cornerstone of scheduling where you go to the Midwest and the Far West and the South and the Northeast and so forth, why, you're going to have to take the best drawing card you can get. I mean finances is always an overriding factor in scheduling.

Q: I would think in one sense, since you do follow that nationwide pattern, that the gambling is more likely to pay off. One team far off is likely to be down one year and up another.

Adm. L.: Well, for instance, we're playing Washington this year. We haven't been to the West Coast for three or four years now. We had to go out to the West Coast well, say five years ago who would you pick? USC, UCLA, Stanford, or California, or Washington. Well, we've played all of those except I don't think we've ever played UCLA, but we've played all the rest of them. And, Washington is a Navy oriented territory with a beautiful stadium out there and they always have good teams. As a matter of fact I scheduled a Washington game when I was Director of Athletics the year we went to the Orange Bowl. We beat them out there on a Greg Mather field goal in the last few seconds--few minutes of play and that year Washington went to the Rose Bowl and we went to the Orange Bowl. There was a lot of pressure to get us to go to the Rose Bowl that year. They wanted revenge. I think that was the only game they lost that year. The attitude was, well we beat them once, why should we play them again. So, we went down and got our ears pinned back by Missouri in the Orange Bowl.

Q: This subject ties in with another, how to keep the service academies, not only the Naval Academy, but the service academies competitive in sports. You have said a few things about it, but I think you can say more.

Adm. L.: Well, Jack, I firmly believe that the time of our being a national power, or the Air Force, or Army is long gone. I don't think we're going to get any really truly blue chip players in here anymore. We're going to get some good ones and we have some good ones, but the five years of obligated service, the specter of pro football, even though a minuscule percentage, say one or two percent or not even that many of all college players make the draft of the NFL, anyone who is a good football player, I feel, he still has that dream up ahead of him.

Q: Riches. The pot of gold.

Adm. L.: And, the days of Staubach and a Bellino, in my opinion, those days are long gone. I don't think we'll ever be able to succeed and successfully recruit an outstanding high school player, anyone who is pursued by the so-called football factories, the teams that have to stand in the first ten every year or the coach gets fired. I just don't think we can compete with them.

Q: It's a built in conflict between-- The purpose of the service academy,...

Adm. L.: It's not only the academic challenge. I think if anyone ever drew a valid comparison between our, the courses and our athletics, all our athletics taken here as compared to any college in the country, why it would almost be laughable. Perhaps you saw in the paper this morning this linebacker who made twenty-five tackles in the Virginia game has a 3.54 average in systems engineering, one of the toughest majors here at the Academy.

Q: I didn't see that.

Adm. L.: And, you look at the number of football players in the country who could not only take that major, but get a 3.54 average and it's just an incredible performance. So, you have the academic challenge most of these people are not ready to face. I mean most of the good football players aren't ready to face. You have the five years obligated service. You have the four years of military life here which a lot of them don't want. You've got the specter, not the specter, but you've got the pro-football dream up ahead of you. So, I just don't think we can compete and George Welsh has been very candid in his remarks since he's been coach here. He said, we can play the Notre Dame's and the Michigan's and teams like that, but not ten or eleven games a year." He said, "We can play, one two, or three or maybe four, but we just do not have the manpower to do this week after week. We can't do it."

If you'll notice the schedule the last few years has noticeabl become, has dropped in severity as far as the quality of football that we play.

Q: Yes. Very uneven in terms of some of our quite potent challenge

Loughlin #5 -211-

Adm. L.: We're down to Kent State and William and Mary this year, and Villanova and Boston College. They are all good teams. Some of them are good teams, but they're not in the top echelon. We just can't play the major teams on a week after week basis. We don't have the talent and we don't have the man power.

Q: I wonder if you have any general kind of statement to make out of your long experience with athletics, your experience with scholastics standards here? Do athletes generally not conform to a high intellectual standard? That's what I'm trying to get at. I'm not expressing it very well.

Adm. L.: Well, the only figure you can use and I can't give you accurate figures, but every year you see some school about the percentage of people who graduate and get a degree that go to the other colleges. Except for attrition here our percentage is, what, ninety-eight percent of people who come here unless they are hurt they graduate in four years. This is unheard of in the big football factories when red shirting was legal.* You know what red shirting is?

Q: Yes.

Adm. L.: Now I understand that red shirting is legal. When I was Director of Athletics, the Superintendent of or President of the college had to sign a statement with the NCAA each year that an athlete was making satisfactory progress toward a degree. So, red shirting was absolutely illegal unless by virtue of an injury. If he got hurt before the first game started and couldn't

---

*Red shirting is the practice of keeping a college athlete out of competition for a year in order to prolong his period of eligibility.

play that year, why, even though you didn't make satisfactory progress they would permit you have to have that fifth year. When you look at the comparison of people who finish their college education in four years and get a degree from any school in the country, any football school in the country as compared to the Naval Academy, why, there is no comparison, absolutely no comparison. You have people who go to college for five years and end up at the grade of a sophmore.

Q: Well, this only bespeaks the fact that the standards have been so low in recent years in our country, the educational standards.

Adm. L.: That's right. The NCAA is somewhat to blame for this. They are under pressure of the big time schools. They have lowered the academic qualifications to such a degree, Jack, that all you have to do is to get a high school diploma and a 2.0 grade average with no subjects, I mean no--as long as you meet the requirements of that particular high school then you are eligible to go to any school in the country. You are eligible. These kids are just not prepared for a college education.

Q: It's predicated on the fact that we seem to think that everybody ought to be entitled to a college education.

Adm. L.: If you're a good athlete.

Q: Now, there was another subject that came up during your tour of duty there and that was the field house. You haven't said anything about that.

Adm. L.: The field house was started after I relieved Ian Eddy within a month or so. It had been in the works for at least two years before and it was killed. Doctor Hanna, who at that time was the President of the Michigan State University, if I'm not mistaken, was on some kind of an advisory board and he personally, at least I was told--

Q: The Advisory Board at the Naval Academy?

Adm. L.: No. It had to do with the Presidential staff.

Q: Oh, I see.

Adm. L.: Or with the Congressional, I don't know whether it was with Congress or with the President. But, I understand that Dr. Hanna, and I think he was on the Board of Visitors too, he almost, personally is responsible for us having the field house item put back in the budget. The work actually started the summer of 1954 and was completed in time for the graduation exercise of 1957. It took just about three years to build it. I lived within fifty yards of it and they drove something like five hundred and thirty five piles and it took about twelve minutes per pile with a pound, pound, pound. You could hear it all over the Naval Academy grounds.

Q: That I'm sure you were able--that was your contribution, I suppose.

Adm. L.: I really had nothing to do with it. I happened to be here when the work was started and when it was completed, but all the gound work had been done before I came here.

Q: Can you comment on its value once it was in operation?

Adm. L.: It was a facility that we had to have. When I was a midshipman we played our basketball games, we didn't even have portable floors in those days. We played on that hard surface in Dahlgren Hall. You know, it wasn't marble, but it was--

Q: Concrete wasn't it?

Adm. L.: I guess it was, but this is what we played on. We had no facilities for indoor track. We had no facilities for basketba We had no facilities for wrestling. The field house was an absolu necessity.

Q: Why was it so difficult do you suppose to get the Congress to consider the need for this?

Adm. L.: I can't answer that.

Q: So many of their members from time to time are on the Board of Visitors and quite aware of the physical plant here.

Adm. L.: I just don't know. It is because I was not here and I don't know what the efforts were to obtain authorization to build a field house.

Q: Well, that leads me to the stadium. The drive was on while you were here. Well, tell me about that.

Adm. L.: I think to put the horse before the cart, I think the decision was made to build the additional wings of Bancroft Hall. You see, all of these things happened about the same time. The fill in the Severn River and Spa Creek, that was authorized and started.

Well, as soon as that was authorized it was obvious that that was going to knock out the stands on that side, on the East side of Thompson Stadium. So, we owned the land, the Naval Academy Athletic Association owned all of Admiral Heights, you know. Not all of it, but a great deal of it.

Q: That was foresight to have acquired that.

Adm. L.: It sure was. Morris Gilmore was responsible for that. So, the decision was made to build a stadium knowing that we were going to lose Thompson Stadium. A lot of people opposed the building of a stadium. But, the answer is, what are you going to do? You're not going to have Thompson Stadium. Are you going to play all your football games away? Which is the only alternative that we had.

Q: You mean, were these townspeople who opposed it?

Adm. L.: No, it was people within the Navy.

Q: Their opposition, I suppose, was financial.

Adm. L.: Yes. We had to finance it ourselves. When I say we, I mean the Navy did. There was no appropriated funds to my knowledge that went into it.

Q: Was there any thought that since the Congress had financed the field house that they might be generous enough to consider the stadium?

Adm. L.: I don't think so because the field house primarily was part of the Physical Education Department. For instance, all of the physical education instructors have their offices, or practically all of them have their offices in the field house. It is used a great deal for intramural activities in addition to varsity track and varsity wrestling and varsity basketball. That's about the only varsity sports you have there. The rest of the time it's used for intramural sports. Whereas the football stadium is solely adjunct of the Naval Academy Athletic Association and therefore no appropriated funds could be obtained and I don't think any attempts were made to obtain appropriated funds to build the stadium.

Q: Now, tell me about your role in this project.

Adm. L.: Very little. My main role was to ask Admiral Smedberg to make Gene Fluckey the head of the fund raising drive. That was the real reason the stadium succeeded.

Q: Yes. That's what Smeddy says too.

Adm. L.: Gene and I are the closest of friends. We made three war patrols together in wolf-packs. I asked him to come out to San Diego where he could take a tender job, and he did, and he got his squadron. I asked him to come back here and we were able to swing it to get him back here and he was the head of the Department of--

Q: Engineering was it?

Adm. L.: No, juice, Electrical Engineering. When I left or just before I left the thing was really starting, why, he reported in, I guess he had been here that year, the first year that Admiral Smedberg was superintendent. At my recommendation Smeddy made him the head of the fund raising drive.

Q: What were your reasons for this selection?

Adm. L.: Well, I just think Gene Fluckey is one of the most outstanding Naval officers I've ever seen if not the most outstanding Naval officer. I knew that if he took it he would succeed. He's got more innovative ideas than you could shake a stick at. He just is full of ideas and they are all practical too.

Now, the mechanics of the fund raising I don't know because I left at just about that time. I know the fleet contributed a great deal. When I got the USS MISSISSINEWA out in the Sixth Fleet there was a terrific drive on by Cat Brown to each ship, the one who had the greatest participation would get a special liberty port some place or some time off some place in the Mediterranean. In other words he waved some little red apples in front of them in order to get the support.

Q: Actually they got the fleets competing with each other.

Adm. L.: I think they did.

Q: Smeddy said that he had to raise 2.2 million.

Adm. L.: I think that's about right. I think the Athletic Association put in a little over a million and the other two-thirds came from private donations.

Q: And, Gates was Secretary of the Navy. Gates was not in favor of this, of making the attempt.

Adm. L.: I didn't know that.

Q: But, Smeddy persuaded him.

Adm. L.: I didn't realize that he was against it. The only reason, I think this is of a little bit of interest, the only argument Gene and I had about this was that the stadium was built according to the plans that were prepared and Morris Gilmore supervised them. But, Gene wanted to build a fifty or sixty five thousand stadium because he foresaw the tremendous boost in population, not only in Annapolis and Anne Arundel County, but the whole state. But, I pointed out that you're only going to draw your fifteen, or eighteen, or twenty thousand people for a weak team. At that time we had the most ideal situation in the world with the Baltimore stadium, with the Park Board up there. I think we only paid five thousand dollars rental. We bussed the midshipmen up there for practically nothing compared to the cost, even of those days, of trains and aircraft travel. We had an arrangement with the Park Board that the Colts could not play, I think it was one day after our Notre Dame game and five days before. In other words, they were frozen out that weekend. They couldn't possibly play on a Sunday when we play Notre Dame on Saturday. We had everything going for us. Of course, that changed, but at that time it was a condition that existed. So, my argument was, why do we need a fifty-five thousand, or fifty thousand stadium here? It would only be utilized for such games that we can just as easily play in Baltimore. Apparently that argument prevailed because we stuck by the original plans, roughly a thirty, of course we went into those memorial seats, I think that cut the seating down a little. Originally it was envisioned thirty thousand as a round figure. I don't believe we have thirty thousand seats there now, it's twenty-eight or twenty-nine. Something like that.

Q: And, it still proves adequate.

Adm. L.: It still is adequate. We've had only, what, five sell out crowds in something like, well when was the stadium opened, 1957, 1958? Some place in there, 1959 maybe. That's almost twenty years and we've had only five or six sell outs.

Q: I would think that there would have been a psychological factor if it had been so much bigger and was never sold out. This would have some bearing on the spirit of the team I would think.

Adm. L.: Well, I just didn't see the necessity of it and I think my forecast was borne out.

Q: Did you have anything to do with the arrangements for the town and the state in order to get the permits and--

Adm. L.: No, no. We owned the land. Of course they condemned the parking lot, the East parking lot. The Athletic Department didn't get anywhere near the fair market value of the thing. That's where the new Court of Appeals building went up.

Q: The state buildings, yes.

Adm. L.: They just condemned it and bang that was it. They paid off, but they didn't get anywhere near the market value of that land. We really didn't need it because the East and West parking lot right now is adequate for even a sell out crowd. That was really wasted land on the other side of Taylor Avenue. So, I don't blame the state for trying to get it, but I think they could have given a better price on it.

Q: Now, the city also has privileges there don't they?

Adm. L.: Well, we've had a running fight with taxes. I think they, that some tax we pay the city is based on attendance. I know Apostle (the mayor) had a run around on that for years. I don't know what the outcome was, but yes they allow the use of the parking lot when there are no football games or something like that. You know they have these shuttle busses for the boat shows and things like that. So, I think the cooperation between the city and the Athletic Association is pretty good now. I don't think it was for a few years ago. I think it is very good now. It makes the city realize just how much the Naval Academy means to them. Every once in awhile you get a downward dip and afterward some people in town say, "We'd just as soon have the Naval Academy move to the West Coast." Anyone in business around here would say, "You've got rocks in your head."

Q: There is always that adversary relationship between the town and the gown. When you were here as Director of Athletics what sort of contact did you have with the permanent faculty? What did you do to encourage a relationship and what sort of ideas did you get from them?

Adm. L.: Well, strangely enough, Jack, I didn't have much relationship with the civilian faculty. You must realize that in those days there wasn't an Admissions Board. The Secretary of the Academic Board really acted as the Admissions Board. He is the one who, based upon the records, decided who was going to be offered an appointment. We had the football sections and we really didn't have any academic problems. I can't recall any first string football player or athlete being discharged for academic reasons. I just can't recall any. Now, whether the kids were smarter in those days or whether they wanted to stay in more or not I just don't know. But, there was really no occasion for me to have personal intimate contact with the civilian faculty, and I didn't. I knew a lot of them, Hap Hepler, because of sailing, and Jeff Jeffries. Individuals I knew, but I did most of my work with the heads of departments. I mean if I had anything to ask or any favor to ask or any request to make, we'd go to Fluckey or Frank Foley or somebody, whoever headed up the Math Department, or headed up the Steam Department, whoever headed up the English department, I'd make the request in that channel which I think was appropriate in those days. At least it was the established procedure.

Now with the Admissions Board and you have all of the civilian professors, I think they have something like twenty-some on the Admissions Board many of whom are civilian faculty and I think the necessity that the Director of Athletics has got to have a personal touch and contact. I know when Carl Ullrich was here he probably knew every professor in the Naval Academy.

He had to arrange for extra instruction and arrange the timing on it so that, hopefully, they could practice and go to extra instruction. So, Carl, I'm sure probably knew every instructor at the Naval Academy.

Q: Smeddy observed that he had fairly extensive contact with faculty and he felt it helped him in that he got so many ideas from them.

Adm. L.: Well, that's the reason I think the Admissions Board per se is probably the best thing they ever did here. One, I think we had taken away the personal touch; in other words Tony Gallaher, who was, and Charlie Brooks who were the two Secretaries of the Academic Board when I was here, you could go in to talk to them and bring out things and you might deter their judgment a little bit or change their judgment as one person. But now you have all these people sitting both in a professional capacity and a civilian capacity as professors and I think this is the reason the quality of our classes has continued to rise. All you have to do is look at the record and look at the attrition figures. There is no question about it the number of candidates are dropping, mainly because of the number of people age wise who are eligible to go to the college at this particular time, this particular era. But, even though the overall number of candidates are dropping, is dropping, why the quality has remained the same or is even higher and the attrition figures are dropping like nothing you've ever seen. When I came here twelve years ago all of the four year attrition figures were over thirty percent. They ran thirty-one, thirty-two, thirty-three, thirty-four.

Q: Sometimes they pushed up in the forties, didn't they?

Adm. L.: Well, not here. They did in the Air Force and the Army. The Air Force is still in trouble with attrition figures and so is the Army, but this year's class is about twenty-six, twenty-seven percent, the first class. My Lord, the other three classes are way down, way down. We have the smallest class this year we've had for years, 1244 and next year's is going to be even smaller. The overall attrition is coming down so fast. That means quality. I mean you're getting better kids at the Naval Academy.

Q: While you were here in that capacity would you say something about the custom of entertaining at your home. How did you view that as a means of promoting your job?

Adm. L.: Well, I did a couple of things that probably were frowned upon. I'm sure they were because they are not done anymore. For instance, I would have, once a year I would have all of the coaches and their wives in for a cocktail party at home. All the coaches.

Q: For all the sports?

Adm. L.: All the sports. After every home football game I would invite Eddie and his staff and selected guests to my home at 3 Porter Road. We did not have the lunches before the game with the exception of the Notre Dame game. The Notre Dame game we played in Baltimore. We had a very, very lavish luncheon at one of the hotels there in which I was criticized by Roberta McCain and other people for. What they didn't realize is that you have to reciprocate on these things. When Navy goes out to Notre Dame Father Hesburgh and Father Joyce, just turn the faucet and everything flows. You're treated just like royalty out there. Lord, if you're going to get that from one school you certainly ought to do it for that school when they come to your place.

Q: Not only ought to, you have to.

Adm. L.: Of course, I never had any financial problems. This is the biggest difference between when I was Director of Athletics and Bo Coppedge right now.

Q: You mean you had funds to do this?

Adm. L.: All kinds of funds. We were making money. You see, travel didn't cost anything or very little, food cost very little, hotels cost very little. We went to a bowl game, what three bowl games in six years. We had sellout crowds for the Army-Navy game every year. Sellout crowds for the Notre Dame game every year. Seventy-five to eighty percent of your football, all of your football income came from those two games. I don't think we wasted money, but as a matter of fact without bragging George Deininger told me once that I was more familiar with the financial workings of the Athletic Association than any Director of Athletics he'd ever served with because I went over it with Morris Gilmore and I went over it with George. I asked what safe guards we had. You know two people have to sign every check. I said, "How can someone really cheat on the Athletic Association?"

They said, "You can't do it. It would take three people. It's going to take you and two people who sign the check."

Then each meeting of, what do you call it, the Executive Committee, why, one member of the Executive Committee went over all the expenditures for promotion of, well for promotions is what we called it which is what it was. So, I don't think we wasted money at all. I think it was a necessary part. You look at what other schools do and what we did and still the comparison is way down.

Q: But you say this is not possible now?

Adm. L.: Well, I think he's--

Q: Reciprocal entertaining?

Adm. L.: They have reciprocal entertainment. For instance, Bo has a dinner Friday night normally for the visiting team dignitaries, the Director of Athletics. Coaches normally don't come there. But the President might be here or the Chancellor or the Director of Admissions. For instance, last year when we played Syracuse we couldn't get a place to have our Friday night event. We always have a dinner Friday night before the annual, before the football game of the weekend we hold our annual meeting. So, I volunteered to ask the officials, Bob

Pirie concurring, I volunteered to ask the official party from Syracuse and the Naval Academy in addition to our trustees and their wives so we would have a place to have our dinner and we picked up the tab for the whole thing. But, normally Bo would have had that from the Athletic Association and entertained his Syracuse counterpart. He does that for every home game. But, I think that's the only thing he does. I think he's knocked off the luncheon before a home game. They used to have the cocktail party at his home after the home games. I don't think he does that anymore. I'm sure it's for financial reasons alone.

Q: Well, Smeddy told me that when he was here as Superintendent a lot of this sort of thing came out of his own pocket.

Adm. L.: Yes.

Q: Not because he wanted to, but because he had to do it and there was no money for it.

Adm. L.: Well, primarily when he was here and Head of the Department of Electrical Engineering I heard him make a flat statement to the Superintendent how much it cost him to entertain when he was Head of the Department of Electrical Engineering. In those days it was a pretty good sum.

I don't know what the contingency fund is for the Superintende In those days he had lots of stewards, six, seven, or eight stewards which helped.

Q: Yes, it helped relieve his wife of a burden.

Adm. L.: One year, or the year I was in the Pentagon, I won't mention the Superintendent's name, but they always put in for additional contingency funds for entertainment purposes. So, I just don't know what the status of the contingency funds are, but there has always been contingency funds. Whether they meet the needs as Smeddy says they didn't meet them when he was Superintendent, why you have to believe Smeddy.

Q: Would you say something about major and minor sports at the Academy.

Adm. L.: Well, in those days they had, they were actually listed a major and minor sports. This had been going on for probably forever. I'm just not sure I told this yarn before, but anyway I think that was a step in the right direction, the abolishment of the differentiation between the major and minor sports. That, and I know I told you this before, making sailing a varsity sport.

Q: Yes, you did tell me that.

Adm. L.: That was a step in the right direction.

When Admiral Boone, Freddie, was Superintendent he had written a letter which, of course, I knew nothing about, to Norman Vincent Peale asking him if he would consider coming down to conduct a service at the Naval Academy. He never got an answer. Somehow it came up, he used to have the heads of departments over to his quarters ever so often. I think it came up at a meeting. But, it so turned out that one of my best friends was a man named Frank Kridel who owned two hotels in New York City. Frank Kridel was, what do you call it, a deacon in the church that he attended. I don't know if the right words is deacon.

Q: Probably.

Adm. L.: In Norman Vincent Peale's church and was a very, very close personal friend of Dr. Peale. So, when I heard this, without even telling Admiral Boone about it, I got on the phone and called Frank. I said, "Frank, do you realize that Dr. Peale had been asked months ago to come down to the Naval Academy and Admiral Boone has not even had the courtesy of reply?"

He said, "I'll call you right back."

He got on the phone with Dr. Peale and found out that there had been an administrative oversight, you know.

Q: I suppose he got thousands of letters all the time.

Adm. L.: But, gee, within a matter of weeks Norman Vincent Peale and his wife were down here at the Superintendent's quarters and spent the night. Apparently Frank told Admiral Boone what I'd done. The Kridels were asked to come down. But, that's how we got Norman Vincent Peale at the Naval Academy through a hotel owner in New York City.

Q: In August of 1957 you took over a big ship command, an oiler. How do you say, it, the MISS--

Adm. L.: MISSISSINEWA. Well that was a disappointment in some respects. What had happened was the USS MISSISSINEWA was supposed to have completed its overhaul and be ready to go to sea either in July or August that year. I was going to join it and deploy immediately to the Sixth Fleet. However, during its overhaul the powers that be decided to convert it to a flag ship for the Service Force, Sixth Fleet which entailed months of additional work.

Q: Where was she being converted?

Adm. L.: The Portsmouth Naval Shipyard in Virginia. So, I went from three years shore duty and then we didn't even get underway until March of the following year. So, I went from three years shore duty here to down there--

Q: How did you occupy your time?

Adm. L.: Well, my family lived in an apartment, but I went to the ship every day. There was all kinds of conversions. See, we had to build office spaces. We had to build quarters. We had to convert to carry atomic weapons and all kinds of things in the fore part of the ship. It was a learning process too just like the USS QUEENFISH during World War II. I had an opportunity to learn the ship.

Q: What about the crew? Did you have a full complement? How did you keep them occupied?

Adm. L.: They were busy red-leading and helping out with the ship's work, ship's maintenance. The construction part was primarily the shipyard's responsibility, but the regular maintenance work and the main engine room and chipping bulkheads, well just like you do in any Navy yard. There is a certain amount of ship's work that is to be done by the ship's complement.

Q: How large a ship is she?

Adm. L.: Oh, Lord, she's thirty-five thousand tons.

Q: Really a big ship for ship handling. Did you have to have special ship handling training?

Adm. L.: No, I didn't take any. I guess all submarine officers pride themselves on being able to handle ships. I tell you it was a real big thrill the first time we got underway. I hadn't been on a big ship since the USS NEW MEXICO way back in 1938 and this is 1958.

Q: And you hadn't had the conn on the USS NEW MEXICO.

Adm. L.: Well, I had been officer of the deck. We got underway from the shipyard and as soon as we got turned around and entered the Elizabeth River the pilot said, "Goodbye, I'll see you this afternoon." So I had to take that tortuous trip all the way down the Elizabeth River to get out to sea.

Q: That's been fatal to some Skippers.

Adm. L.: It was a big thrill, I'll tell you that. Then coming back the same way the pilot boarded us just before we got--we had to have a pilot that took you out of the Navy Yard and brought you back in. That's common throughout the whole country, any place, any Naval base or ship yard. I think that's one of the biggest thrills of my life having the conn of this monster, having been on shore for damned near four years, four years and nine months.

Q: Well, were there any bugs in her that had to be corrected when you were having your shake down?

Adm. L.: No, the only untoward incident that happened was when we left the shipyard or left Norfolk for Guantanamo for our shake down training period. Of course, the ship had been in overhaul for over a year, I guess, and a brand new crew, or most of them were new, and some emergency came up and for the life of me I can't recall what it was. But, we were diverted to refuel a division of destroyers who, incidentally, were under the command of Claude Ricketts. So, we refueled them in an expeditious manner which surprised the bejesus out of me. I had never seen a refueling exercise before. About all I had to do was maintain a steady course and speed and then the deck crew was the one who did all the work. I had a wonderful chief boatswain and a wonderful deck crew. I told, at that time, Captain Ricketts by phone, I said, "We're on our way to Guantanamo and this is the first refueling the ship has done in over a year and it is the first time I've ever seen a refueling."

He smiled or laughed on the phone and said, "Nice job and good luck."

So, we turned around and then we went on down to Guantanamo and went through shake down training. It was arduous, again, because never having operated a ship like this, a lot of it was brand new to me.

Q: What was the complement of a ship that size?

Adm. L.: I can't tell you exactly. I had about twelve officers, ten or twelve, and I'd say around a hundred and seventy-five to two hundred crew. No, I guess I only had about eight officers, Jack. I remember the names of most of them. I guess I only had eight officers.

Then we came back to Norfolk and had an administrative inspection which bugged the living bejesus out of me because we weren't ready for it and we were trying to get loaded and get ready to deploy. We had a deadline date to leave Norfolk to get over to the 6th Fleet and they gave me a speed of advance. The ship would only make twenty knots and they gave me a speed of advance of eighteen knots and this is what we made. We averaged eighteen knots from Norfolk over to Naples.

Q: Pushing.

Adm. L.: The 6th Fleet, the Service Force staff was on a tender and they had to shift to the USS MISSISSINEWA and the timing was very, very tight so we had to get there on a certain date so they could shift from the tender to the USS MISSISSINEWA which they did. Then the rest of the deployment and it was very short because I didn't get there until April and I was detached in August. But we had several things happen. The Lebanon incident took place at the time.

Q: Oh, yes!

Adm. L.: Pete Galantin, whom I'm sure you know, he and Tom Moorer were the first two four year early selectees in the whole Naval Academy promotion system. Well, Pete had been sent over to be on Admiral Briscoe's staff in Naples. He and Ginny were very good frineds of ours. My wife was there and our daughter and we were staying with the Galantins at the time. They woke me up at three o'clock in the morning and said, "Hey, get back to the ship. You have to get underway at five o'clock."

Well, we actually didn't get underway until seven. That's when Admiral Burke said, "Get going."

Fortunately we were full up with fuel and we were the only oiler in the Mediterranean, just because of circumstances, that was completely filled with fuel. The darned 6th Fleet was going around twenty-five knots. I don't know if they were worried about submarines or not, but finally Bill Nelson who was my Commodore, the Commander Service Force-6th Fleet, and Bill Ellis, I think, was Chief of Staff to Admiral Anderson, his carrier division, said, "Hey, look we've refueled every destroyer and the cruiser in the 6th Fleet," in about three days because they were going at twenty-five knots.

Q: You got lots of practice at that point didn't you?

Adm. L.: Yes. We'd refueled ships before that, but this was not at the beginning of the deployment. This was a couple of months later. But, they did lower the speed down to fifteen knots. That eased the situation to some extent.

I guess that was the only real crisis we had while I was there as far as international crisis is concerned. The operations were kind of arduous because they had electronic silence, no radar, no communications and running a darkened ship. I don't know if you are familiar with how merchant ships operated in the Mediterranean, but they put the iron mike on and if anyone is on the bridge, even at night, it's a miracle. You see a ship coming down and you have the right-of-way you just didn't take a chance. What I'd do if I had the right-of-way I'd make a full, long ahead of time, I'd make a full circle around, just turn away from him. Go all the way around and go back astern because you just didn't know, they kept barreling right on through. Lord the Straits of Gibraltar, I don't think you could ever go through there without seeing eight or ten or twelve ships, even today probably.

Q: Plus the current and all the rest of it.

Adm. L.: Then we made several transits of that, what's the famous straits there between Sicily--

Q: Messina.

Adm. L.: Yes, the Messina Straits and that was a thrill because even that big ship, heavily loaded, when that current hits you, why your bow would fall off fifteen or twenty degrees and there was nothing you could do about it. You'd catch it all right, but it just moved you. If you're passing a ship there you had to be extremely careful and cautious. That is one of the most wicked currents I guess I've ever seen.

Q: You had a home base in Naples?

Adm. L.: We were home ported in Cannes and our home port was changed to Naples. We had to go up to, oh yes, we went to Naples and just stayed there overnight or two nights in order to unload cars and things like that. Then we went up to Villefranche and that's when we took on Service Force Staff. You see, their home port was in Villefranche and then it was changed from there to Naples. So, we got them aboard up there and then went down to Naples and that became the home port.

Q: Is that where your wife was?

Adm. L.: Yes. Well, she was in Villefranche actually when we arrived there. She was staying with friends when she moved down to Naples.

Q: Did you touch any of the North African ports?

Adm. L.: The only port we went--in those days the Turks and the Greeks were, even then having their trouble. We had a trip to Izmir which was cancelled. We did have two weeks in Piraeus, the port for Athens. But, the only port we saw the four, five, six months I was there was Villefranche, Naples and Piraeus. Then, what's the place in Crete? Suda Bay? Which isn't a port. So, those are the only two places we saw the time I was over there.

Q: At that time in the Mediterranean there was no evidence of Russian Naval force?

Adm. L.: I never saw a Russian ship in 1958. They hadn't really- I don't think they had started down there.

Q: It was actually an American sea at that time.

Adm. L.: Yes, it was.

Q: The British had moved out somewhat.

Adm. L.: Yes. We had, I'm pretty sure we had two carrier groups there. Com 6th Fleet was in a cruiser I know that. George Anderson had a carrier division before he became Com 6th Fleet. I'm sure there was another one there because he was in Athens when--

Q: Now, Holloway was there too.

Adm. L.: Well, he was CincNelm. Then he was sent down to take charge of the Lebanon crisis. And, I think Red Yeager was Skipper of the tender. But, they actually moored right in, what's the main port?

Q: Beirut.

Adm. L.: Beirut. But, Admiral Holloway was in charge of that operation.

Q: This command of a big ship was sort of a truncated command for you. So, then you go back to a real one.

Adm. L.: Well, you say a real one. I think there were more challenges the short time I had the USS MISSISSINEWA than on any ships I've ever been on.

Q: Oh, really?

Adm. L.: I had no officer help. I had what is called a TAR commander who was a very nice guy, but useless. Therefore I did all the ship handling myself and practically did all of the executive work myself. The officer assistance, to me, was very limited. Fortunately I had a good chief engineer, I had a good engineering crew and I had a marvelous deck gang, you know, for fueling. But the administration of the ship, particularly with the ship staff aboard was close to---.

Q: Were they Naval Academy men?

Adm. L.: None of them were. That was the common cry in those days, and long before those days. The Service Force really got the short end of the deal. It's just like the Mine Force. the Mine Force and the Service Force have never really had, I think, adequate strength and they certainly haven't had the officer talent that the other branches of our Navy have.

Q: But, both services are essential to the Navy. The Service Force and the logistics, this is the life-blood of the fleet.

Adm. L.: But, they have never had the quality of personnel that they should have, in my opinion. And, I would venture to say they still don't. Amphibious Force the same way.

Now, when I got aboard the USS TOLEDO which is the next step in this chain, goodness, I don't know how many officers I had, twenty-five or thirty and a wonderful Exec. All the heads of departments except one were outstanding officers. All the junior officers, Ned Oldham who was the Captain of the football team here was one of my junior officers. It was just a pleasure to go from the USS MISSISSINEWA to the USS TOLEDO and have all of this help which I did not have on the USS MISSISSINEWA. And, I wasn't alone, I mean, my situation was not unique at all.

Q: Well, it certainly added to your experience, however as a Naval officer.

Adm. L.: Yes, and it also really helped me in the USS TOLEDO because I went from the Sixth Fleet--can we go on to the USS TOLEDO now because I was detached.

Q: You went to her in August of 1958?

Adm. L.: Yes. I have one interesting story just before I was detached. My wife had rented a villa over in Ischia, which is a little island near Capri. Ischia is within sight of Capri. Through the Galantins, Marjorie rented a villa over there for a whole month. Well, I got in port one night while she was there for the month and went over and spent the night there. We were getting under way, supposedly, at seven o'clock the next morning. My gig took me over there and brought me back. We were refueling the ship that night and the Italian on the pumps went to sleep.

Q: In the process?

Adm. L.: And, the line broke. We finally had the ship cleaned after all the dirt that accumulated in a navy yard over haul and there was this beautiful ship, black fuel oil from the top of the mast all the way down over the bridge, over the deck house, over everything. I almost wept because I was being relieved within a week. I almost wept. So, I asked the commodore for a few hours delay getting underway and turned the whole ship's crew, engineers, everybody to get the stuff at least off the superstructure. But, I bet there is still evidence of that oil spill.

Q: It's sort of indelible.

Adm. L.: So, I was relieved a week later. It was the first and only time in my life we took a commercial ship the SS CONSTITUTION, as I recall, back. We were able to get aboard that with our car. We landed in New York and left immediately to cross the country and reported aboard the USS TOLEDO.

Q: Well, that was a brief vacation anyway.

Adm. L.: I had no leave. I just had the travel time. We landed in New York and visited her mother on route across country and drove straight into Long Beach and took over the USS TOLEDO.

Q: What was her state when you took her over?

Adm. L.: Excellent, excellent. Harry Reiter was the Skipper and he is an excellent officer. That's when I had all of this help aboard. When did I report aboard? August.

Adm. L.: Well, we operated in fleet exercises, normal routine operations until, as I recall, shortly after Christmas.

I had a six month deployment and I came back. When was I detached?

Q: November of 1959 from the USS TOLEDO.

Adm. L.: June, July, August, September, well maybe that's right then. Well, I reported in Thanksgiving Day, if I remember right. Red Yeager--that would be June, July, August, September, October, November, that's probably right then.

Q: So it was June of 1959 when you went to the Seventh Fleet? But, were you attached to the First Fleet before that or what?

Adm. L.: Yes and Charlie Melson, as I recall was COMFIRSTFLEET, or Smeddy, I'm not sure which one was which. I think Smeddy was. I'm sure he was.

Q: What sort of a charger was Smeddy?

Adm. L.: Well, Smeddy was in Coronado or San Diego when I was stationed at Long Beach. So, we really never had anything to---you see I had a Division Commander aboard who was really my immediate boss. G. Serpell Patrick was the Division Commander and then he was relieved by Corky Ward in Pearl on our way out to the Seventh Fleet. So, I really had nothing to do with Smeddy. Actually Frank Virden was CruDesPac. So, the chain of command went from me to the Division Commander to ComCruDesPac and stopped there. In other words, CruDesPac is the one.

Q: Well perhaps you could answer that question about Smeddy and what kind of a charger he was by reverting back to the Naval Academy and telling me what he was like as Superintendent.

Adm. L.: He's a charger and he hasn't changed a bit. He sat right behind me at the Virginia game last week and he looks the same as ever and he's just as enthusiastic, just as vibrant, all kinds of energy. Well, Smeddy is just a wonderful person to work for and with. No question about it.

Q: He's one who has an idea a minute too.

Adm. L.: I was here at the Naval Station, Jack, when he was the head of the department. So, I got to know him quite well then. That was from 1949 to 1952. Then after two years with Admiral Boone I served one year with him as Superintendent in my last year here 1956, 1957. He's really responsible, well I'm just a little ahead of my story now. Well, I guess not, he's really responsible, I think, for my being selected Admiral because when they brought me back--you see I never had any Pentagon duty. Denny Daspit, who is a submariner, asked Red Yeager, Red was losing his deputy in this Op-001 Bravo, this ASW readiness section directly under Admiral Burke and Herb Andrews from the class of 1931, as you recall, had to retire by 1 November 1959 in order to take advantage of the tombstone admiral bit. Well, Herb had not been selected that year, and he didn't want to take a chance, so he got out. I wasn't going to get back until Thanksgiving, but Daspit talked Red Yeager into taking me into that job. So, I'll skip over that because we'll come back to it.

Anyway, when I didn't get selected that year Smeddy called me in on this one Saturday morning briefing. You know Admiral Burke still had the Saturday morning briefings in those days.

He asked, "How would you like to go down and work for Admiral Dennison on SacLant staff?"

I said, "Gee does he want me or will he take me." I'd just met Admiral Dennison once.

He kind of looked nonplused for a minute and then said, "Yes, he will."

So, I don't know whether-he obviously had to talk to Admiral Dennison because my predecessor Bill Groverman had made admiral in the job.

Q: That was a good spot to get into.

Admc. L.: Smeddy was trying to take care of me I'm sure. But, you asked me about Smedberg so I'd thought I'd just bring that up.

Q: Let's revert back to the USS TOLEDO and out on the West Coast during those months when you were there on exercises--

Adm. L.: Just fleet exercises operating the carrier. Just normal training exercises, gun practices, short range battle practices, long range.

Q: It was kind of a low period in the Navy, wasn't it, out on the West Coast? The Korean conflict was over.

Adm. L.: There was really nothing going on. I mean no crisis. Well, we had the crisis between Taiwan and Red China from time to time, but that was the only trouble on the horizon in that particular era. So, we just had normal peace time training exercises.

Loughlin #5 -243-

Q: With the knowledge that you were going to deploy to the Seventh Fleet?

Adm. L.: Yes, we knew that we were going to deploy to the Seventh Fleet.

Q: Who was the commanding officer of the Seventh Fleet at that point?

Adm. L.: Kivette, Admiral Kivette.

Q: So, you went out there in June of 1959. Tell me about your duties out there?

Adm. L.: I'm trying to think now. You see I had another tour of duty just two years later when I made Admiral as CruDesFlot Commander.

Q: You said Corky Ward was out there?

Adm. L.: Well, Corky relieved Serpell Patrick in Pearl and then we deployed and went right to Yokosuka. We were there for a short period of time and then somebody, either Admiral Kivette or Corky, dreamed up an exercises where we operated with a U.S. submarine and I think three Japanese destroyers. We left Yokosuka and we completely circumnavigated, we went in at Sasebo, made a port stop up on the Western Coast of Japan, went up to Hokkaido, came back on the East Coast to Sendai, and ended up in Yokohoma and Yokosuka. A marvelous, marvelous educational visit because I had never seen any of those places. We worked with these three destroyers and the Japanese people---

Q: Basically to train them was it?

Adm. L.: That's exactly what it was.

Q: They were part of the Maritime--

Adm. L.: Self Defense Force. But, the Japanese people couldn't have been more pleasant, more wonderful. We were royally entertained every place we went. I guess this was the first time a cruiser had been in some of these ports, Sendai and Hokkaido.

Q: Some of those narrow passageways.

Adm. L.: Yes, well that passageway between Hokkaido and Honshu is nothing like the Messina Straits. Matter of fact, we went through this passage at night. We had no trouble at all.

We ended up at Sasebo another time and had our battle practice short range and normal range. I guess we had three turrets and I think eight five inch guns and I don't know how many 40 millimeters. We put "E"s on all the turrets, all of the five inch guns and I think half of the other armament. Corky sent a message back and reported it and I got a very congratulatory dispatch from Admiral Burke personally from him. So, I was very proud of that.

Q: You were really proving your mettle weren't you?

Adm. L.: Well, as I said, I had a good ship, I had a good ship.

Q: Did you get over to Korea at all?

Loughlin #5 -245-

Adm. L.: No. The only ports we made are the ones I mentioned. Well, we did get to Okinawa.

Q: And Taiwan?

Adm. L.: No, the Philippines that trip. I made a subsequent trip. So, we had a very successful cruise.

Q: Did you get involved with the Japanese local authorities in these various towns?

Adm. L.: Yes, we did. We got to know the Japanese CNO, through Corky, of course, and being the commanding officer of the flag ship why, I mean being commanding officer of the ship in which he was embarked, why I was normally included in all of the official things that he did.

Q: He really enjoyed all of those contacts, didn't he.

Adm. L.: Yes. Oh, wait a minute, I left out the most interesting thing of the whole trip. I tell you, I get mixed up between the two deployments because they came so quickly. We made a state visit to Saigon. We went up the Saigon River which is a hairy, hairy, hairy experience because it is so narrow against the current. You have to have a pilot and we had the first- We had the first South Vietnamese pilot, I mean it was the first time he had ever been on a heavy cruiser. They had taken over from the French. You had to have one because you couldn't follow the middle part of the river. You had to know, just as you pointed out, where the silt was and where the shoal was and there is such a current there that they never have dredged the thing to the best of my knowledge because it just scours out this thing, but it changes the channel. The only thing that was hair-raising about it, well, the two things was he used too much rudder, and it's such a narrow river you just don't want to use too much rudder in case it jams and then you're in trouble. So, as we approached Saigon which is on the port hand he said, "Well, now this is," he spoke very good English. He said, "Well, this is a real tricky thing to do. What we do is we go past the dock, the city. Then we make a right turn and put our bow up against the mud bank and then back and twist and back and twist until we get turned around. Then we are headed down river and moor starboard side too." You follow me on this?

Q: Yes.

Adm. L.: We were there by ourselves. Well, I had the thing all worked out and he was going to let me know when he was going to put the rudder over. We were making twelve knots and all of a sudden without any warning what-so-ever he said, "Right full rudder." Making twelve knots and, hell, the river wasn't more than fifty yards away. So, I said, "All back emergency." Boy we hit it with a bang. If I hadn't stepped in right at that moment, I mean five seconds later it would have been too late. We would have been high and dry on that damned mud bank. There was a noticeable jar when we hit the bank.

Q: At least it was mud.

Adm. L.: At least it was mud. So we finally moored. We had the mos marvelous eight day visit there. Diem was there. He and Corky hit it off quite well. I didn't have one minute to myself the whole eight days we were there. We were doing something official every single minute of the day and night, until it was time to go to bed at night. I never saw the town. We did make one trip out, automobile trip out to some church out of town. The rest of it was just official visit after official visit. It was, not a headache, because it was most enjoyable.

Q: What was your impression of Diem.

Adm. L.: I was very impressed with him. He was very quiet, soft spoken, looked you right in the eye. I guess it was his sister who really--

Q: His sister-in-law.

Adm. L.: His sister-in-law, well she made an official visit to the ship. She was quite an impressive gal too. But, just before we got underway, why, they called Corky and me up to, I guess, the palace where he lived and he gave Corky one of the most beautiful paintings I've ever seen in my life. Corky was smart enough to write the State Department and get permission to keep it. He still has it in his house up in Severna Park.

Q: I've seen it.

Adm. L.: Isn't that a beautiful painting though? So, that really was the high point, that and the trip around Honshu which were the two high points of the trip and the gun shoot where we did so well.

Then, the time went by, again more fleet exercises, you know, working with carriers. We ran into a couple of typhoons. Not too bad, I mean we ran into the fringe of them.

Q: What sort of weather reports did you have at that point out there?

Adm. L.: Pretty good. The Weather Central was in Yokosuka. We were there in the typhoon season. We were able to circumvent them. We never got it real bad, just the fringes of them.

Q: The Seventh Fleet has a healthy respect for typhoons.

Adm. L.: You're darned right. So, eventually the time came to come home and we went back via Guam.

Q: Had you taken your wife out to Japan?

Adm. L.: No, not that time.

Q: It was too short a tour.

Adm. L.: Yes. We had Gay in high school so she couldn't go out there. But, we came back through Guam and I had a very interesting experience there. The Cousteaus and Walsh had the deep submersible TRIESTE. You know, the one that went down thirty-five thousand feet.

Q: The bathysphere?

Adm. L.: Yes. Well, they took us through it, or what they could show us of it. Shortly after we left, incidentally, they went out and made their thirty-five thousand foot dive in the Guam trench or whatever you call it there. I don't think I'm getting confused with the two deployments now. This was when I was on the USS TOLEDO.

Then we came back through Pearl and back to Long Beach. I picked up Joe Williams in Pearl and he rode the ship from Pearl to Long Beach. I had my orders back to OPNAV.

Q: So, you were finally going to get Pentagon duty?

Adm. L.: I'll tell you a story about that too. But, anyway, Joe relieved me and unfortunately they decided to decommission the ship within a month.

Q: Oh really. Was she ever recommissioned?

Adm. L.: I don't think so. So, Joe was very disappointed because it was really an excellent ship. In good shape, good condition. Those were the days, if you recall Jack, when the Navy was on a missile binge. They were taking all the guns off the cruisers and putting nothing but missiles. I remember Johnny Davidson who was a DivCom, and Corky and all of the DivCom's and Skippers said this is stupid to remove all the armament on a cruiser and have them solely dependent on missiles.

I'd like to go back when I first took over the USS TOLEDO or shortly after I took over, the USS TOLEDO was a REGULUS missile heavy cruiser. You remember the REGULUS II.

Q: Oh, yes.

Adm. L.: The firing range was off Point Sur towards the South whatever the range was, I can't remember what the range was now. But, we'd go in to Monterey overnight because the swells were pretty heavy up there. Arthur Beaumont came up and rode us one time. While we were anchored in Monterey there is a sketch he made of the USS TOLEDO which I'm quite proud to have. We stopped in Guam and then went to Pearl and back to Long Beach and then Joe Williams relieved me.

Q: So, in November of 1959 you came into the Pentagon for the first time. Your first duty there as Deputy for Anti-submarine Warfare, the readiness section.

Adm. L.: Admiral Burke had set this up himself because Admiral Yeager, Red Yeager, reported directly to Admiral Burke not through Op 03, not through anybody, a direct chain of command to Admiral Burke.

Q: How did that happen?

Adm. L.: Well, I guess Admiral Burke wasn't satisfied with the ASW Readiness throughout the fleet.

Q: One of his innovative things.

Adm. L.: Yes, he just set it up. It was set up long before I got there. They had some outstanding officers. We only had about five, or six, or seven officers and I was a Deputy.

Q: That certainly bespeaks well for you.

Adm. L.: Well, it was through Denny Daspit who had asked Red if he would take me. I'd known Red for years, in particular when I was Director of Athletics. He was very interested in

Loughlin #5 -251-

athletics. Red was a very easy person for me to work for. He was kind of rough on junior officers, but he and I were good friends to start with, so, I never had any argument with Red.

It was a real instructive year for me because my ASW experience was really limited to what little we did in the submarines.

Q: That was on the receiving end.

Adm. L.: And, we didn't have any on the USS TOLEDO, obviously. I didn't know anything about the patrol planes the VP Squadrons. Whitey Taylor at that time was in charge of the ASW CincLantFleet. I went to Norfolk and we went down to--I didn't know anything about SOSUS, you know the sound surveillance system.

Q: Well, that was fairly new wasn't it?

Adm. L.: Well, fairly new, but we had the installation. As a matter of fact, I went to Cape Hatteras and Whitey took me down by helo from Norfolk. So, really being a novice, I really tried to learn. I wasn't much help to Red I'm afraid, but we had a good staff there. They were all afraid of him. Everyone I think just shook in their boots. Red could be awful rough you know. He could be awful rough on junior officers.

Q: You mean he was abrupt and demanding?

Adm. L.: Yes.

Q: Was he a perfectionist?

Adm. L.: No, not per se. He was a perfectionist if anything went wrong. He would get it corrected real quick because he was working directly for Arleigh and--. And Red was striking for three stars. He was a Rear Admiral and he got his third star in that job. But, I was a kind of buffer between Red and the rest of the staff because they knew that he would ask me and I got along well with him. All of their problems instead of going to him they would come to me and I would go to Red and try to smooth things over. It worked out pretty nicely.

Q: The diplomat at work again.

Adm. L.: Well, it was. That's exactly what it was, diplomacy. But, I never will forget, I don't think I told you this. Right after I arrived Bob Pirie had a cocktail party and lived over at the Navy Yard. He was Op 05 at the time. I walked in with Marjorie and the first two persons I saw were Fred Boone, who'd been on the selection, head of the selection board the previous year when I had the USS TOLEDO, and Page Smith who was Chief of the Bureau of Personnel. I can't recall whether it was Page Smith or if it was Fred, but they looked at me and said "Well, it's about time you got to Washington for duty."

I said, "Admiral Smith if you'll look up my preference cards,(which you submitted in those days,) you'll notice that the last four consecutive cards I've submitted I've requested duty in OpNav. And, they have finally got around to ordering me here."

Neither one said a word after that.

It was almost actually mandatory that you had to have duty, that is the reason Denny Daspit prevailed upon Red Yaeger when I didn't make it the year I had the USS TOLEDO, particularly after we'd done such a fine job in the USS TOLEDO, he said, "You've got to get back in the Pentagon or you are never going to make it."

Well, I didn't make it that year either. So, to show you how much policy comes into it and here I'd only had one year in the Pentagon, never had had duty there before, so Smeddy sent me from the Pentagon right down to CincLantFleet to work with Admiral Dennison. And, I did make it that year.

Q: Not only did you learn something about Anti-submarine Warfare during that year, but there must have been other happenings too.

Adm. L.: Since the head worked directly for Admiral Burke there was a lot of interaction, interplay between the civilian secretaries. That's where I met Jim Wakelin. For instance, incidentally Lloyd Mustin relieved Red in that job when Red made his third star. Lloyd was a master. He is just as smooth as silk and very, very smart, Oh, boy, he's one of the smartest--I think Lloyd stood four, five, or six in his class and very, very intelligent. He was so smooth. He would brief the Secretary of the Navy and all of his staff, I think at least once every two or three weeks on ASW development. So I got to know Jim Wakelin. He was the Assistant Secretary of the Navy for Research and Development. Chick Hayward, Charley Martell were in the Op 07 branch there. Chick had been a friend of mine since I was a midshipman. I didn't have much to do with the secretaries but Wakelin became a good friend. Let's see was Bob Baldwin there then? I forget who, I get it mixed up with when I became Commander of the Naval District. I did get to know the workings of the secretariat branch of the Navy as well as the Op Nav branch because I represented Red at, I went to all the morning briefings and then whenever Admiral Burke would have a regular meeting, which was once a week, with all of the Op's there.

Q: That was his CAB.

Adm. L.: Yes. Why, I would sit in for Red on those because he was doing a lot of work over on the Hill, legislation. So, it was a real learning and interesting experience. The hours were horrible. I had to get there early enough to get all the dispatches and stuff ready to brief Red by twenty minutes of eight or a quarter of eight. So, that meant I got there at seven ten or seven fifteen. He had to be in the briefing room by five minutes to eight in the mornings. He worked until five-thirty, six, six-thirty every night including every Saturday. So, it was not the easiest year in the world, but it was a very rewarding year. I learned an awful lot.

Q: Burke himself set the pace for all of you.

Adm. L.: Oh, he certainly did, he certainly did. And, Jim Russell wasn't far behind as Vice CNO. Admiral Russell, incidentally, he's a classmate of Bob's and I think he's one of the finest gents I've ever met. Do you know him well too?

Q: Well, what professional connection did you have with Jim Wakelin in terms of research and development.

Adm. L.: He just would come to all the briefings and I just got to know him. Personally I had nothing to do with him really professionally, but he would attend all of the briefings. We had people on the staff who would brief him from time to time. I wouldn't but we had two or three really outstanding young officers there who really knew about ASW, both from the destroyer point of view and from the air point of view. So, we just had frequent contact with him.

Q: What were the overall objectives of ASW at that point in the late 1950's?

Adm. L.: I think they were just trying to improve the state of the art. For instance they thought they had an unknown submarine cornered down in the Key West area. It later turned out to be, I guess a false--

Q: Whale or something.

Adm. L.: But, for two days, why they had all kinds of forces down there trying to find out who it was or what it was and make it surface. The ASW state of the art in those days was not too good.

Q: The threat of Russian developments in that area was not great at that time?

Adm. L.: No. no it wasn't. It was just sonobuoys. I think they were relatively new then. That's about all I can say, Jack. I think Admiral Burke was not satisfied with the state of the art of ASW and he set up this ASW Readiness executive outfit more or less to, well we didn't have any real authority, but, I mean we were able to keep abreast with all of the developmen I don't think we initiated anything of relevance there in that shop. We worked pretty closely with Chick Hayward's outfit and Charlie Martell who was the head, who was Op 07 and Charlie was his deputy. They were classmates. We worked closely with Op 31 the submarines. Red Ramage had that job. Admiral Beakley was Op 03. As I said it was a real educational experience for me to see how OpNav worked and I was in the best position in the world to see it and to learn in a year how it worked.

Q: Indeed you were. You want to say something about Burke as CNO since you had a close view of him at the time? It seems to me that he was into so many different areas all at once. I mean, he was just everywhere and this in contrast with other CNO's whom I've known.

Adm L.: Well, I'd hate to compare him with Rickover, but he probably is as hard a worker as Rickover is. Rickover is my number one choice in being the hardest working man, not a genius, but the hardest working men I've ever served with in the Navy. I would say that Admiral Burke was not more so, but certainly either a close second or an equal one. Of course, whereas Rickover responsibiities were somewhat limited, Admiral Burke's covered the whole spectrum of Naval warfare. And, I agree with you

I just don't see how he could devote so much energy to so many things because he was in on everything, everything. He wrote me a couple of weeks ago. We write letters to the class officers when we designate these honor scholars each year. And, I wrote two separate letters, one because one was a girl and one was a boy. He wrote back and said, "I see that you left out the girl and I'm sure it was inadvertent" or something like that because it appeared in the newsletter. He said, "Now, don't do anything about it." I don't know why he said that. So, I sat right down and said, "Admiral Burke I learned back in 1959 one thing when you were the Chief of Naval Operations, don't ever cross the boss unless you know what you're talking about." I said, "I wrote you two letters Admiral Burke, both dated the same day, one with Mary Jane Chipkevich and the other whoever this other guy was." Well apparently, he'd gotten the first one and hadn't gotten the second one at that time that he wrote me the letter. I flatly contradicted him because I enclosed a copy of my letters.

Interview No. 6 with Rear Admiral Elliott Loughlin, U.S. Navy
(Retired)

Place: Annapolis, Maryland

Date: October 8, 1980

Subject: Biography

By: John T. Mason, Jr.

Q: Well, sir, we're about to have another very interesting chapter and this one, especially so I believe considering where you went and with whom you worked and the events that transpired. You went on August 6, 1960 to become Director of Plans for SAC LANT. SAC LANT at that point was Admiral Dennison who had taken over the job in February of that year.

Adm. L. He relieved Admiral Wright I believe.

Q: Yes. So, would you tell me about the nature of this job and some of the details.

Adm. L.: Well, it's, SAC LANT is a very unique organization in the country, Jack. As you know, its a NATO command, and Admiral Dennison at that time wore two hats. He was Cinc LANT Fleet on the national side and he was SAC LANT, the Supreme Allied Commander of the Atlantic Fleet on the NATO side.

Q: Then he took on another hat, didn't he? In the Cuban missile crisis he--

Adm. L.: Yes, I guess he did. Something that very few people know about the SACLANT job is that the charter or whatever you call it of NATO provides that a U.S. admiral will be SACLANT. It doesn't say that for the counterpart over in SHAPE. That can be anyone. It's always been a U.S. officer, but it's not specified in the charter. But, the charter does specify that the Supreme Allied Commander of the Atlantic Fleet will be a United States Naval Officer.

Q: And the rationale for this was?

Adm. L.: Because we had the greatest number of units undoubtedly.

Q: And, it was a matter of some contention that the British also---

Adm. L.: It could have been, it could have been. I would think though the contention would be with the Supreme Allied Commander of Europe rather than with the Atlantic because there are so many more forces there. I would think the total number of forces of Europe would exceed the U.S. forces. I would think, but I'm not sure. I'm talking about right now.

Q: In aggregate they do, yes.

Adm. L.: At that time we, the U.S. Naval forces certainly exceeded the aggregate of all other Naval forces in the alliance. So, as I said, it was a very unique organization. It had, oh, some headaches because you had a few officers who had both national jobs and NATO jobs. Of course, the NATO officers enjoyed the liquor mess there. Tax free liquor and I think tonic cost more than Beefeater's Gin, as a matter of fact. So, we had our perks there.

Q: Yes, I remember the story of how this was achieved. I think Herb Riley had a hand in it.

Adm. L.: Probably. And, we had other things, like the Canadians had their own little mess for cigarettes and things like nobody else could buy except the Canadians. But, I found it to be one of the most enjoyable and one of the most pleasant tours I've ever had although I can't recall, all NATO countries did not have Naval officers on the staff. Obviously Iceland didn't, but Turkey and Portugal, and Norway, and Denmark, there were so many countries that had Naval officers there that I had never been closely associated with that it was just, really, a delight. They really sent their top officers to those jobs. I had a very international small staff under my direction as Director of Plans and also had the opportunity to visit and attend the big NATO meetings over, at that time, headquarters in Paris. The meetings were in Paris. It's always a delight to go to. So all-in-all it was, just like my one year in the Pentagon, it was very educational as I'd never been with anything connected with NATO before. It was just an absolutely outstanding year in every respect. We lived in Virginia Beach. I rented a beautiful home down there and commuted back and forth. In those days the traffic wasn't that bad. I remember one Saturday I went, of course we worked on Saturdays, the U.S. officers did on the

Loughlin #6 -261-

staff. Nobody else did, I mean on the NATO staffs. I remember once I timed it deliberately and I was able to go from Virginia Beach to SACLant Headquarters and made every traffic light. That's impossible these days, but I did it one Saturday morning.

Q: Virginia Beach isn't Virginia Beach any more.

Adm. L.: No. We lived right on the beach, right on the beach at about 56th Street. I think.

Q: For the most part the SACLant staff was quite different from the CinCLant staff.

Adm. L.: Oh, yes sir. There were only two or three officers that had two hats and they primarily were on the CinCLant staff, not SACLant.

Q: Well, now, as Director of Plans what did you plan for? The joint operations? Exercises?

Adm. L.: Well, actually it was not an operational job, Jack, it was more with keeping up with the plans. For instance, the convoy system and all of the massive regulations on how to run the convoy systems was within my bailiwick. I had a Royal Canadian officer who was in charge of that section, absolutely magnificent. When Admiral Page Smith relieved Admiral Dennison he read this whole thing that, I say, we had prepared; I didn't prepare it but Bob Timbrel did. He said it was far superior to anything that CinCLant people had ever put out. So, it was mostly a planning future, not for current operations. At that time we didn't have any current operations, NATO operations. It developed when I was there, either that tour or the next tour, when we set up this force of destroyers which I think still exists. Four or five countries put destroyers in and they have exercises involving four or five navies. I think they have been doing this ever since 1962, 1963. This particular force was only a destroyer force. They have combined exercises. This was a task force set up to operate as a task force and it only consisted of destroyers.

Q: Was that the Strike Force? What they called the Strike Force?

Adm. L.: No., the Strike Force involved the carriers and everything else. The name of this particular small group is Standing Naval Force Atlantic. It was just to orient the various navies, and different countries participated in different years. The U.S. was always in it. Other countries would come in one year and then somebody else would come in the next year. It was just a question of orienting the signals and tactics. As a matter of fact, it was a very worthwhile thing. I didn't suggest it. It was developed when I was there, but I really didn't have anything to do with the origin of it.

We mentioned before the interview started that Admiral Sabin was the Chief of Staff of SACLant and one of the finest gentlemen I've ever served with. Just an absolutely magnificent man. The Deputy was always a Royal Navy Vice Admiral. Sir Charles Evans was there when I arrived. I think this anecdote will illustrate a couple of things. I'd always heard about the British reserve. I'm sure most people have this impression. Well, the day I reported in after I'd been introduced and made my calls, Sir Charles asked me to go over to the SACLant mess to have an afternoon drink which I did. As we finished the first drink I said, "Sir Charles will you have another drink?"

He said, "Elliott" I'd never met the Vice Admiral before, he looked me right in the eye and said, "Elliott, you never ask a gentlemen if he will have another drink. You always say 'Would you have anything to drink?'"

Well, I learned my lesson that day and I don't think I've ever asked anyone if they will have another drink based upon that experience.

Q: Yes, that's assuming too much.

Adm. L.: But, it really was a marvelous year. It was a short year because I happened to be selected that year. And, Jim Davis out of 1930 a submariner was my boss and an old friend of mine. It just so happened that I hit it off with all of the allied officers, not only in my section, but in the whole division. It just couldn't have been more pleasant. I learned a lot and did a lot of traveling. I went up to Norway and watched an exercise up there. I made several trips to Paris with Admiral Dennison. Of course, Admiral Dennison, I think is really one of the smartest, brainiest, most intelligent Naval officers we've ever had. He just was a magnificent man to work for.

Q: Tell me about the Paris meetings.

Adm. L.: Well, Lord Mountbatten was in his prime then. He really was the power behind the throne. And, Norstad was the senior officer in SHAPE. And, Norstad tried to be the center of all meetings because he was held, you know, in very, very high esteem by all of the European NATO countries. But, I think Lord Mountbatten just towered above everybody. Anything that came up, you always went to Lord Mountbatten, you didn't go to General Norstad.

Q: His whole stature, presence, everything.

Adm. L.: As he walked in the room he just commanded attention. He was such a nice person. He would have a reception at some huge home in Paris at every meeting to which all attending officers were invited. He was just a most genial person as a host and professionally. I think Admiral Dennison certainly respected him and admired his judgment. There isn't any question about that. I think they were very close to each other. I think Lord Mountbatten respected Admiral Dennison very much, which well he should.

Q: Did Montgomery put in an appearance?

Adm. L.: No, sir. He was not in the picture then. He was out.

Q: What about Norstad?

Adm. L.: I was never fond of General Norstad. I mean, I can't say professionally because I never served with him. I didn't like him, I think he had an overbearing attitude and he had a couple of strategic concepts which none of us really bought.

One of them was the mobile missile thing. He wanted to put missiles on, just like the same thing we're doing out here in the midwest. Supposedly put them on railroad cars and be able to move them here and move them there. He also had a concept which I personally disagreed with that you could have a tactical nuclear war without having a nuclear war. Jack, I just can't buy that.

Q: One leads to the other.

Adm. L.: I think when one goes off, who knows whether it's strategic or tactical. I just never bought that concept. I could be wrong and maybe I'm in the minority, but I think when the first one goes and then everything is going to go. That's my personal opinion.

Q: Well, is that in lieu of building up the conventional forces?

Adm. L.: We always, at that time we had a heck of a lot more conventional forces than we have now. I think it was well understood and agreed that if we ever got into a conventional war that, even in those days, Europe would be overrun very quickly. And, I think the same pertains right today. I don't think there is any question about it. I don't think we could hold out in any conventional war. I think this was General Norstad's thrust on this type of war that if a conventional war did develop he wanted to have the resources which, perhaps, could turn the tide and perhaps he was right. I don't know. He's an awful lot smarter than I am. But, you know he had his uniforms made specially and he was a very imposing figure and a handsome fellow, and I would say, arrogant. He certainly was not the type of warm personality that Lord Mountbatten was.

Q: You say you visited Norway, what was their attitude in NATO?

Adm. L.: They were a part of NATO. I went up to Oslo and visited the various installations there. Ira Nunn, as I recall, was the Naval Attache then. I saw Admiral Nunn. It was during the winter, so I didn't see much of--I remember the sun probably got five degrees above the horizon for an arc of thirty degrees. It would come up here and go down over there. The rest of the time it was dark.

One of the things, that has nothing to do with NATO, which impressed me about Norway was that there were several cocktail parties and dinner parties the few days I was there. One of the young Naval officers who kind of took charge of me when I was there, he and his wife, I can't remember their names, but they were a very nice couple, but, as you perhaps know, Norway is, at that time and is perhaps still is, the toughest country in the world on drinking and driving. You'd get caught no matter who you were. If you get caught driving, not under the infleunce, but just drinking having alcohol on your breath, you were thrown in the jug. Whether you were a Naval officer, a foreign Naval officer or not. So, it was just standard SOP, Standard Operating Procedure, if the couple went to a party, if the husband drank then the wife drove. If the wife drank, even beer, then the husband drove. And, they did that all the time. They would never go out with both of them taking drinks at the same time at the same party. They really had strict enforcement on that. It would be interesting to see what their accident rate shows compared to the U.S. or any other country.

Q: The Norwegians are part of NATO were or have always been somewhat careful members haven't they?

Adm. L.: Yes.

Q: They are not full hearted.

Adm. L.: Well, they are, they are in a very precarious position being up there. North Cape and--

Q: Did you have anything to do with the Dutch and--?

Adm. L.: Only on the staff. I'm very fond of them. They had one hard-headed guy who was, Hans was his first name. He was a submarine officer. He wanted to argue. He argued all the time. But, he was a very, very capable Naval officer. I think they only had one or two Dutch officers on the whole staff.

Q: I was thinking of the NATO problem with them in terms of exercises because of their unions. All their sailors are unionized.

Adm. L.: Yes. Well, we ran into that with the haircuts and uniforms and stuff like that. But, it didn't seem to bother the Dutch too much. I don't think the officers liked it, but it didn't seem to bother their efficiency too much.

You see, I was in a planning outfit. I wasn't in the operational part. I never saw how the ships operated, Jack.

Q: Did you have anything much to do with Dennison himself?

Adm. L.: Yes, I did. My predecessor was one of Admiral Dennison's favorite people, Bill Wylie, who had been selected the year before.

I relieved Bill Wylie. Bill was a planner of the first order and was very adroit and very clever and very good in setting forth positions. So, he and Admiral Dennison had a very close relationship or liaison in the tiny outfit. I did not have Bill Wylie's ability to put thoughts on paper. But, Admiral Dennison, whom I had known briefly before, but apparently was sympathetic to my position. Admiral Sabin was of tremendous help as was Jim Davis. This may sound like conceit again, but when we would have a conference in Admiral Dennison's office when I came in, every time, I don't think he ever missed once he would say, "Good morning."

I'd say, "Good morning, Admiral."

He always spoke to me first. Every time I was ever in his office he made me feel very, very good. So, my personal relationship with him was most pleasant although I don't think I contribut a great deal as Bill Wylie did. I must confess that. I had never been in a planning job before and it was difficult to adjust my thinking and put my thoughts on paper because I didn't have, really, the ability that Bill had. But Sabe was a tremendous help. He could write things down. He just ran the thing just beautifully. I think Rivets Rivero was Admiral Dennison's National Deputy Chief of Staff there.

Q: Yes, in CinCLant.

Adm. L.: Wally, the one that committed suicide.

Q: Beakley.

Adm. L.: Beakley, well he was Chief of Staff on the national side. I had known him the year I was in the Pentagon, well the year before when he was Op 03 and Beakley couldn't have been nicer. He was a wonderful man. His wife was crippled, you know, at that time and we made our normal call on them. She was in bed and we'd sit next to her bedside. I guess we called on them two or three times.

Q: Did SACLant down in Norfolk entertain VIP's very much?

Adm. L.: Yes, sir.

Q: What sort of a program did you have in that area?

Adm. L.: Well, all of the Naval Attachés, or the representatives in Washington would come down once or twice a year to get briefed on SACLant policies and plans. Admiral Dennison would have a group in. As a matter of fact, we did too. Even as a Captain and later on as an Admiral. But, we had these briefing teams of which I was a member which came to the Naval Academy and would go up to Washington and various places to brief various organizations on SACLant things. That was an interesting part.

Q: That was an educational part also.

Adm. L.: Yes sir. I really didn't participate in the briefing. I accompanied the briefing team. The people who worked for me were really the briefers, but Admiral Sabin, for instance, and I would always go with the team. He would make opening and closing remarks and I was present to see that everything went all right.

Q: Did the Russian Naval Attache come down? Was he invited?

Adm. L.: Only NATO. Later on I got to know the Russian Naval Attache fairly well when I was Commandant of the Naval District, but he was never in Norfolk to my knowledge. Obviously, he would never be at any of these meetings, but I don't think he was ever even in Norfolk.

Q: You said Iceland did not have a Naval representative on the staff. Did you visit Iceland?

Adm. L.: No, I never got to Iceland. As a matter of fact Iceland was a non-participant in all NATO affairs.

Q: A reluctant member of NATO, but important in terms of bases.

Adm. L.: In terms of geography. I don't think Iceland ever had representatives in the big meetings in Paris. I don't think they participated one iota. They were just a name only. In other words, they had our NATO protection, but they contribute nothing except Keflavik. I think that's the name of the base isn't it?

Q: Keflavik. You were with the plans section for only a year.

Adm. L.: Just a short year. The selection board in those days met, I believe in July, I was selected.

Q: Did you have some kind of celebration upon selection?

Adm. L.: Well, it was kind of an unusual afternoon. it so happened that day I went up to Washington with Whitey Taylor who was the ASW commander for a conference. A national conference not a NATO.

Joe Grenfell, who was ComSubLant at the time was on the selection board. Well, I noticed that everybody was real pleasant when I walked into this, my old job ASW Readiness Executive. Lloyd Mustin still had the job. Well, they are always pleasant. It just seemed to me to be a little bit different attitude. When the conference was over we got ready to go back in Whitey's plane and Joe was supposed to be with us. I said, "Where's Admiral Grenfell?"

They said, "Oh, he's gotten held up. He couldn't make it."

So, we got back to Norfolk and I got in my office. Well, I'd no sooner gotten in my office than the phone rang and it was Admiral Dennison. He said, "Elliott, congratulations you've just been selected."

I said, "Admiral, are you sure?"

What had happened was the President hadn't signed the darned thing and Admiral Dennison had told Joe to stay up there until the list was approved by the President.

So, Admiral Dennison personally called me. The next couple of days were pretty much euphoria. This was my last crack. As you know I got the general court martial.

Q: And, this was in the background and this is why they were so pleased.

Adm. L.: Well, I asked Joe later on, I said, "Joe, what happened? How was the SS AWA MARU handled in the deliberation?" I knew him well enough to ask him this.

He said, "Elliott, it never came up. Somebody did mention it once and then somebody else said, 'Well he sank a lot of Japs didn't he?'" He said, "That was the only mention of the AWA MARU."

The other strange part about that particular selection board, according to Joe, was they, let's say thirty-two were selected that year. I don't know maybe it was thirty-three or thirty-one. We'll say thirty two. He said, on the very first go around they got down to thirty-four officers. So, all they had to do was eliminate two which I think is most unusual for a selection board.

Q: Apparently so. You hear of them struggling over a fairly large list.

Adm. L.: That's right. But, the first vote taken the list was down to thirty-four from, how many were on the list? I haven't the slightest idea. Several hundred I'd think.

Q: Well, that meant that automatically you had to move out of that place.

Adm. L.: No, it didn't because I wouldn't make my number and I didn't make my number, actually, until the following spring. So, I fully expected to stay there at least until the next year. But, all of a sudden a phone call came and said, "Hey, we're going to give you CruDesFlot 9, Admiral, Long Beach. So get your bags packed."

Well, I had just a few days notice. Not a few days probably a couple of weeks notice. I was rather surprised to get orders so quickly because I knew I wouldn't make my number until several months had passed.

Q: It was a prize command wasn't it?

Adm. L.: Yes.

Q: Tell me the scope of it.

Adm. L.: Well, I was embarked on the USS OKLAHOMA CITY as the flag ship and had two destroyer squadrons, either two or three. Unfortunately all of whom were down in San Diego, but I was stationed in Long Beach. The reason for that was there were two Admirals there. I think Red Baumberger or Draper Kauffman, I forget which one, was the other one. And, he was deployed, so they had to keep an Admiral in Long Beach in a cruiser-destroyer organization. So, even though most of my ships were in San Diego, or all of my ships except the cruiser, I was in Long Beach until I deployed.

Q: The First Fleet was based in San Diego?

Adm. L.: San Diego, yes. I think Charlie Melson had the first fleet, if I'm not mistaken. And, Frank Virden was the boss. He was ComCruDesPac. He was in San Diego. They had two CruDes Flots down there, so they had all kinds of flag officers on tap in San Diego, but I was the only afloat flag officer in Long Beach at that particular time.

Q: Now, what was your relationship with CincPac?

Adm. L.: Very little. We worked directly for CruDesPac who in turn worked for either CincPacFleet or First Fleet depending upon whether it was a training exercise or it was a deployment. So, the chain of command was just right up the line and Frank Virden was my boss at that time.

Q: Well, tell me something about your duties, I mean your deployment.

Adm. L.: Well, it was really just a housekeeping job in Long Beach because I had no ships. I'm trying to recall now when we deployed. You corrected me on the first time when I had the USS TOLEDO. I'm pretty sure this time we went out in January, didn't we? I think.

Q: October 1961 you took command.

Adm. L.: I think it was January. Well, actually I spent a lot of time in San Diego making inspections. That was one of my big jobs to get the squadrons ready who were going to deploy.

Q: Before they were deployed were they under First Fleet then?

Adm. L.: No, they came directly under CruDesPac. So, I know I went down many, many times with my staff and had an inspection of the ships to be sure they were ready to deploy and to help out in any way that we could.

I'm sure it was in January, Jack because Hank Miller was Aviation Carrier Division Commander. He had been selected a year ahead of me. So, he was the senior. We all deployed from San Diego to Honolulu with Hank overall in charge and I went out in the USS HENRY B. WILSON which was a DDG. Don Griffin had been promised that the USS OKLAHOMA CITY would be his flag ship for the Seventh Fleet when he had that command. The USS OKLAHOMA CITY went out to Yokosuka and became Bill Schoech's flag ship. He was Com Seventh Fleet. I went out on a DDG and had nothing to do at all because Miller was the officer in charge going out to Honolulu. I just was along for the ride. We were there for a week or so and then I deployed from Honolulu to Yokosuka with two squadrons plus some smaller ships that were not in my command. We had a real fine transit from Honolulu to Yokosuka with no incidents and got there overnight and left immediately and went down to Sasebo where I joined the USS ST. PAUL. That was my flag ship there the remainder of the deployment.

Q: A very, very good flag ship.

Adm. L.: Yes. Al Church was the Skipper. He is a marvelous person out of 1938. He had a real unfortunate accident later on in Yokosuka. But, I rode the USS ST. PAUL from then on. We just operated in fleet exercises. The normal Seventh Fleet employment for the rest of the deployment. No particular long cruises like we had before. We never got to Taiwan. Of course we went to Hong Kong. My wife, fortunately, was able, my daughter was in her fifth high school in four years. A senior in high school in Coronado. But, Johnny Hack and his wife took her into their home and Marjorie came out for a few months in Japan. She hated Japan, had hated Japan from World War II.

Q: You mean because they were enemies.

Adm. L.: Yes, and because I was out in a submarine fighting the war and she wanted no part of it. She really thoroughly enjoyed Japan. We had lots of time and were able to make many trips. We visited Kyoto. The ship went into Nagasaki for a visit. We got to Sasebo. I forget the place north of Tokyo in the mountains up there. A magnificent mountain. I can't remember the name of it now. Buddy Yeomans was Commander Naval Forces Far East. Buddy and Helen had been two of our friends of longstanding. They occupied the quarters of a Japanese admiral in town. They were not on the base.

But, Buddy and Helen lived in a beautiful Japanese home right in the middle of Yokosuka. They had Japanese servants who had been there with the Japanese admiral before the war. I have a lot of fond memories of Japan. They always treated me, both as a Captain when I had the USS TOLEDO, and when I had the CruDesFl there were no unpleasant incidents the whole time I was there. Very friendly people, I thought.

Q: Did you have any contacts with former Japanese Naval officers of the Imperial Navy?

Adm. L.: Yes, quite a bit. I can't remember the name of the CNO, but we went to several parties with the Japanese Chief of Naval Operations. There was a retired Japanese admiral who had this battleship memorial which is moored in Yokosuka. I can't remember either his name, but the MIKASA is a memorial in Yokosuka. We met several Japanese civilian people. I think one of the most fascinating visits we had was we had a reception in Yokohama with the USS ST. PAUL and a lady came aboard who had been the secretary for Mikimoto. She had a pearl shop in Yokohama and she was the only person in all of Japan who owned this shop that could use the name Mikimoto. In other words, she was not part of the Mikimot family or the dynasty, and she owned this shop and we became friendly with her. At this reception, she brought a Japanese friend of longstanding who lived in Yokohama and whose home had been taken over, not by MacArthur, but by whoever MacArthur's number two guy was after the war. They just appropriated it and that's where the American general lived until we got out of Japan. Then this particular family moved back in. Well, they invited us out for a Japanese high tea the next afternoon after this reception. I think it was the most magnificent occurrence we've ever had. The living room was Western style, but everything else was, I mean they had chairs and tables and everything, but everything else was Japanese. We had the high tea and after that, we thought that was going to be the end of it, but after that we went outside and gosh he had food and liquor and everything you'd ever want to see. It lasted the whole afternoon. It just so happened that we fell into this because of the reception and because of our friendship with this gal who ran the Mikimoto shop right in Yokohama.

The other interesting experience which I had was I got the gout which I didn't know about and suffered pretty severely coming back from Hong Kong.

Q: In your foot?

Adm. L.: In my right toe, big toe. We got back to Yokosuka and there was a big parade, or Yokohama. So, Bill Schoech designated me to lead the parade. I marched around the city for about two and a half hours in agony really. I didn't know it was the gout and the ship's doctor didn't know it was the gout. I just thought I had a sore big toe. But, I got through it. I had the Japanese robes on and all of this paraphernalia. I think Marjorie still has pictures of some of it.

We were coming back from a fleet exercise, and there was this incident.

Q: This was still in the Far East?

Adm. L.: Yes, sir. In Yokosuka. And, Al prided himself, and rightly so on handling the ship and he wouldn't use a pilot. He had a pilot aboard, but he wouldn't, he made his own landings. He was landing, trying to make a landing of the USS ST. PAUL and it was a pretty high wind velocity and he turned too quickly, or too soon, and the wind just threw him up against the USS CORAL SEA with practically no way on it at all, but with the angled deck on the USS CORAL SEA, the carriers back into the piers so if they have to get underway they can just shoot out. So, the angled deck and he was pushed into the USS CORAL SEA he was going this way and the USS CORAL SEA was headed this way. The angled deck extended out, if you follow me.

Q: Yes.

Adm. L.: With very little way on, why, this angled deck just acted like a knife and sheared off about three five inch guns and did considerable superstructure damage to Al. Unfortunately, Admiral Schoech was witnessing this and I had to be the investigating officer. Actually the biggest contributing factor was they had these camels alongside the USS CORAL SEA which they had not removed because they had just docked just before us. If they hadn't been there, I think Al might have avoided either all of the damage or some of the damage. But, I had to investigate the thing and it was pretty hard because I was very fond of Al and I did everything I possibly could to not find him at fault, and I didn't find him at fault. I got overturned. I'm sure this was a big contributing factor that Al didn't get selected for Rear Admiral. He was a very, very fine officer.

Shortly after that we were sent home. This is a strange thing the way aviators do things. Again I was riding the USS HENRY B. WILSON home, the DDG. We all got underway with the USS CORAL SEA and Tommy Booth all in formation. The next morning, no USS CORAL SEA. Gone. They had been sent out to do a mission or something in the Aleutians. Tommy didn't let me know. He didn't say a damned word. I guess it was a top secret thing or something. I proceeded merrily on my way with the sixteen destroyers back to San Diego. I never did see the USS CORAL SEA again.

Q: Did you ever find out what it was?

Adm. L.: No. It was a classified mission. But, the type of mission it was I don't know. But, we never saw him again and we had a most uneventful trip.

Q: You mean she went on her own without an escort of any kind?

Adm. L.: No, she had her own squadron of destroyers with her for plane guards. They were not in my command. I had sixteen ships. We had a very uneventful trip back to San Diego.

Q: Were the Russians in evidence in the Pacific at that time?

Adm. L.: No. Then when we got back I was relieved shortly after that and had gotten orders to go back to SACLant staff again to relieve Jim Davis.

Q: They liked you there?

Adm. L.: Well, Admiral Dennison was still there. And, I called Jim on the phone because really it was a crisis, I mean nobody knew what the heck was going on. You remember the thing I'm sure clearly. Jim had orders to go to Guantanamo. He said, "Elliott take your time coming back. You have thirty days leave if you want to use it. There is no sense in coming here, this place is a mad house and I'm stuck. They won't let me go down to Guantar until this thing is over one way or the other."

I said "Are you sure? Can I be of any help?"

He said, "All you're going to do is sit around and do nothing. So, you might as well enjoy yourself cross country."

So, I took him at his word. It happened to be the truth. Marjorie and I went up to San Francisco. I had my dog with me. We visited my sister in Saratoga and stayed three or four days in San Francisco. We had a marvelous time there. Then a leisurely trip across country. We picked up her mother in the western part of Pennsylvania and eventually got down to SACLant staff. Jim was still there. This was shortly after Thanksgiving, I guess the last week of November.

Q: So, the real crisis had passed?

Adm. L.: Right. Shortly after I got there John McNay Taylor had relieved Sabe, I guess. This was the SACLant Chief of Staff.

Loughlin #6 -281-

He was mixed up on the national side with the crisis. Well, you know, it was resolved. So, Jim went to Guantanamo and I relieved him, obviously before he went to Guantanamo and spent the next year there as Deputy Chief of staff for SACLant.

Q: What about the immediate aftermath to the crisis?

Adm. L. Well, see, SACLant really didn't enter, the SACLant staff itself didn't really enter into this too much. It was strictly a national exercise, if you want to call it an exercise, Jack.

Q: It was more than an exercise.

Adm. L.: No, but I mean the deployment of ships was, as you know, controlled by McNamara and George Anderson. I've talked to Admiral Anderson many times about this and I know one of the things that led to his downfall was when they started shifting ships individually as to what station to take. He publicly remonstrated with McNamara and said, "Look, Admiral Dennison is one of the most capable officers we have and is most capable of handling the situation. You tell him what to do and then let him do it the way he wants to."

Well, McNamara and the hierarchy didn't go for that. They had to do every little, they would be shifting the ships, this is all hearsay on my part for I wasn't there at the time. But, they would tell a destroyer to take such-and-such station. I think it was a pretty unpleasant time for Admiral Dennison too. He had the tools, but he didn't have the authority to use them. It was done by the war game people in the Pentagon and DoD, and the White House.

Q: It was an unpleasant time for them. It also was an unpleasant time for Corky Ward who had the Second Fleet whose destroyers were involved.

Adm. L.: I imagine it was. I can well imagine that.

Of course, that--I must have been there two years, I guess. Yes, I was there two years because President Kennedy, he was assassinated the following year, 1963. So I had two years of duty there.

Q: You were again in Plans and Policy?

Adm. L.: Yes.

Q: Was it similar to what you did before?

Adm. L.: Well, except I had all of the sections. The other ones I just had, what they call, C32, which is a particular section. As Deputy Chief of Staff and head of the Plans and Policy I had everybody on the staff concerned with Plans and Policy under my command.

Q: Did the plans begin to change with the impact of the missile crisis? It was a watershed period in terms of defense.

Adm. L.: They actually didn't, Jack, as I said, I guess it's hard to explain it, but this was strictly a national thing between Russia and the United States, nobody else entered into this argumen

Q: They were more than just witnesses however.

Adm. L.: Well, they were concerned, but there wasn't a hell of a lot they could do about it. It was out of NATO's sphere of influence. You see Cinc East Lant had all of the waters around Europe and this was out in the middle of the Atlantic which was strictly CinCLant, CinCLant Fleet bailiwick. NATO really had no part of this operation. It just wasn't in this area of operation.

Q: What about the organization of Latin American states? They got involved in this because they wanted to.

Adm. L.: Well, we never, as far as SACLant, again were out of the sphere of the influence of NATO. I mean the NATO staff never had anything to do with the South American plans. They were concerned only with the areas of operations which concerned NATO in case we ever went to a war of NATO's responsibility, of which West Lant was not. Although there was a Cinc West Lant NATO had, occupied by U.S. Naval officers. Only U.S. ships would have been concerned with operations in Cinc West Lant, or in West Lant.

Q: Did Plans have anything to do or any concern with the possibility of joint operations where you had language differences and customs?

Adm. L.: No, because English was still the universal language as far as the top echelon was concerned. For instance, all of the NATO officers, and I don't know how many we had on the staff there, we must have had thirty or forty spoke fluent English. So, from a staff point of view language never offered any difficulty. English was the language spoken at all of the NATO conferences in Paris. Of course, interpreters, you know people wore ear phones and they would all be duplicated in French by some interpreter, but English was the language spoken. As far as in the field is concerned, perhaps that's one reason they had this small group of ships that they formed which rotated together was to solve the language barriers they might find. I never operated with them because, as I said, I was in plans, I was not in operations I'm sure the Skippers and the signals were in English, I'm posit of that. The Turkish, the Greeks, we didn't have any Greek offic on the staff. We had Turkish officers in Portugal. But, they all spoke English.

Q: Was IBER LANT in being then?

Adm. L.: It was in being, but there was no IBER LANT command. Infrastructure was the only part of the plan that had been implem I did make one or two trips to Portugal and inspected the infrastructure, the ammunition depots and the proposed site for IBER LANT which did take place later on. Gene Fluckey was there, it was his last job, I guess, as Cinc IBER LANT. It was a command but it had not been activated as such.

Q: I think the reason for that was because of the contention betw the U.S. and Britain over who was going to have the top job.

Adm. L.: We had an awful lot of contention. The in-fighting was pretty terrific particularly between Great Britain and the United States. Then, of course, De Gaulle came to the fore during that two year period of time. He pulled his people out of NATO. Shor after that SHAPE moved up to Brussels. They had several French officers there, but two in particular, one I had met once way back in 1949 when he was here at the Naval Station when he was the Assistant Naval Attache here in Washington. His first name was Pierre and I can't remember his last name. The other one was de la Husse who had married an American girl. They both later made admiral. They were trying to be loyal to De Gaulle, but off the record they were just sick at heart. It put them in a most embarrassing predicament on SACLant Staff, to have De Gaulle just pull out of everything which he did.

Q: That I understand has generally been the attitude of the French Navy. They have wanted to continue.

Adm. L.: Well, we did work out a degree of, not a treaty, but an agreement of cooperation. We did work it out even with De Gaulle's administration, but it was never publicized. In other words, if we had gone to war, if it had been a crisis, the French Navy would have cooperated with us and Great Britain in the areas contiguous to France which was their primary responsibility, even under NATO plans. So, they would have cooperated. I think they would right now, frankly.

Q: But always without any public acknowledgment of the fact.

Adm. L.: That's right. Apparently the commands were set up when NATO was established, or when SACLant was established, were set up, and rightly so in my judgment, depending upon the forces available. Therefore, the U.S., this is undoubtedly the reason they wrote in that SACLant was to be a U.S. Naval officer. Great Britain had the next greatest Naval forces and, therefore, they had the next top commands.

Q: Which is a practical approach.

Adm. L.: I think this is what rankled France is that they never had a real high Naval command in SACLant. I think this is what rankled them.

Q: When you were in Plans there for SACLant did you have to take into consideration the difficulties with communications, especial when you got out into that area up around Norway? The interference with communications where communications became a real problem, I understand. Atmospheric interference.

Adm. L.: Yes, I'm trying to think when the station in Maine was activated. You know the very low frequency station we have up in Maine that is primarily for the FBM, but I don't know when that was activated. I really don't think we had, I can't recall having too many NATO exercises involving NATO forces up in the North Cape, up in the northern part of the Northern Atlantic.

Q: I remember one when Admiral Wright was in the Atlantic and they had terrible problems with communications because of the Aurora Borealis. It almost ruined the exercise because they coul communicate.

Adm. L.: Well, I'm sure the difficulties existed, but, because during my tenure there we really didn't have any combined exercis up in the far north.

Q: Where were yours centered largely?

Adm. L.: Well, we didn't really have many operational exercises. It was kind of frustrating because it was really a planning job.

You planned for contingencies, but the contingencies never developed. In other words, I mentioned this before, the whole convoy system was set up, but they never executed a convoy exercise.

Q: And, as a planner you hope to see some of your plans in operation.

Adm. L.: Yes. You'd like to. But, I guess money made a difference, materiel made a difference. I don't think we had too much resources to spare on combined NATO exercises in those days. I think this is the reason we didn't implement any of these plans.

Q: Also, we were occupied otherwise, not only with the missile crisis, but with the developing problems in the Far East.

Adm. L.: The Far East and the Soviet threat, the submarine threat. I'm sure that took a lot of men and money on the national side. As you well know the Soviet submarines, both their nuclears, well primarily their nuclears are making patrols all over the Atlantic. This was one of the big headaches we had was to try to keep track of these Soviet nuclear submarines.

Q: Now by the time you were there for plans our POLARIS submarines were becoming operational; now, did they figure in any of the NATO plans?

Adm. L.: No, sir they were never included in NATO plans. They were strictly a national deterrent. As a matter of fact, it caused quite a bit of hassle at SACLant Headquarters. On a visit from the UK staff several of them came over and a couple of them were pretty senior officers. Hal Shear, who later on was a four star admiral, was Admiral Dennison's FBM Operational Officer, so to speak. The British tried their best to get Admiral Dennison to, at least notify them when our FBM's were going to transit the Strait of Gibraltar. The answer was, "no."

Q: At that point the British didn't have any POLARIS submarines?

Adm. L.: No. They had started one. My next tour of duty when I went down to Charleston, at that time they did not have the missiles nor the POLARIS submarines. They got their missiles from us, you know. They built their submarines, but they got their missiles from the United States.

I never will forget this conference I sat in. Hal Shear was speaking for Admiral Dennison and they said, "Suppose we detect them? How do we know if it's the U.S. or a Russian, or who it is?"

Hal just said, "We'll just have to take that chance."

We would not notify the UK forces in Gibraltar when our submarines were going back and forth.

Q: Now, what was the rationale in back of that?

Adm. L. I think--the FBM operations are really a closely held thing and it's strictly a national force, they are not earmarked for NATO in any respect whatsoever. The communication, the methods of communications, the methods of operation, the patrol areas were closely held and the United States would not divulge them to anyone.

Q: But, the British, it would seem to me, might be asking for this information in terms of, not as a NATO partner, but as somebody who stood guard at the Straits.

Adm. L.: I agree, but I wasn't making the decisions.

Q: At the same time had we not already negotiated for a base up in Scotland?

Adm. L.: Yes, Holy Loch. We were already in Holy Loch.

Q: So, it was a bitter pill for them to accept?

Adm. L.: I would think so.

Q: They were a partner in a sense in providing space, but not a partner in actuality. Maybe this is one of the things that inspired them to get on with a POLARIS program of their own.

Adm. L.: I think they started off with three, didn't they? I know the missiles were built in the United States and were loaded down in Charleston when I got there in my next tour of duty.

Q: And, I believe Mountbattan had something to do with this, swinging this program.

Adm. L.: Probably. No, I certainly can well understand the British point of view on this. They were responsible for the defense of the Gibraltar Straits and if I were responsible for defense, I think, I would like to know who was going back and forth. Perhaps one valid reason, Jack, is we just didn't want them to know how many FBM's we had deployed in the Mediterranean. That information certainly would have been very closely held. If you're going to notify them anytime anyone goes in or out of those straits, why, it doesn't take a mathematician to figure out how many boats you're going to have deployed there.

Q: Two and two make four.

Adm. L.: And, that's the reason, I think that's one reason they shifted around instead of having everyone in Holy Loch going up into the North Cape area they started sending submarines down in the Mediterranean from Holy Loch in addition to the ones from Rota. And, they started sending ships from Rota up into the Nort Sea, North Cape just to keep anybody from counting.

Q: Yes, multiplying the force.

Adm. L.: And, our boats in Charleston, later on, in the next tour of duty some of them would go to the Mediterranean and some of them would go to the North Cape. You see, we had four squadro We had one in New London. We had one in Charleston, one in Rota, and one in Holy Loch. They criss-crossed to keep somebody from counting how many boats we had there at any one time.

Q: In going back again to your job as a planner for future things you had to rely, you had to include in your plans atmospheric conditions and all that sort of data, hydrographic information, did you treat it as a static matter that you had all the informat that was available or did you think in terms expanding or includi more knowledge?

Adm. L.: I think more or less static, Jack. It's very hard to dissociate yourself from your national hat and your SACLant hat. I knew about the new communications station up in Maine. And, as I said, I can't remember when it became operational. I knew our own capabilities as far as communications were concerned. I didn't know and do not know to this day what the capabilities of the other NATO countries were. I'm afraid that's one area where we didn't lay too much importance on it.

Q: You mean it wasn't communicated to you by them?

Adm. L.: I don't think that--because of the lack of operations involving NATO ships, which were practically nil during my time there, I don't think this problem was ever resolved or really recognized. Admiral Wright, as you say, recognized it. But, to my knowledge I can't recall until two years later that we ever had a combined NATO exercise, an operational exercise during the time I was on the staff. Therefore I think there had to be problems which I wasn't aware of and which were not emphasized and which never really came to light.

Q: What about the existing knowledge of weather conditions and that sort of thing at the time? Was that adequate?

Adm. L.: Well, it was from the national point of view. Again, from the NATO point of view it was never emphasized. I think that's one of the main disadvantages, and I tried not do to it, but it's hard not to do it, and even the NATO officers on the staff, it's hard to disassociate yourself from your national objectives and from your NATO objectives.

Q: Trying to be two different people.

Adm. L.: I mean the French, for instance had two wonderful captain on the staff. I know that their whole concern was what's going to happen to the French Naval forces under De Gaulle? And, they did their staff work on the SACLant staff, but their hearts were back in the French Navy. And, I'm sure the UK officers were the same way, and I'm sure the Dutch officers were the same way.

Q: So, you put your finger on one of the tremendous weaknesses of a NATO force.

Adm. L.: Absolutely.

Q: There are two loyalties and the stronger one is the national one.

Adm. L.: It is the national one. No question about it. Isn't the same way with SACLant, CinCLant Fleet. His main concern is with the national forces, not with his NATO forces. Now SACEUR is different.

Q: In what sense?

Adm. L.: Well, one the predominant land forces are not even the U.S. forces. He is truly a unified commander.

Q: A multinational commander?

Adm. L.: A multinational commander with all of these various land forces, tanks, and planes, missiles, and everything. I think that Norstad and General Lemnitzer both felt that they were over in Paris, they weren't sitting back in the United States. They

Loughlin #6 -293-

weren't responsible for the United States national objectives. They were responsible for NATO objectives, SACEUR objectives in Europe.

Q: But, at the same time this weakness that you point out, in terms of Naval forces, it seems to me would be inherent in the land forces. For instance, use this as a hypothetical thing. Say, the Dutch lowlands are being invaded by the enemy. Dutch troops under NATO command wouldn't be very happy serving in the south of France at that point. They would want to be up there defending their own land. So, isn't it the same thing?

Adm. L.: It's the same thing, but he really has more resources than SACLant has. Who's going to bear the brunt of the fighting in a Naval war? The U.S. forces.

Q: But, set this at the NATO command up against, as it must be set up against the Warsaw Pact nations it seems to me that they might have a more unified effort, a demonstrated unified effort because the ideology that's back of it. There is an attempt, as one understands it, to obliterate really, the national boundaries in terms of the ideology.

Q: Well, I think SACEUR can do that so much easier than SACLant. Their plans call for the deployment of the various multi-national forces, the actual deployment of it. They have exercises where they use this, training exercises. We don't do that in SACLant. Our plans may call for the deployment of forces to protect convoys, but I've already said I don't think they are ever going to be made available even though they are earmarked. But, they are available in Europe. You can't pull our X number of divisions we have over in Europe and get them back to the states, or get them some other place in the world in the event of a NATO war. They are there for a NATO war. Our forces are not there for a NATO war, in my opinion. They are there to protect the national interest.

Q: Well, I hope you're right in terms of the military aspect of Western Europe.

Adm. L.: They have exercises all the time which the Naval forces don't have, Jack, where they utilize the various countries they have, the land forces available. All of their contingency plans call for deployment of these forces to certain areas.

Q: Now, thinking in terms again of your planning operation what part of the plans developed under the aegis of SACLant had to do with the traditional concept of the Navy transporting troops and so forth? Getting them to hot spots?

Adm. L.: The same thing. We had ear marked forces, ear marked Marine divisions, ear marked Army division, ear marked transports ear marked escorts. When I say ear marked, I mean this is indeed what the plans envisioned-that in the event of a NATO war, why, the Marine divisions, the Army divisions, the transports, and the escorts would convoy these troops over to Europe. But, agai I just can't envision a NATO war without involving the national interest of the United States. I just can't envision it.

Q: Of course it is an inherent part of it, of NATO.

Adm. L.: But, I mean Russia is not going to have a land war over in Europe without involving us in other parts of the world. Look at the development in the Persian Gulf now. What happens if they invade Poland or invade part of Europe? What do you think we're going to do? I think we're just going to build up as many forces as we can down in the Persian Gulf.

Q: Now, I think we'll turn our attention to your command of Submarine Flotilla 6 which happened in the year 1964.

Adm. L.: I had been out of the submarine service, really, since I had my squadron in 1953. This is, what, eleven years later. And had had no nuclear training, had not even ridden in a nuclear powered ship.

Q: They weren't in being, actually.

Adm. L.: Well, until later on. I guess the USS NAUTILUS was what, 1953 or 1954. But, Joe Grenfell, who was ComSubLant wanted me to go down and take over ComSubFlot 6 and frankly I demurred. I said, "Gee, Joe, I've been out of submarines for eleven, twelve years and I've never had any nuclear training." I knew what my responsibilities would be down there.

    He said, "No, I want you to go down anyway."

    So I went.

Q: With any special training, any special course?

Adm. L.: No, I called on Rickover.

Q: Did he give his blessing?

Adm. L.: No he didn't. He runs his own little nuclear program, you know. He didn't care who was in operations.

Q: You were not a part of that?

Adm. L.: No. Nobody is except Rickover. ComSubLant's not part of it. But, I knew what the responsibilities entailed at that time, Jack in the period of 1964 to 1966, I stayed there for two years. The apex of the FBM building program was reached. This is when most of the forty-one submarines were built during those two years. I had, actually, operational command, not operational command, I had command of all FBM submarines from the time they were commissioned until the time they deployed to their parent squadron.

Q: What period of time was involved in that?

Adm. L.: All of their shake down training and all of their missile training.

Q: That was a matter of what, months?

Adm. L.: Oh, months. Several months. This really entailed, this really resulted in the most interesting experience of my life. I was obliged to and wanted to go down and ride each missile submarine, FBM submarine, both the blue and the gold for their missile shooting at Cape Canaveral. During the period I was there I think I saw something like forty-one or forty-two missile shoot I had to miss some, so forty-two would be twenty-one submarines and I missed some, so during those two years at least twenty-five or twenty-six or twenty-seven FBM submarines were built and deplo during a two year period of time.

Of course Squadron 18 was activated during my two years there which is one of the four Polaris squadrons. As I said, one in Charleston, one in New London, one in Holy Loch and one in Rota. So, when Admiral Lowrance relieved Admiral Grenfell, they split the, they divided the submarine forces up, really, into two parts. They had an admiral up in New London who had the New London squadron of the conventional submarines, the New London Polaris submarines and the Holy Loch submarines. And, I had the Charleston conventional submarines, the Norfolk conventional submarines, the Key West conventional submarines, the Polaris squadron in Charleston, and the Polaris squadron in Rota. So, it was split right down the middle into two parts. Of course, once the Polaris submarine deployed he became directly under the operational control of ComSubLant. Nobody else was in on that. The operations orders and everything and the same way with the SSN's when they went out on their special missions, which I'm sure you're familiar with, their operation order, even under the squadron commander had nothing to do with it. It came directly under the operational control of ComSubLant. All the squadron commanders did, and all I did in Charleston was to provide logistics support and training and be sure the crews were ready to deploy. Once they deployed, why, the squadron commander not I, neither one of us, were ever in the planning, even in the planning of the mission. As I say, it was just a marvelous experience because, without bragging, I'll make this statement to my dying day, the Polaris submarine force had the cream of the crop of the U.S. Navy. There is no question in my mind whatsoever. These people, they just were superb Naval officers to start with. And, Rickover has just done a magnificent job even though he runs a taut circle, why look at the accidents. The lack of accidents we've had in the nuclear program in the Navy, Jack. There has been one or two maybe close calls, but never has a submarine been forced to curtail a mission because of a nuclear problem, never.

Q: It's a wonderful record, but it's a protected one too. In case we did have something happen that's a blackeye to the whole program.

Adm. L.: Well the USS THRESHER, we've lost the USS THRESHER and the USS SCORPION. I think I know what caused both of them, but it certainly wasn't a failure of the nuclear component, in my opinion. I had a long talk with Admiral Libby,-

Q: Austin?

Adm. L.: Count Austin who was in charge of both investigations and the findings have never been published.

Q: Did you know that he didn't see the final report either?

Adm. L.: No, I didn't know that. But, I'm convinced in my own mind, I was in Norfolk at the time the USS THRESHER went down. I was still on SACLant staff. I'm convinced in my own mind that he was down at test depth and he was going at a very slow speed and, I'm convinced, that something jarred away a fitting or a line or something carried away in the engine room which caused them to take an up angle. Of course, he tried to increase speed and blow his main ballast tanks. This we know. But, at that depth the high pressure air was so wire drawn through the narrow apertures leading to the main ballast tank that he wasn't able to get enough water out of the ship to compensate for the water that was coming in plus the fact that the standard operational procedure at that time called for a shut down of the nuclear power plant in case something went wrong with the nuclear power plant. From all indications that I've been able to find out, I think the nuclear power plant was shut down which meant they lost power, which meant they just went down this way and were probably going sixty miles an hour when they hit six thousand feet. And, they changed all of that after this thing. That's the reason I think what I'm saying is probably the truth. For instance they had a multi-million dollar program on, not only the SSN's, but the FBM's, the Polaris submarines and the regular attack submarines, where they had a central manifold and they had these huge pipes where you could push one button and all of the high pressure air would just go through this big opening to the ballast tank rather than be wire drawn. Boy, they practiced this thing. Even a Polaris submarine will pop to the surface in practically nothing flat because they had thousands of pounds of high pressure air going into the ballast tank. It really gave you a real fast ride. As a matter of fact, one of the Skippers down in Charleston had this modification done and he hit the button, deliberately as a training exercise and there was something wrong. He took about sixty degree list and practically scared the living be-jesus out of everybody on the ship. The submarine surfaced all right, but it came up with about a sixty degree list. That's an awfully uncomfortable feeling.

Q: I guess so. It would be a sense of out of control.

Adm. L.: Now, the USS SCORPION is a different thing. I have no information to go on except my chief of staff, my first chief of staff in Charleston subsequently became a squadron commander in New London. During that tour of duty he was sent out to the Azores on an ASR to try to locate the USS SCORPION which he did. You know how the USS SCORPION was located? The general location was determined by an Air Force triangulation on an explosion, not by our own SOSUS outfit, to my knowledge. They went out there and, by God, they located the USS SCORPION and, what was it, six thousand feet again.

Q: Great depth.

Adm. L.: And, they took hundreds and hundreds of pictures from a submerged camera. I talked with Jim Traylor after he came back and he doesn't think that it was an interior explosion at all because he said the hull was intact. I think what happened was that they were handling a torpedo in the fore torpedo room, had pulled it out of the tube, and had, I think, what we call a "hot run," in the torpedo room. I think the torpedo took off and went through the bow, and shutters and it went down. In other words, the water came through and they couldn't catch it in time. But, anyway, that's theory. They are the only two losses that we've had and neither one of them, really entailed a nuclear reactor accident supposing my hypothesis is correct that they did shut down the plant because of, not something that was in the plant, but something outside the plant caused them to shut it down.

Maybe you could say that was a nuclear accident, but I don't think so. With all the hundreds of submarines, well not hundreds. I guess we're up to forty-one Polaris and must be up to some sixty some odd nuclear now I think are still running. I think that's a record that speaks for itself.

Q: How did you acquire an intimate knowledge of this subject?

Adm. L.: In those days, and perhaps still, we had to ride a submarine a certain number of hours in order to get submarine pay. This was easy for me becaue I was down at the Cape every month practically. I guess I was down there every month. So, all of the riding I did, both at the Cape and with transits from Charleston down to the Cape and from the Cape back to Charleston were on the nuclear submarines. All I did was talk to the Skipper and talk to the people who ran the base down there and tried to educate myself.

Q: It was a practical course.

Adm. L.: That's right. Another thing I started, which I think is well worthwhile-with Rebel Lowrance's permission we had a debriefing from the Polaris Skippers after every patrol in Charleston. And SubLant would send an observer down and Levering Smith's outfit, Special Projects, would send an observer down. In other words instead of having several debriefings we'd have one right in the Headquarters in Charleston. That was an education in itself too.

Q: Yes. Did they also have debriefings up in New London?

Adm. L.: I don't know what the Admiral did up there. This was just my own idea and I received the blessing of Rebel Lowrance. I did it.

Q: Was Rickover interested in that phase of thing?

Adm. L.: No.

Q: He had his own debriefings.

Adm. L.: All he was concerned with was not the patrol procedure, which was my concern, but whether they had any maintenance proble with the nuclear plant. His interest is solely in the nuclear plant, solely. To hell with the missiles, to hell with the navigation, to hell with anything else.

Q: So, with all of this going on it didn't take you very long to really get a massive education.

Adm. L.: That's right. I'm certainly not an expert. There was a lot I didn't know when I left. But, I knew a lot more when I left than when I got there. I was able to talk the language with these Skippers and became firm friends with every one of them. Incidentally it went by the board as soon as the guy relie me, but I saw every crew off from the Charleston Air Force Base and I saw every crew return from patrol to the Charleston Air Force Base whether they got in at two-thirty in the morning or three-thirty in the morning or whatever it was.

Q: That was the Nimitz habit.

Adm. L.: Well, I don't know. But, nobody else did it before and nobody has done it since.

Q: So you were concerned about the personnel.

Adm. L.: Absolutely.

Q: And, there were problems with personnel and the long tours.

Adm. L.: We had problems and we had customs problems.

Q: Customs problems?

Adm. L.: Yes. The kids would come back at two-thirty in the morning and sit around the waiting room for an hour waiting for Customs to examine their luggage. So, I went down and spoke to the officials in Charleston. I said, "Look," --you see I was out there so I knew what they were--here they had gone on a sixty day patrol and their wives were waiting, everything was waiting at two-thirty in the morning. I said, "Isn't there some way we can beat this thing?"

They said, "Sure."

I've never seen more cooperative people in my life. They said "Have the Executive Officer and the Skipper inspect and certify before they leave Rota," this is the only one I was concerned with, see, because the submariners came back to New London, I mean to Charleston, "before they ever leave Rota have a certification made that there are no articles in this personal baggage or cruise boxes or anything that are subject to customs. If they are, have the declaration all made when they come in."

We put that into operation.

Q: At the same time you have to have a Customs agent there to receive it?

Adm. L.: That's right, but we put it into operation and ten minut[es] after they debarked they were on their way home to their wife and family. It is the best thing that ever happened for morale. It's horrible though to have that long flight back after sixty days of patrol and then sit there and wait for an hour or two Jack.

Q: Well, that was an inexcusable delay. How did you deal with the morale problems that were involved with the sixty day detail When they are out for sixty days?

Adm L.: There weren't any morale problems. No. The thing that very few people realize, Jack, is that the schedule is set up, unless it's an accident, and we've had one or two accidents. I think one FBM hit a rock and had to come back early from Holy Loch. But, a guy knows two years ahead of time if he's going to be home for Christmas, if he's going to be home for Easter, if he's going to be home for his birthday. In other words, they know what their rotation is on patrols. It's cut and dried. It's a certain number of finite number of days on patrol for refreshing training, for transit, for everything. There is an awfu[l] lot of time on patrol to study. We had the highest rate of advancement of any unit in the fleet mainly because they have this time. Ninty percent of the time on patrol you're not doing anything.

Q: They not only have the time, they have the facility.

Adm. L.: Right. We had the highest percentage of people that went into what they call NESEP, Naval Scientific Enlisted Program.

In other words, they go to college for two years and get a degree.

The only morale problems we had was excessive length of sea duty, not the patrol itself. In other words, we didn't have enough officers to give them a normal sea-shore rotation. I had one commanding officer that made admiral who had a hundred and eight consecutive months of sea duty. A hundred and eight. We had people who would make three or four years of sea duty before they could get rotated off to shore duty.

Q: They have to make a complete career, they have no family.

Adm. L.: Indirectly that's one reason why they had to go to this bonus business which I think you may be familiar with. They had to give these kids thousands of dollars.

Q: To re-enlist.

Adm. L.: Mostly officers in order to extend and not get out of the Navy. The enlisted personnel wasn't quite as bad a pinch as the officer personnel. You had more enlisted people. In other words, you didn't have the norm of four or five years of sea duty with enlisted personnel as you did with officers and, that's what caused a tremendous morale problem There was nothing I could do about that. I couldn't do one damned thing about that.

Q: No, that's a much bigger problem.

Interview No. 7 with Rear Admiral C. E. Loughlin, U.S. Navy
(Retired)

Place: Annapolis, Md.

Date: 21 October 1980

Subject: Biography

By: John T. Mason, Jr.

Q: You said, last time, Elliott that you went out on all the Nuke subs as they came into Key West.

Adm. L.: Cape Canaveral.

Q: Cape Canaveral, yes. And I just wondered whether there were any reportable incidents that were interesting.

Adm. L.: Actually, Jack, there weren't except for the various dignitaries of people from big companies like Jones Laughlin Stee and people like that got clearance to make what they called the DASO shots. But, I can't recall and I think I saw either thirty-nine or forty, or perhaps, forty-one missile shots and I can't recall a single, anything that went wrong with any one of those missile shots. It was a routine operation that had a bunch of experts that worked for Raborn in what they called SP's, Special Projects. A retired Captain, who lives here in Annapolis, Pappy Sims, was in charge of this team. They were just absolutely supe technicians. By that time the crews were pretty well trained. As I said, everything went according to clockwork. There were no Russian submarines around, no Russian trawlers.

Q: So you had the whole area to yourself?

Adm. L.: Well, we only went about thirty miles away from the dock there. Twenty-five or thirty miles to get the square marked off for triangulation so they knew where we were and then, of course, they had the thing where the landing area was. They triangulated it. I think they were all A-3 shots though at that time. In other words, three separate warheads so they had to triangulate each one of the three. But, as I said, there was no diving incident and to the best of my knoweldge, to the best of my remembrance rather, I think every shot we made when I was there was successful.

Q: This operation you were involved in, those various bases in the Caribbean--

Adm. L.: No. This was what they called DASO. It was just a readiness exercise to be sure that the Blue and Gold crew could get ready. See, they were on the regular patrol routine. In other words, they didn't make the missiles ready until, I think, it was a half an hour ahead of time. They started thirty minutes before they were to fire. Then they fired right on the button.

There was one interesting incident too which I had failed to recall. If you remember or perhaps you remember, one of our space ships was orbiting and, I think, they went to the Air Force and tried to get an ICBM fired for the space ship to observe. Well, it had to be split timing obviously you know how fast they travel and how fast a missile travels. And, the Air Force turned them down. At least this is the story I got. So, we hopped on it. It had to be absolutely split second timing. So, we went out. I forget which one of the space ships it was. Three of our astronauts were onboard. Let's say it had to go off at 10:12 02, whatever it had worked out to the actual second. So, you work from 10:12 02 thirty minutes and start making the missile ready and at 10:12 02 it went off and they saw it from the space ship.

Q: They did?

Adm. L.: Yes, sir. A perfect exercise.

Q: One up for the Navy.

Adm. L.: One up for the Navy. I guess the Air Force just didn't have enough confidence that they could get the thing off in a split second timing, which they had to do. But, we did.

Q: Well, that's great. Did Raborn ever come down there?

Adm. L: Yes, sir. He came, he made all of the inital shots. I don't think Admiral Raborn was aboard--as a matter of fact--

Q: He was no longer--

Adm. L.: Levering Smith came down.

Q: Did you make a trip to Rota?

Adm. L.: Yes, I made several.

Q: Tell me about Rota.

Adm. L.: Well, I may have mentioned this before, but we had four FBM squadrons. There were two in SubFlot 6 and two in the SubFlot up in New London. And, New London had one based in New London and one in Holy Loch. The two I had were based in Rota and right there in Charleston.

Q: Yes, you did explain that division of interest.

Adm. L.: So, I really had nothing to do with the operational part of the exercise of Rota. Our job in SubFlot 6 was to be sure they had the training faciliites and the refit facilities, I mean recreation. After they had finished a patrol they came back to report and were there for thirty days or whatever it was and then they went back to Rota and took the ship out again after the ship came back on the Blue and Gold.

But, Rota, at that time was a thriving establishment. We had a big air station there, and I guess an Elint station, a communication intelligence outfit, a tender. Of course, we've been kicked out now you know. They are down in Georgia. We don't have a squadron there anymore. As a matter of fact Bill Mott, a classmate of mine, just went to Rota within the last two weeks and he said it just makes you sick to see the state that the base has been reduced to. He said it's no maintenance, nobody there.

Q: Well, is that because we didn't renew our treaty?

Adm. L.: I don't know what the basic reason for not renewing the lease was in Rota. I just don't know. As far as I know, I think, we still have the air base at Madrid. But, they wanted the nuclears out of there apparently and they won because they are not there.

Q: That's isn't quite as hampering now is it?

Adm. L.: I don't know what missiles the submarines now based in Georgia have, whether they are POSEIDON or not. I presume they are POSEIDON and therefore they have longer range. But, certainly the transit time has been greatly affected whereas in Rota you could get in the Med in a day and a half. Once in a while we did send submarines up to augment Holy Loch and north. But, most of the runs made by the Rota submarines were made in the Med and the ones in Charleston either went to the Med or went up north. ComSubLant exercised sole control over the area assignments and who went where. So, I wouldn't know actually until the submarine came back when we got debriefed.

Q: When we were still actively using Rota we were limited to Rota we couldn't go into any other Spanish ports could we?

Adm. L.: I don't think so. We never--once they were commissioned and made their first run they never went into any port anyway. The only place they ever went was on patrol and then back to their refit base. They never visited, they did in training exercises before they ever made their first run. Remember I told you, we brought on into Charleston where I had my change of command. But, that was before he became operational and went on his first patrol. Bill Antle, who later died of a heart attack, one trip I made there, we heloed out to the submarine and spent two or three days on one during the training exercises that they put the new crew, the one that had just come back to R&R. It was a very interesting operation. Antle and Pappy Sims and the other--later Pappy became a Squadron Commander. Phil Beshany was there when I first arrived and he was relieved by Antle who was relieved by Pappy Sims. So, I was there, really, with three of them.

Q: Phil has told me about visits to Rota. For the sake of the record you might talk about the Blue and Gold arrangement.

Adm. L.: Well, the purpose with forty-one submarines, the purpose was to keep a maximum number of boats on patrol at any one time. I think it came out to be either twenty-five or twenty-eight out of forty one were on patrol all the time. The only way you could do this was to have two crews. One crew, let's say was leaving, say, from Rota. They would be on patrol for, say, fifty six or fifty eight days. I think it normally came out to be around fifty eight days. Then they would come back to Rota. In the meantime the crew that had finished the previous patrol had finished their R & R in Charleston. That was their home port. They were flown over to Rota. Then as soon as the crew came back from patrol, say the Blue crew for instance, they immediately were flown from Rota to Charleston. The other crew having arrived, well I say immediately, I think they had a day or two turn over to go through whatever defects, maintenance had to be done. But, with a minimum turn around time the crew that had just finished patrol were flown back to Charleston and the crew that had just finished their R&R took over and immediately started their training period. I forget what it amounted to. Probably six or eight days. Then

Loughlin #7 -312-

they would go on patrol. Then you would just continue that process on all four squadrons, Charleston, New London, Holy Loch and Rota. The big advantage of it was unless you had a tragedy or an accident two years ahead of time you knew that you were going to be home Christmas, or home on your birthday, or home at Easter, or you're going to be on patrol on your birthday, or Christmas, or Easter.

Q: Your wife could plan accordingly.

Adm. L.: That's exactly right. The schedule was very inflexible unless you had an accident.

Q: That's a very happy system. Who dreamed it up? Submariners?

Adm. L.: I'm sure they did. I don't know the individual responsible for it.

Q: You've had a real experience with both the nuclear subs and the diesels, would you talk about the merits of one against the other? Sometimes, you see people who are advocating a return to the production of diesel submarines and that they have a real place in the Navy.

Adm. L.: I think with the budget that is not austere as we've had in the past few years that a good case could be made for diesel submarines in an ASW capacity. You could build a barrier in certain areas. They are very quiet. They can hover. They can just sit there without, virtually immune from detection unless someone with active sonar picks them up. And, I think a case could be made for a barrier ASW screen. But, other than that, their lack of mobility certainly would preclude putting them in a class with the nuclear boats even though they may snorkel they are subject to detection when they are snorkeling much more than a nuclear is. It's going to take them a long time to get there on station, a long time to get back. Their time on station would be limited. compared in size to a nuclear submarine--

Q: By virtue to the weapon itself they are not--they don't constitute a shield to the nation in national defense.

Adm. L.: No it would be really an ASW mission in my opinion. that would be the main advantage if having some diesel subs. See, I forget what the FBM's carry, probably not more than four torpedoes. They did carry a minimum number for self defense whereas a diesel could carry, what, twenty-four to twenty-eight. We carried twenty-four on the USS QUEENFISH. I think they did get up to twenty-eight on some of the later boats. So, I don't think you could make a case for the diesels under the present environment, budget environment. But, I think if you had, not an unlimited budget, but if you had more money to spare, you probably could make a pitch that if we had enough warning or if we were going to get in a war with somebody.

Q: They are useful too in the sense of convoy aren't they? Can't they be?

Adm. L.: Well, I have trouble--their snorkel, they wouldn't be able to keep up with the convoy, probably with convoy speed and in the event they were going to have to be on the surface if they did that. And, you always have the question of identity too and you have trigger happy people and in these convoys I wouldn't want to be a submarine Skipper going along with a convoy and you know that a Russian or enemy submarine could be in the same vicinity. Submerged identity is still a very difficult thing to do, very difficult. As you know, we had at least two that I know of our own submarines in World War II sunk by our own ships and planes. I'm sure of two. And I think it's just as much of a problem now as it was then. Once you are submerged there is no way to commun to them. You depend on sonar signals or flares or something like that.

Q: Now, those were two great years you spent in Charleston weren' they?

Adm. L.: I think the most fascinating part was being intimately associatiated with the brand new submariners. I may have mention before, and I'm certainly not being parochial on this, but I don' think there is any question about the fact that in those days, at least when we reached the apex of the FBM program, building program, which happened during that 1964-1966 period, these were the finest young Naval officers that I have ever been associated with in my life. This was really the joy and pleasure of the job. It was not only riding the boats, but when they were back for their rest and rehabilitation, the R&R period, as I told you we would be briefed by the skippers and I had an opportunity to see them on a day-to-day basis. And, the junior officers, I told you also, I met every one as they came back. I got to know not only the Skippers and the Exec, but many of the junior office and it was a real exhilarating experience.

Q: When you reflect on it what makes them so superior? You yourself are part of a group of superior officers, submarine officers in World War II.

Adm. L.: Well, I think their technical ability coupled with their operational ability. Many of us, including myself, were qualified and we knew how to run the boat, but the technical aspect of a nuclear submarine is so much greater in magnitude than a diesel submarine; I didn't run into any Skipper who couldn't solve any problem on that darned boat. I mean he really had to be an expert in navigation, in fire control, in the missile compartments, in engineering, particularly in engineering. Their technical knowledge is just almost frightening. Not frightening, that's not the right word, but I mean it was so far above anything that I had ever been associated with in the Navy. So far above. I don't doubt that the Skippers of the USS BAINBRIDGE and the USS LONG BEACH--for instance, Wilkinson, you remember, was the first Skipper of the USS LONG BEACH and I don't think there has ever been anyone in the Navy who's been more technically proficient than was Wilkinson So, I'm not trying--the only thing is we had so many more than the surface ships did. We had forty-one plus at that time thirty to forty nuclear attack submarines and the same degree of proficiency existed in the nuclear attack submarines as they did in the FBM's.

Q: Now, this great degree of efficiency is dependent upon the kind of training received, the thoroughness of the training. Has this had its reflection and its influence on the Navy as a whole? The fact that you have such a superior group of men who are trained?

Adm. L.: I don't think it has for one reason and that's Admiral Rickover. Whether you like Admiral Rickover or not and a lot of people don't like him. They respect him. I happen to like him. I not only respect him, but I like him. But, Admiral Rickover exerts an iron hold on anyone coming into the nuclear program, any officer. He's responsible for the training and he's responsible for the nuclear power, the engineering plant after they get commissioned, because one of the things that really I question, and I know it drove the Skippers wild, were all of these inspections that Rickover and his outfit made. It really was--he must have considered it necessary or he wouldn't have done it. But, it really played havoc with the crew. I mean, two or three days in a row they would be up night and day getting ready for this thing and the inspection itself lasted two or three days. But, I think it paid off. I know it paid off because, to my knowledge, I saw Ned Beach here at the parade last week and I think Ned had a minor casualty where he didn't actually surface, but I think he had an enlisted man who had to be transferred. He got sick on his round-the-world-cruise submerged. I believe he came, not to the surface but he came with decks awash and I think they removed the guy by helo, I think. That was many, many years ago. But, other than that here is a nuclear submairne that traveled all the way around the world submerged without any surfacing. We had one of them that went aground, that hit a rock or something in Holy Loch and darned near lost the ship. I think we've had a collision, probably, with a merchant ship in the Strait of Gibraltar. But, when you consider literally the hundreds and hundreds of patrols these forty-one submarines have made since the USS GEO

WASHINGTON made the first one in 1960 and here it is in 1980 and you can count incidents on one hand of all of those, literally in the thousands now patrols. I think you have to give credit to Rickover for the training these guys get. I think the main disadvantage of his system is he didn't or couldn't get enough people in the program where we had this rapid buildup of both FBM's and SSM's. I know I've thrown this out before, we just could not give the Skippers and junior officers, we could not give them a normal sea and shore rotation and it played havoc with morale. All these Lieutenants and Lieutenant Commanders and contemporaries going to PG school or get their two years shore duty and being home with their families. They would make six, seven, and eight runs. I told you this one Skipper had a hundred and eight consecutive months of sea duty.

Q: It takes an iron man to hold up under that.

Adm. L.: I give Admiral Rickover full credit for the training and the selection of the nuclear people. I give him full credit. I think he's in trouble now.

Q: What's your prognosis when he fades from the scene?

Adm. L. It depends on who relieves him. I just don't know who he's got and I don't know what his hierarchy is. Most of the bright people who worked for him got out of the Navy. They are in Westinghouse. The manager of the Three Mile Island was a nuclear trained submariner. I think the head of Westinghouse, I know was Rickover's right hand for several years. I just think industry attracted these people and they are making hundreds of thousands of dollars instead of thirty or forty or fifty thousand each year So, who he has left to fall back on I don't know. I just don't know. I would presume it would be an Admiral.

Q: And, somebody who has been through the mill.

Adm. L.: Has been through the mill and on active duty. I assume that's who it would be. I don't know.

I do know he's in trouble recruiting people because, as you probably know Jack, last year the CNO, I think, under duress and protest permitted a quota of two hundred and fifty midshipmen graduating Ensigns to go into the nuclear power program and they had to draft either seventy-six or seventy-seven to meet their two fifty. That's the first time that's happened to my knowledge

Q: And in the case where they are drafted some of them are reluctant-

Adm. L.: Very, very reluctant.

Q: And this may affect their performance too.

Adm. L.: Very reluctant. Of course, it's all hearsay, but I've talked with several people who had put in for the nuclear program and took the majors which would prepare them for it and Rickover turned them down and yet drafted seventy-seven people who didn't want to go into the nuclear power program. Undoubtedly he had his reasons for turning them down, but it seems rather strange to me for someone who volunteers for this program, who had done well academically, has taken the majors to prepared himself for the nuclear power program, and he's graduated from the Naval Academy, therefore he's got to have something on the ball. It seems rather strange to me he would turn that person down and take a non-volunteer.

Q: It came time for you to give up your command and this was in 1966. You must have done it reluctantly?

Adm. L.: Well, I did because I went, I thought personally I had done a good job as a flag officer. I know I had as far as fitness reports are concerned and I was rather chagrined at going back to or to go to a Naval District job which is historically or has been the last stop on the line. I went in to see Admiral McDonald. Admiral McDonald who is a good friend of mine now and who is one of our trustees. I said, "Is this the end of the line?"

He said, "Oh, no, if you do a good job here, there is no reason why you don't have a crack at making Vice Admiral."

It just so happened that Pierre Charbonnet, who was a Commandant down in New Orleans, did make Vice Admiral during that two year period. So, he was basically being honest.

Q: And you were near the seat of power. You were in Washington.

Adm. L.: But, I didn't make it. Of course as a Commandant or any officer, any flag officer if you don't make Vice Admiral, you have to get out. In those days we had seven years in which I had before I retired whreas now it's much less. I think you come up to two selection processes now. I think one is at the end of either three or four years. I think we have had many selected Admirals who have had only four years active duty as an Admiral before they had to get out.

Q: Well as things worked out it seems to me you got something pretty favorable anyway.

Adm. L.: This is no sour grapes at all, Jack. The best thing that ever happened to me was actually not making Vice Admiral because here I've had this marvelous job for twelve years.

Q: With tremendous influence.

Adm. L.: It's interesting, it's challenging and I have a chance to work with these youngsters. It just so happened that Kenny McKee is the only Superintendent I had never met before he came here. I became very good friends with him immediately because he, being a submarine officer, knew about me although I didn't know about him. But, that didn't make any difference.

Q: Well, first tell me about the Washington assignment. You were there two years. What was the scope of your command?

Adm. L.: It was a very interesting command. I had what they call in those days area coordination. The Naval District, Washington was the area coordinator for all of these installations throughout the whole Washington area and there was literally hundreds of them.

Q: It reached over here to Annapolis.

Adm. L.: To Annapolis, down to Dahlgren and NOL at White Oak, the Sound Lab, the Taylor Model Basin, the communications station in Cheltenham and even the Naval Air facility at Andrews Air Force Base came under me for area coordination.

Q: A lot of the research facilities of the Navy.

Adm. L.: And, the Office of Naval Research, well, not the Office of Naval Research, but the big research installation just below the Navy Yard. We probably had a hundred outfits here and I was required to inspect them, so, again, it was a heck of an educational process for two years to not only be involved with the Pentagon with all the various OpNavs. I went to all the briefings over there and all the conferences. But, to go around to all these technical organizations and installations. I never ran into any animosity even from the aviators who were at Andrews Air Force Base. I don't think the aviators particularly liked have an 1100 officer exercising any area coordination, but I made it a point to tell them, "Hey, look the only reason I'm inspecting is to see if I can help you or not. I'm not here to criticize you or to find fault." As a result we had a really marvelous relationship between my staff and myself and all of these various outfits.

Jimmy Dempsey (who has subsequently died) whom I relieved as Operations Officer of ComSubLant, was my immediate boss. He worked for Rivero. Rivets was Vice Chief and Jimmy was Op 09-B (Bravo). In other words, he was the administrator. He handled all the administration in the Pentagon and OpNav. He was my immediate boss as he was for all Commandants. He had been a close personal friend of mine, and the working relationship couldn't have been better. It couldn't have been better.

Then another interesting facet was I was one of the unofficial hosts for all the Naval attaches in Washington.

Q: Where did you live?

Adm. L.: Tingey House, the same one the Chief of Naval Operations is in right now. The most beautiful set of quarters in the Navy. Far better than the Superintendent's quarters out at the Naval Observatory in my opinion.

So, the social life was also an enlightening activity because I became very good friends with many, many of the Naval attaches.

Q: And, was intelligence gathering in that sense wasn't it?

Adm. L.: A little bit.

Adm. L.: We still go up practically every year, if we can, to visit Stuart Paddon who was the Canadian Naval Attache at that time. He lives up near Ottawa at a lake up there in the summer.

Q: What kind of an allowance did you get for that aspect of your job?

Adm. L.: I can't remember what it was. It was sufficient though. I didn't have to dip into my own pocket except for my own personal entertainment.

Q: This really put a burden on your wife?

Adm. L.: It did, but we had three steward's mates. One of them was a Chief who had worked for Admiral Russell, and other four star admirals at the famous place over in Naples. I can't remember the name of it, but Admiral Russell came by and we invited him for some function once. Beltran was the Chief's name. I told him that Beltran was now my chief steward. He said, "Oh, I've got to see him," and he dashed right back to the kitchen. They had a great reunion. Beltran was a marvelous, marvelous guy. He was married to a Spanish girl and I was able to get him back to Rota for his last tour of duty before he retired.

So, that takes care of the professional aspect of it and the social aspect of it. One of the most interesting things that happened was that at some party, I think at the Finnish ambassador's home, I got to be very good friends with the Finnish ambassador. He was a wonderful, wonderful guy. He was a businessman. He wasn't a diplomat.

I met George Abell; his first wife divorced him and married Drew Pearson. He was a Deputy Chief of Protocol at the State Department. He called me one day and said, "Hey, the Prince of Nepal is going to be in town. He's making a tour of the United States. If we furnish the liquor and the food and everything, could you swing it to give him a cruise on your barge up and down the Potomac?"

Well, that was a little bit out of my line so I--

Q: It was out of the Prince's line too, wasn't it?

Adm. L.: So, I cleared this with Jimmy Dempsey. We took him out and spent three or four hours. It happened to be a beautiful day. George told me after the thing was over that of all the things he'd done in the United States he had enjoyed this the most. He is now King of Nepal.

Q: It is a landlocked kingdom.

Adm. L.: Some months later his father came over, the King, and gave, I think, probably the most magnificent party at either the Shoreham or one of the big hotels. Mr. Johnson was the President at the time. He made an appearance. And Marjorie and I were asked primarily through the State Department protocol because we had been nice to the young prince. I guess of all the incidents that happened, that stuck in my mind because it was such a pleasant occasion.

And the USS LIBERTY incident took place in those days. You remember the one that got bombed by Israel? Joe Toth's son was killed. The Skipper got a Congressional Medal of Honor. I think Mr. Nitze was then Secretary of the Navy. I conducted the ceremony for the presentation in the old sail loft.

Q: Did anything interesting develop in the scientific areas under your jurisdiction at this time?

Adm. L.: No, because I was not really in the chain of command, Jack. Very few people know, and even I didn't know exactly what is the area coordinator. What are his responsibilities? Well, it was never really laid down. The only thing I did was to visit these outlying places. There were all kinds of different OpNav people, and really to see if I could be of any help. Having been in the submarine force this is what you do. I mean, if you can help the squadron commander, the Skipper--

Q: If he's got a problem--

Adm. L.: If he's got a problem and you can help him. So, all I did was talk with them and educate myself and find out if I could be of any assistance. And I think this is the reason that this very tenuous relationship worked out so well for those two years. They could see that I wasn't trying to superimpose any authority over them.

Q: With that sort of command, a lot depends upon the personality of the Skipper doesn't it?

Adm. L.: Yes sir. The Skipper and the Commandant.

Q: I mean the Commandant.

Adm. L.: Well, on the Skipper too. I mean, if he gets a bug in his shoulder. But, I never ran into that, with any of them. So, I can't answer that question because I really wasn't in the technical aspects of their various projects. They would discuss it with me, but I don't remember any earth shaking event that happened those two years.

Q: So then you chose retirement?

Adm. L.: Well, I had to get out. I was asked to get out since I wasn't on the list for Vice Admiral. There was no sense in keeping a Commandant on for an additional year or another two star job. There was just a glut on the market.

I happened to be in Rota at the time when I got the word. I was disappointed at the time. This was in January or December and I didn't get out until August.

Loughlin #7 -326-

Q: August of 1968.

Adm. L.: 1968.

Q: Then how soon thereafter did you get this job?

Adm. L.: Well, what had happened was Bill Allen who was running the Marine Corps Residents Foundation then, Vinson Hall. I was on the board as Commandant. So, when Bill learned sometime in the spring that I was going to get out he offered me the job that Jack Alford has. He still may have it, I'm not sure. And, I accepted it.

Q: With Vinson Hall?

Adm. L.: Yes. At that time Vinson Hall had not been built.

Q: You didn't realize that you were stepping into big headaches, did you?

Adm. L.: Yes, I did. But Marjorie wanted to stay in Washington. I didn't see any prospect of anything I wanted to do. I said, "Well I'll take this." Well, gosh, it wasn't more than a week or two later Bob Pirie called me up and said, "Hey, Bud Bowler's going to have to give up one of his two jobs he's been holding for two years. He's got more equity in the Naval Institute than he does in the Foundation, so he's going to give up the Foundation. Would you be interested in it?"

Well, I'd been a board member, I'd been on the Foundation* Board of Trustees ever since I was Director of Athletics, I guess.

*This reference is to the Naval Academy Foundation, which is where Admiral Loughlin actually wound up working. It should not be confused with the Marine Corps Residents Foundation, which he accepted briefly and then declined when offered the position with the Naval Academy Foundation.

Q: So, it wasn't anything new?

Adm. L.: So, I had to call up Bill and tell him. I didn't do it for about three days because I was so embarrassed. When I did call him he laughed and said, "You'd be stupid not to take it."

I said, "Oh, gee Bill you don't know how happy I am to hear you say that. I thought you were going to be so damned mad at me."

He said, "Oh, that would be ridiculous. Go ahead and take it and God bless you."

Of course that put a different light on the whole thing. We had been looking for a place, not a house, but an apartment in Washington. And, with the two dogs that was very difficult to do. I asked Marjorie to come on down to Annapolis and find a place to live. And, she wanted to come here too. It was the best move we ever made. We have a house here on Cumberland Court that I wouldn't trade with anybody in the whole city of Annapolis. The darned thing had been on the market, I think, for a year and nobody would meet Ed Mather's price. We took one look at it and we met it.

Q: It's an old house, is it?

Adm. L.: No, it was an old house and he tore it down completely and left about two bulkheads standing with a fireplace and then added on to it including an upstairs. It's probably worth four or five times what we paid for it. It's in the most desirable location. We're only three feet from the Paca Gardens at the end of a cul de sac. Cumberland Court only runs from Maryland Avenue down to our house. We put a lot of money into it and a lot of improvement in it, but I just wouldn't trade with anybody in the city of Annapolis. Anybody. I can walk back and forth to the office.

Q: Tell me for the record, the scope of the foundation job.

Adm. L.: Our most prime mission in life is to locate and identify and determine the qualifications of young men and women who need an additional year of academic preparation to enter the Naval Academy. We do this through a variety of means. If they are not qualified by virtue of the standards the Naval Academy sets and we select them, we send them to one of sixteen prep schools. If they are fully qualified scholastically but just don't stand high enough in competition the previous year to get an appointment we sponsor them and give them a certain amount of money to go to the college of their choice.

Q: The prep schools are scattered throughout the country?

Adm. L.: Yes. They run from Bridgton, Maine down to Harlingen, Texas and out to Culver Military Academy. And, some of the best in the country, Deerfield, The Gunnery, Northfield, Mt. Herman, Admiral Farragut, Kiski School, Wyoming Seminary. You name it. Marvelous, marvelous schools.

There are two major developments since I took over the job. One is that we've had since the very beginning we've had one hundred percent cooperation from the Department of Candidate

Guidance who furnish us names each year with people, whether they are qualified or not, that they think will be good candidates. The biggest change was made two years ago when the Admission Board came up and said, "Hey, we don't like these people coming up where we have never looked at them before." By looking at them they have never seen their record before. So, they said, "How would you or would you object if we looked at their records before you ever sponsor them? Then we will indicate our recommendation for sponsorship or not."

Factually from a pragmatic point of view if they ever do turn one down we're not going to sponsor them because the same people that are looking at their record are going to be the same people next March who are going to make the appointment or not. But, the point is we've got everything going for us. Once on the cover sheet they put their initials down and say they recommend for Foundation sponsorship because they came up before the Board, unless they dropped their bricks completely during their school year, they say, "Heck if this guy was good enough for us to recommend for sponsorship and he's qualified and he's done a good job in school, so let's appoint him." So, the results the last several years, we get between eighty-five and ninety percent of our kids in the Naval Academy. It's mainly due to, really, the degree of cooperation which starts with the Superintendent and Commandant. Bob McNitt was on Gene Fluckey's ship and I've known Bob since 1938. He's the Dean of Admissions and runs the whole outfit. I know they had a reorganization where he's in charge of nominations for appointment of candidates and everything.

So, it's just the most--I just am the luckiest fellow in the world because we just get a hundred and ten percent cooperation from everybody we work with.

Q: They are all working for the same end, of course.

Adm L.: And, of course, I was Director of Athletics and sat on the Academic Board for three years. I was at the Naval Station, so I know the Naval Academy probably better than any one retired officer in the country. Having had two tours of duty here, the type of tours that I had, one from a logistic and sailing point of view and the other from the athletic point of view, and then sitting on the Academic Board for three years.

Q: How does this tie in with the Congressional appointments?

Adm. L.: Well, that is our big headache right now. Up until last year the Athletic Association because--well, go back for just a moment Jack. The NCAA put us out of business back in, roughly, 1960 or 1961 because I think we went to three bowl games in five years. In those days the Athletic Association paid for the tuition bills which, incidentally, was legal. But, we only had athletes in the program. Maybe thirty, thirty-five or forty.

Q: And the Foundation covered them?

Adm. L.: Yes. They all either went to Bullis School or Wyoming Seminary for prep. Well, they put us out of business and said, "No institutional funds can be used for prep school education." So, for two years, I think, the Naval Institute picked up the tab so they were not institutional funds. Then through Charlie Minter and Charles Kirkpatrick a new set of rules were formulated which the NCAA accepted. The main one provided that we had to help nonathletes, people who were not recommended on athletic ability as people with recognized athletic ability, in the approximate same ratio as the number of the Brigade of Midshipmen to the number of people on varsity squads which happens to be around four-to-one. So, out of eighty people we could have, say, twenty good athletes.

Q: Do you manage to do that?

Adm. L.: Never have in the twelve years I've been here. Never.

Q: With no concerted effort to do it?

Adm. L.: Oh, yes. Now this year we've gotten more than we've ever had because the football coaches have given us around seven or eight recruited athletes this year. The first time we've done that in the twelve years I have been here. Then we have other recruited athletes also. I would say this year we have a hundred in the program and we probably have, well, I'm waiting for a list from Dave Smalley now. I'd say we probably have twelve or thirteen out of a hundred who are good enough to be recruited in the various sports.

Q: Now, on the average, what does it cost you to send a boy or a girl to school?

Adm. L.: We have different ways of doing it. For the college portion of the program, and they are the ones that scholastic qualified don't stand high enough, (Incidentally remind me to get back to the nominations for this is what I started to talk about). We just give them up to a thousand dollars, if required. Most of them go to junior colleges or to a state college where the thousand dollars, I mean nobody is going to go to Cornell or a place like that unless they can get a lot more money. And, for one year in college they are not going to get any scholarship money unless they go to ROTC. Now, we have several people each year who are in ROTC. Once they are offered an appointment to the Naval Academy that takes precedence over their ROTC obligation.

For the prep school we have several ways of doing it. The normal way is that we ask the parents to contribute within their financial capability. Then the school and the Foundation divides the remainder if any. Now, mind you several four, five, six, seven or eight families each year are so happy to have their sons or daughters sponsored by the Foundation that they pick up the whole tab. But if they don't, then we subtract the parents' contribution from the total tuition costs including uniforms and books in the case of a military school and then the Foundation and the school reach an equitable arrangement in dividing that amount. This year our tuition with a hundred people, which is the most we've ever had. Ninety-one two years ago, I think. Now, we have a hundred exactly, which incidentally we are authorize The Superintendent has authorized us to sponsor one hundred people each year. Our tuition bill this year is roughly a hundred and twenty-five thousand. It's never been over ninety thousand before.

Loughlin #7 -333-

But, to get back to nominations, two years ago Army, the way I heard the story is some GS 8, 9, 10, 11 or 12 in the War Department found out about this and actually it's illegal. By illegal you're supposed to live in a state or congressional district in order to get a nomination from that Senator or from that Representative.

Q: That's the law, yes.

Adm. L.: But, for years, ever since the Foundation started in 1944 and probably before that, I know before that because Bill Mott a classmate of mine got in on an out of district nomination. There are certain Representatives particularly who are in districts where they cannot fill their nominations. See, they are allowed to have ten nominees for every vacancy they have and they are allowed to have five people in the Naval Academy at any one time. So, if they have one vacancy they can nominate ten. If they have two they can nominate twenty. Well, the Athletic Association, hell, I've got off the track. Since we had been nothing but an athletic factory, really, legal red shirting for the Naval Academy Athletic Association for all of these many years they offered to get us out-of-district nominations for anyone of our young men and women who could not get their own nomination. Now, we do require (and we've done this ever since I've been here) we do require them to write both of their Senators and their Representative requesting a nomination. We stress how important it is, even a Presidential. We stress how important it is to get a nomination. But, if they didn't, up until last year Carl Ullrich got us out of district nominations if we needed five or eight. I think the most we ever needed was nine out of, say, eighty some odd. We would get out of district nominations. Well, this Army guy wrote a letter to the Army Chief of Staff and said this is illegal and we shouldn't do it. Well, the Army Chief of Staff went up to see Goodpaster and Goodpaster says, "Yep, it's illegal we shouldn't do it." So, he talked the Air Force into it and he talked Bill Lawrence into it. So, last year for the first time the policy is that no one that is connected with the Naval Academy, which includes the Foundation, because the Superintendent is really responsible for the Foundation performance to the NCAA. I mean, if we violate something then he's and we're in trouble. The Superintendent said, "Nobody associated with the Naval Academy can initiate anything for out-of-district nominations." Now, he didn't close the door. In other words, if somebody not associated with the Naval Academy can go to Marjor Holt or go--well, Marjorie is out because she always has so many that she can't even take care of her own district. So, kind of off-the-record we had three people last year who could not get nominations out of seventy-seven. Someone whose name I won't mention is an administrative aide to a Congressman for many years and is now in his own business here. But, he knows every Congressman on the Hill and one phone call and he got three out-of-district nominations which were accepted by the Naval Academy. But, it is a problem. It's not only a potential problem, but it's a hell of a problem because if they ever decide that they will not accept an out-of-district nomination, then that means that whoever doesn't get a nomination is not going to the Naval Academy

Q: Is there any likelihood of the law being changed?

Adm. L.: They are working in alternatives. They are trying to get the Vice President to have more nominees. They are trying to raise the ten up to twenty. They are trying various alternatives.

Q: Is that what the Vice President has, ten?

Adm. L.: No, he can have, this is a funny story, I think he can have twelve each year, but apparently the Army and the Air Force don't know that he's not limited to the number of nominations he can make. So, we, this year, we had all of our people write the Vice President asking for nominations. You see if you get a nomination that makes you a bonafide candidate and then let the Naval Academy decide if you get an appointment or not. If you get an appointment, they have to find a way to get you in.

Q: What about the Presidential appointments? How many are they?

Adm. L.: There are a hundred Presidential and there are eighty-five U.S. Navy and eighty-five U.S. Naval Reserve and they pool them. That gives you two hundred and seventy. And, NAPS take care of a lot of that although people at NAPS are also required to write their Representatives and Senators. But, they have an automatic Presidential by enlisting in the Naval Reserve or an automatic Presidential by being in the U.S. Navy. And, of course, anybody who's the son or daughter of an officer who has drawn retired pay, in other words who has had twenty years of active duty or who is on active duty automatically gets a Presidential nomination.

Q: Now, how does this tie in with the Civil Service exams that are held at the behest of Congressmen?

Adm. L.: Well, I don't know how many people do it. Most Congressmen have a review board which reviews the qualification of their applicants. Most of them now use the board scores, I think, rather than the Civil Service exams, Jack.

Q: Oh, they do?

Adm. L.: Yes.

Q: What is the review board?

Adm. L.: Well, normally retired Army, Navy and Air Force officers sit on a review board that reviews the qualifications. Marjorie Holt does it. Review the qualifications of these candidates. Let's say she has one vacancy for ten nominations she may have a hundred and fifty or two hundred people that are requesting nominations from her. And, this review board looks it over and then makes their recommendations to her as to the ten top people. Now, she doesn't have to follow that and I don't think she--

Q: It serves in an advisory capacity?

Adm. L.: Yes. It's not statutory or anything like that because I happen to know that a kid last year who got a late appointment, he got appointed two days before the class entered. He was far superior--we were going to pick him up and send him to school this year. But, he was so far superior to another person who got one of Marjorie's nominations that it was obvious that she did it for other than strictly equal--

Q: I suppose politics enters in. I mean, you have to face the ballot box every two years.

Adm. L.: This guy is a state policeman and it was his son and she gave him a nomination. For instance, Mr. Brooke, Senator Brooke used to--there are three different ways of doing it. Most of them use the ten competitive nominations. In other words, they give the Naval Academy ten names and the guy who stands number one, who is scholastically qualified and medically qualified automatically gets the principal. Then the other nine go on what's called the qualified alternate list, if they are qualified. The second method is the principal and nine alternate appointments.

Q: Gosh, one, two, three, four, five?

Adm. L.: Yes and the top guy who has the highest multiple scholastically and medically qualified gets the principal. Now it could be the third alternate. It could be the fifth. One year we had people, ten people in a competitive status and he was the only one of the ten who was scholastically and medically qualified. So, he automatically got the principal.

The third method which is not used very often is a principal and nine competitive. This is where your politics comes in. And, Senator Brooke used to do this. In other words, he would nominate somebody as his principal nominee.

Q: With the full intention that he was going to get--

Adm. L.: Well, if he qualified he would get in automatically. Then the other nine, he would give nine names to the Naval Academy and they would decide numerically where they stood.

I think politics to a great extent has been taken out of this, Jack.

Q: Well, it certainly should. This review board I think is a great idea.

Adm. L.: I think the answer is the attrition figures. I don't know how well you keep up. I keep up very closely with it. This year's class is going to be about the same as last year, maybe a little bit worse. But, the other two classes, it looks like the Plebe class is going to be awfully good too. You're going to have the lowest attrition for the four classes as a whole this year as we've ever had in the history of the Naval Academy.

Q: That saves money for the government.

Adm. L.: The biggest joy we take in our program is for the last several years we've had a lower attrition rate overall than the class as a whole. That's what I call the bottom line. If more of our kids stay in and graduate than the class a a whole, then I think we're doing our job and this is what Bill Lawrence feels, this is what Scott McCauley feels, this is what Bob McNitt feels. If we can just keep this performance and this is where I have no objection whatsoever to the Admissions Board reviewing these records because we don't want--we can't interview everybody here, Jack. We just can't do it. It's too expensive to bring them all back here. So, if the Admissions Board sees something in the record which makes them give a little caution or a warning flag to them they say, "Hey, we don't think you ought to sponsor this guy," I'm all for it because that just keeps us from losing that guy. So, I think that's one reason why our success ratio has been so high plus the fact that, I think, our attrition has been so low because not only do we give them a thorough screening, but the Admissions Board gives them a thorough screening.

Q: Do you have any provisions for keeping in touch with these men and women after they graduate? To keep them in the service?

Adm. L.: Well, I've run into this thing and I've fought Freddy Boone and other people really. They are not as close to the situation, not as they were at one time. Jack, it's just like Plebe year-I keep close tabs on these people Plebe year. Once they finish Plebe year then I'm with the next class that comes in as Plebes. It depends on the Commandant. It depends on the Company Officer. It depends on the First Class. It depends on your squad leader. I remember I was, I had so many, not so many, but I had several run-ins with my company officer which completely soured me on the Navy when I was a midshipman. And, there are so many tangible and intangible things that affect someone. His deployment, whether he's married or not, whether his wife likes the Navy or not. It has nothing to do with Foundation sponsorship. I mean, it really--there is no direct communication and, Jack, these are the things that are making these kids get out at the end of five years. Not the fact that we sponsor them or that we didn't sponor them. This is the point we try to make.

Q: All you can do is hope they are mature enough to face the issues as they develop.

Adm. L.: We had a kid that resigned without letting me know after he finished his Plebe year with a 3.6 something average. He got mixed up with a girl and she didn't want him to be here. A week after he resigned his father called me up in tears and said "Is there any way you can get him back in?"

I said, "I wouldn't get him back in for anything. I went to bat for this kid in order to get him in in the first place."

We had another kid whose father called me and said, "He's mixed up with a girl. He's known her for three years and she's broken up with him. He wants to get out."

I said, "For God sake why does he want to get out if this gal has broken up? What good it is going to do to get out?"

Q: All he can do is find another one.

Adm. L.: So, I called the Company Officer and he said, "No, he's changed his mind."

I've tried to get him and he's tried to get me three times in the last four days and I haven't had a chance to talk to him yet.

Q: It's a question of maturity or lack of maturity.

Adm. L.: Yes. The ones we lose, primarily, Jack are the ones that go to college and are in an ROTC unit and they like the college, they like the having of a car, they like the beer, they like the girls, and they say, "The heck with it even though I

I said I would accept an appointment if offered. I've changed my mind now. I'm going to stay at college." We lose one or two or three that way a year.

Q: But, the younger ones at prep school.

Adm. L.: Very rarely at prep school. The others we lose, the ones who have not demonstrated to the Admissions Board their capability of doing college work. They have dropped the bricks either in college or at prep school. If they don't do well, and I emphasize this, throughout the whole year I say, "Try for A's and B's. Don't mess with C's or if you get any D's, E's, or F's, why you're out. So, if you can get all A's, and B's and do well on your board, why, you're way, way ahead of the game."

Now last year out of seventy we lost seven people, I guess, who did not do well. Six of them in college and one in prep school. We actually had seventy-four out of eighty-three offered appointments. But, seventy-seven we had offered appointments and four of them declined. It was the greatest number of declinations we've ever had since I've been here. So, we actually ended up with seventy-three out of eighty-six. Although seventy-seven out of eight-six were offered appoinments, which again is about ninety percent. We had one resignation Plebe summer. So, we had seventy-two at the end out of seventy-three. That is, we had an attrition of one so far.

Q: Well, I suppose as long as there is such a difference between life at the Academy and the freedom of life at the university-

Adm. L.: But, we try to impress upon them to make up their mind. For instance we make them sign an agreement, both the parents and the kids. One of the chief points of the agreement is that you won't voluntarily drop out of school unless for reasons over which you have no control like death in the family. That you will do your best to qualify. And, three, that you will accept an appointment if offered.

Q: Now, this is asking for a degree of integrity in these young men.

Adm. L.: If they are not willing to accept those three conditions, then we don't want any part of them. Yet, we had four last year who declined appointments and who had signed the statement. So, I think we are better off without them.

Q: What is your estimate of the degree of integrity among young people today? I mean, as you observe it through this connection?

Adm. L.: Well, it's hard to say because although I interview roughly half of them and form my own personal opinion I really go by their performance in school; the remarks of the head master, and the correspondence, and how they respond to what I tell them to do. This year, it seems to me that the group we have have shown more interest than any other group we've had. In other words, we go out with a letter and tell them what to do, the very first letter about writing their Congressman and their Senator. A month or six weeks ago every one of them had written both. The hundred had written both their Senators and their Representative. That is the first time it has ever happened. We say as soon as your senior year is over get your transcript or have the school send it to me. If you send it to me, I'll get it in the file. We've got some seventy some already. We should have had a hundred percent, but we don't have it.

Q: Your experience with all these wonderful prep schools would enable you to comment on what a prep school contributes over and above what public schools contribute to the education of the young person.

Adm. L.: Smaller classes. More proficient instructors or tutors or professors or whatever you want to call them. Most of them are boarding schools where they are under pretty close supervision, dormitories. All of them have been experienced now, since I've been here, most of them we have one or two new ones within, I'd say, the last five or six years. Their experience is what is expected of them to get these kids ready to get into the Naval Academy, not only curriculum wise for I tell them what to do when I review the transcript. I tell them what subjects to take. But, also get on them and be sure and take the board scores if they haven't gotten them up high enough or to get them even higher. There is only one disadvantage and I've had several fights with people and I win everytime because they really don't have a leg to stand on. Some of the schools lay more stress on meeting their own graduation requirements than they do in getting the kids in the Naval Academy. I say, "Look, the only reason we sent this young man up here is to get into the Naval Academy." I said "I could care less whether he graduates from The Gunnery

School. He's already graduated from high school. I don't care whether he gets your diploma or not. But, I want him to take chemistry. I want him to take Calculus. I want him to take English composition, literature and a history course. Now, if you want him to take something else, that's up to you. But, I think this is enough load for any kid to carry in prep school. He's got to take these courses in order to get in the Naval Academy."

Well, they rebel. They want him to take music, art or some such damned thing. That's really the only complaint I have with the preps. I don't have that with Mercersburg Academy. I don't have that with Kiski. Admiral Farragut School is one. Peddie is one that does it. The Gunnery is one that does it. Deerfield is one that does it. Mt. Herman to a certain extent does it. But, most of them--see I write the same type of letter that I send the kids telling them everything they have to do and I send a copy of this to the guidance counselor and request that they read this thing and please see that he gets this curriculum and please see that he does this, and this, and this. And, most of them do it.

Q: Do you run up against any anti-military attitudes in some of these schools?

Adm. L.: Not now, not now. In 1968 we did a little bit, but it never got to me directly. I think it was peer pressure more than it was the school.

Q: Do you run up against any drug influence at any of the prep schools?

Adm. L.: I question the headmasters about the thing in general. We've had isolated cases. You know they have to fill out a questionnaire and if they answer it honest, have they ever taken drugs? If they answer it "once in a while, " someone says, "Yes, I did smoke a marijuana cigarette when I was a senior in high school, but I've never touched it since." If he is being perfectly honest about it, the Naval Academy just disregards that. They don't consider that.

We have never had anybody kicked out of school for drugs since I've been here. And, I'm sure the schools are particularly strong on that. I mean highly enforce it.

Q: Tell me how you really finance this wonderful effort part of the Foundation? You talk about a hundred thousand or a hundred and twenty-five thousand in tuition.

Adm. L.: The main source of funds is obtained, the main sources of funds are obtained by the creation, establishment, of what we call Honor Scholarships for twenty thousand dollars and can be done in various manners. We establish an honor scholarship or a memorial honor scholarship in the name of an individual or a class. The procedure up until this year has been when the class enters in July, a member of that class is designated as the honor scholar for that particular scholarship. Well, we're reaching a point now when we have more scholarships established than we have entering plebes. Accordingly, this past year we had five (5) unfilled scholarships. So what we do is the ones who have not lost anyone by attrition, this year I had to pick out five and we did not designate an honor scholar in those names. Now, next year I don't think that is going to happen because we have a hundred in the program. If it should happen, however, if it's one or two or three then we pick three more and not pick the five that we picked this year. I hope with a hundred people in the program we won't have this problem for two or three more years until the scholarships continue to build up. That's the main source. For instance, when I got here, I think, in 1968 we had three hundred and, say, fifty thousand dollars on what we call the Scholarship Endowment Fund. It's now 2.7 million. The proceeds from that can be used only for tuition purposes.

Q: You have some financial outfit handling your funds?

Adm. L.: Morgan Guaranty Trust. We have our own Vice President Morgan and financial advisor John Parker who I was talking to when you came in, is chairman of the finance committee. We meet at least once a year and go over our investment policy. We're realizing roughly a hundred and seventy five or a hundred and eighty thousand bucks from that fund alone.

Mr. Castera, George Castera out of 1923, left us roughly six hundred and seventy thousand dollars years ago. We can't use the corpus on that, but we do get the proceeds from it as long as the Foundation is in business.

Q: Are you subject to that stipulation of the Internal Revenue that foundations have to spend five percent of the principal?

Adm. L.: No, no we've got the highest public supported classification that you can get.

That's the two main sources of funds. A guy named Chezak who is an ex-chief petty officer left something like sixty-seven thousand dollars to the Naval Academy Athletic Association while he was living. When he died, he directed that it be given to the Foundation and we could reinvest it or use it in any way that we wanted to.

Q: What was his interest?

Adm. L.: He was just a chief petty officer who loved the Naval Academy.

Q: How do you spell his name?

Adm. L.; C-H-E-Z-A-K. We call it the Chezak Fund. We get various bequests. Dundas Preble Tucker out of 1925 died. About 1970 he came in and said, "I don't have any family at all. No wife. No children. No cousins. No nothing. I want to leave my estate to the Foundation and it will probably be in six figures."

It came to two hundred and ninety-seven thousand dollars. This just happaned a year ago.

A man named Tony Rorschach out of 1925 was instrumental in the class of 1925 starting an honor scholarship. He died and his wife died shortly thereafter, seventy-four thousand dollars to the Foundation.

Now, that's mostly scholarship, I'm talking about now. So you can see that we have more than enough money for tuition purposes.

The Society of Sponsors of the U.S. Navy has been a wonderful supporter, giving us about $10,000 each year to support candidates they choose to sponsor. So, what my concern is how do I meet operations? The Trustees, we just went from a hundred and forty to a hundred and fifty, most of whom give at least three hundred dollars or more. That's unrestricted funds. We get from fourteen to sixteen thousand dollars from our twenty-five hundred members. The dues are nominal, three dollars. Many give six, eight, ten dollars, twenty-five, fifty, a hundred. We have two insurance programs. One is ordinary life run by or underwritten by the Valley Forge Life Insurance Company. The president of the company and an outfit called AGIA, Associated Group Insurance Administrator Ray Dufour, a very wealthy man, is a trustee. He not only gives us a thousand dollars a year as a contribution, but we get roughly eleven or twelve thousand out of that program. There are still about sixteen to eighteen hundred insurees. We get a portion of the administrative premiums.

Junie Clark runs an insurance program and they use our name. It's called the Naval Academy Foundation Insurance Program. Junie has the same thing with NJROTC, ROTC, Army ROTC, and the Coast Guard, the Merchant Marine and the Naval Academy. We don't get any out of the Naval Academy. We roughly get between eight and nine thousand a year and that's been going on since 1959. It's added up to two hundred and two thousand dollars since 1959.

We get what's called "other contributions". These are contributions made which are not specifically designated for scholastic purposes.

Q: It's just to the Foundation.

Adm. L.: It's just to the Foundation. For instance Olga McNeil, widow of the former Assistant to the Controller of DoD.

Q: Yes, he died last year.

Adm. L.: Yes. He was chairman of the Finance Committee before Floyd Akers. He left Olga a sum of money to be distributed to such charitable organization as she saw fit. She just sent us a check for a thousand dollars. Again, that's "other contributions".

So, we break even at least every year that I've been here. I have two things to fall back on which I haven't done as yet. The Scholarship Endowment Fund is broken down to restricted and unrestricted funds. The restricted being that, those sums which have been contributed directly for scholarships. If we invest and make money that goes into the unrestricted funds. That's roughly one fifth of the total sum. I can use that, in other words if we get a hundred and seventy-five thousand dollars I can use one-fifth of that money.

Q: Yes, that's out from under the restriction?

Adm. L.: Yes. But I haven't had to do that. The Castera Fund is between forty-five and fifty thousand dollars a year. The sole trustee, the Pacific Security National Bank, we wrote and requested that we be authorized to use twenty percent if required of that annual proceeds for administrative purposes incident to the granting of these scholarships. This was granted. I haven't had to do that yet.

Q: Well, the scholarships are dependent on being administered.

Adm. L.: I mean there was no complaint on their part at all. So, we're in good financial shape. We're in good financial shape.

Q: It certainly is a thrilling kind of a set up.

Adm. L.: We're doing some good.

Q: That's the thrilling part of it. I mean, you're doing some good and you're training young people to serve their nation.

Adm. L.: Well, the biggest question we have to answer (and Bill Busik is one of them, not now, but originally), "Why do you need the Foundation? You have seven thousand candidates each year for twelve, thirteen, fourteen hundred entering. Why do you need the Foundation?"

Well, for years we needed it for the athletic point of view. That went down the drain until this year. But, the main thing is, I say, we're getting the kids that the Naval Academy wants, that the Admissions Board wants and the Candidate Guidance wants--as long as we keep the attrition below the class, which we have consistently done, almost consistently for the last eight or nine years. Scott McCauley is the most enthusiastic Commandant I've ever had, ever seen. He just wrote me a letter this week. He said the Foundation is doing an excellent job. "I'm so pleased with the performance with the Foundation sponsorshi of midshipmen."

Q: You're building up a cadre of midshipmen somewhat similar to the cadre of officers in the nuclear program.

Adm. L.: They are scattered throughout the thirty-six companies and they are scattered by classes. I think the classes keep together. For instance, maybe twenty or thirty Plebes came in with their parents on Parents' Weekend, perhaps even more. Several of them, like four of them are in one particular company and they happened to win the color competition this year. Well, each of the four knew each other being in that particular company. But, those four probably didn't know other people in other companies because with thirty-six companies you don't see them too often. So, we're really not building up anything that's a separate entity within the Naval Academy. It's not that close and we don't want that.

Q: Tell me about how the women fit in the program?

Adm. L.: We went into the women really against the protest of several of our trustees. The only point I made was I said, "Hey look all somebody has to do is bring up a discrimination case and you're going to jeopardize our tax exempt status. Once we do that, we're out of business."

So, what I did was to take the percentage that the Naval Academy uses. It's roughly around 7.2 percent of the incoming class are women. It's a little bit more this year. They have 1244 and they have taken a hundred, so what is it? It's about eight percent. So, I say, if we are going to take ninety for the class, seven times ninety is sixty-three, so we will take up to six women. We count a hundred this year so seven times a hundred is seven, we'll take seven. Well, we don't have them. We only have three or four.

Q: But, you can't be accused of discrimination?

Adm. L.: No. We didn't get the applications and two, they didn't meet the qualification and standards. So, we'll take up to what the Naval Academy takes if they apply, if they are selected by us and by the Admissions Board. We'll take up to that percentage.

Q: It is on a merit basis the same as everybody else?

Adm. L.: The same way with Blacks. We go out of our way to get Blacks and practically no success. There are two good reasons for it. One of them is if they meet our standards and qualifications to be sponsored by the Foundation, the odds are they are going to be offered an appointment by the Naval Academy.

Q: Yes, I can see that. The second. Sought after really.

Adm. L.: The second reason is that the ones that really want to come in are so bad that the Admissions Board won't approve them. I mean they are so low.

Q: And, is this actually because of the kind of public schooling they have had?

Adm. L.: I don't know what it is. They haven't had the subjects. You look at their transcript and you can see that, no. In two cases we have sent kids to two years of prep school. Paid the full amount with the school. One of them ended up as being Captain of the track team. A guy by the name of Elijah Turner.

His father was an ex-chief steward in the Navy. But, we paid an awful lot of money and sent one of them for two years at Marine Military Academy. Unfortuantely he bilged out. We sent Elijah Turner to Marine Military Academy and then to the New Mexico Military Institute. He got in and finished. He graduated. So, if the guy has qualities we're looking for and he requires two years, we'll take him for two years.

Q: But, you can't coddle him.

Adm. L.: No. Two of our Blacks we got in last year bilged out Plebe year.

Hispanic, yes, we have a little better luck with Hispanics. Asian Americans, Mexican American. You know there are all kinds of Hispanics that are combinations. We've got two or three of them. One is a girl who is an excellent candidate this year. She is going to get in. I think we have five.

I think one of the reasons for our success, Jack, is that we have such, we have gone up, I think, from eighty trustees when I took over to a hundred and then a hundred and ten, to a hundred and twenty, and now we've gone up to a hundred and fifty.

Q: You mean this is the enthusiasm of the--

Adm. L.: The point I'm trying to make is they range from people like Admiral Burke and all the CNO's subsequent to him except Zumwalt, are trustees. Gus Long, a Naval Academy graduate, he was president and chief operating officer of Texaco. Duane Andreas who was Hubert Humphrey's angel for years. He just sent us another two thousand dollars last week but he didn't send us any last year. So, he must have a pretty good secretary. Shelton Fisher who is Chairman of the Board of McGraw-Hill. But, there are many people who have no ties to the Naval Academy whatsoever like Will McNeal. The enthusiasm and we're getting more and more younger people. This is one thing, we're getting much too old. We're trying to get the younger people to come in. And, gosh, we have two meetings a year, the spring meeting and the fall meeting. We have anywhere from eighty to a hundred trustees to show up for this meeting.

Q: It's an event.

Adm. L.: Oh, yes sir and the enthusiasm. The Superintendent always comes. He always talks-is always here. The Commandant is always here. The Dean of Admissions is always here. The Academic Dean is always here. It's just a going concern.

Q: You almost have to hire a hall to have a meal.

Adm. L.: We have it over in Hubbard Hall. Fortunately we're able to get that. We've had as many as a hundred and fifty people for a luncheon over there. We would invite the wives to a luncheon before the game.

Q: Do you have any women on your Board now?

Adm. L.: Yes. Winnie Collins who was the first Wave Captain. And we have Mary Ellen Hanley who just finished being the first Chairman of the Board of Visitors of the Naval Academy. We have the President of the Society of Sponsors of the United States Navy. A gal by the name of Dorie Cochran. So we have three women on the Board now.

Cuts down Bob McFarlane's jokes at the meetings.

Q: I suppose it does limit him. Well, it's a great story and I hope you keep on doing this job for many years.

Adm. L: I'll be seventy-one next year.

Q: I can see that your personality is a very important aspect of this.

Adm. L.: I appreciate that. I attribute a lot of our success to the fact that without conceit I, and I've mentioned this before, my background with the Naval Academy. Having had two tours of duty with the Naval Academy and, as I said, being Director of Athletics here and in charge of the Naval Academy sailing squadron, the Commanding Officer of the Naval Station, sitting on the Academic Board. So, it encompasses admissions, curriculum discipline, sports, the works. I think that's one reason for our success.

Q: Yes. Bob Pirie certainly made a good selection when he beckoned to you. Well, thank you very much Elliott. I've certainly appreciated this.

INDEX

REAR ADMIRAL CHARLES ELLIOTT LOUGHLIN

Air Force, U.S.
  Its recruiting efforts have resulted in Navy doing away with shipboard qualification of naval aviators prior to flight training, pp. 41-42.

AKITSU MARU (Japanese merchant ship)
  Sinking of by USS QUEENFISH, 15 November 1944, pp. 106-107.

Aleutian Islands
  Williwaw approaches when USS NEW MEXICO there for fleet exercise during 1930s, p. 36.

Anderson, Admiral George W.
  Difficulties with SecDef McNamara while serving as CNO during Cuban Missile Crisis in 1962, p. 281.

Annapolis (Maryland) Naval Air Facility
  As part of naval station, p. 163.

Annapolis (Maryland) Naval Station
  Loughlin serves as executive officer from 1949 to 1951 and commanding officer, 1951 to 1952, pp. 161-174; personnel problems, pp. 161, 164-165; engineering experiments on hydrofoils, pp. 167-168.

Antisubmarine Warfare
  Loughlin's tour of duty in the ASW readiness section of OpNav, 1959-1960, pp. 250-256.

ARKANSAS, USS (BB-33)
  Midshipman cruise in early 1930s, pp. 8-9.

ASW
  See Antisubmarine Warfare

Athletics
  Basketball played by ships' teams in 1930s, pp. 38-39; varsity basketball team with Plebes at Naval Academy, p. 170; Naval Academy record football, p. 186; sailing made eligible for varsity letter, p. 188; means of supporting athletics, p. 209; problems of "football sections," p. 204; understanding special demands of Naval Academy players and coach, p. 204; "red shirting," p. 211; athletics and education, pp. 211-212; field house, p. 213; Naval Academy stadium, p. 214; expenses of, p. 224; major and minor sports in, p. 227.

Athletics in the career of Rear Admiral C. E. Loughlin
  Tennis as midshipmen in 1929, p. 4; basketball as midshipmen, 1929, p. 4; State Championship 1932-33, p. 4; All-City championship in Basketball, 1932-33, p. 4; continuing influence

1

on, p, 6; Tennis matches at Naval Academy, p. 10; National inter-collegiate, inter-scholastic ranking, 1932-33, p. 10; Loughlin's basketball records at Naval Academy held until 1948-49, p. 11; Second team All-American, 1930, p. 11; Thompson trophy in 1933, p. 11; TENNESSEE's basketball team, p. 38; basketball team representative in 1949, p. 168; Commander of Board of Control (Executive Committee), p. 169.

Aviators, Naval
No longer have qualification period prior to flight training because of competition from Air Force, pp. 41-42.

AWA MARU (Japanese merchant ship)
Sinking of by USS QUEENFISH on 1 April 1945, despite being given safe conduct by U.S. Government, pp. 120-135; interviews of Loughlin by Japanese, pp. 137-139; not a factor when Loughlin considered for flag rank, p. 271.

BARB, USS (SS-220)
In wolf pack with USS QUEENFISH and USS PICUDA in Yellow Sea and Formosa Strait in late 1944, pp. 86, 105, 115-119.

BASS, USS (SS-164)
Crewmen killed by battery fire while submarine was operating off Panama, 17 August 1942, p. 66.

BATFISH, USS (SS-310)
Sinks Japanese submarines in vicinity of the Philippines in February 1945, p. 109.

Bathythermograph
Use of to find temperature gradient so submarines can stay on station without use of power, pp. 158-159.

Beakley, Rear Admiral Wallace
Impressions of while serving as Admiral Dennison's chief of staff in 1960, pp. 268-269.

Bennett, Lieutenant John E.
On board cruiser SAN FRANCISCO when damaged at Guadalcanal in November 1942, p. 86; attended submarine school, then reported to USS QUEENFISH, p. 86; rescues POWs from sea and reads burial service for those who died, p. 101; officer of the deck of USS QUEENFISH after sinking of AKITSU MARU in November 1944, p. 107; notifies Loughlin of sinking of AWA MARU, p. 125.

Beshany, Vice Admiral Philip A.
Former S-14 shipmate of Elliott Loughlin; eager to get submarine command right after World War II, p. 140.

Boone, Rear Admiral Walter F. ("Freddie")
Superintendent of Naval Academy in mid-1950s with whom Loughlin had difficult working relationship, pp. 192-194, 197-199;

invites Dr. Norman Vincent Peale to preach at Naval Academy, pp. 227-228.

Brockett, Rear Admiral William A.
One of several USS NEW MEXICO division officers in 1930s who later made flag rank, p. 25; best man at Eliott Loughlin's wedding, p. 27.

Bruton, Captain Henry Chester
As Loughlin's defense counsel at AWA MARU cort-martial in 1945, pp. 128, 130, 133.

Buchanan, Captain Charles A.
Served with Loughlin in USS NEW MEXICO in 1930s; as Naval Academy commandant, had a hand in selecting Loughlin as athletic director in 1954, pp. 182-183; difficulties with football coach Eddie Erdelatz, pp. 185-186.

Burke, Admiral Arleigh A.
Dissatisfied with U.S. Navy antisubmarine warfare while CNO in 1950s, p. 256; description of personality, pp. 256-257.

Burlingame, Captain Creed
Submarine squadron commander in Panama after World War II, forced to revert from captain to commander along with rest of his Naval Academy class, pp. 152-154.

Church, Captain Albert T., Jr.
Skipper of cruiser ST. PAUL, p. 275; career hurt when his ship collides with carrier CORAL SEA in early 1960s, pp. 278-279.

Classmates of Elliott Loughlin at Naval Academy
Tommy Peters, p. 32; Selby Santmyers, p. 39; Charlie Duncan, p. 40; Joe Enright, p. 50; Penrod Schneider, p. 91; Otto Spahr, p. 181; Bill Mott, pp. 309, 333.

Coppedge, Captain John O. ("Bo")
As Naval Academy director of athletics in 1970s, pp. 224-226.

CORAL SEA, USS (CVA-43)
Hit by cruiser ST. PAUL at Yokosuka, Japan, in early 1960s, pp. 278-279.

Courts-Martial
Trial of CDR Elliott Loughlin, skipper of USS QUEENFISH in 1945 for sinking of Japanese AWA MARU, pp. 127-134.

Crawford, Captain George C. ("Turkey Neck")
As COMSUBLANT chief of staff in June 1944, helped conduct short-notice inspection of USS QUEENFISH, pp. 148-149.

Cruiser-Destroyer Flotilla 9
  Commanded by Rear Admiral Loughlin in early 1960s, pp. 272-279; in USS OKLAHOMA CITY on West Coast, pp. 272-274; in USS ST. PAUL in Far East, 275-279.

Daubin, Rear Admiral Freeland
  As COMSUBLANT in spring of 1944, conducts short-notice inspection of USS QUEENFISH, pp. 148-149.

Dawson, Lieutenant (junior grade) William L.
  At Loughlin's wedding, p. 27.

Daughters
  Birth of first daughter on Memorial Day, 1936, p. 37; birth of second daughter, July 1937, p. 39.

DeGaulle, General Charles
  Pulls France out of military participation in NATO alliance in early 1960s, pp. 284-285.

Dempsey, Rear Admiral James C.
  While serving as OP-09B in mid-1960s, was immediate boss of Loughlin and other naval district commandants, pp. 321, 323.

Dennison, Admiral Robert L.
  As Supreme Allied Commander Atlantic (NATO command), 1960, pp. 263-264, 268-271; during 1962 crisis, p. 281.

Diem, Ngo Dinh
  As president of South Vietnam in early 1960s, description of personal characteristics, p. 247.

Dornin, Ensign Robert E. ("Dusty")
  As junior officer in USS NEW MEXICO in 1935, p. 28; member of outstanding group of students at submarine school in late 1930s, p.45.

Doyle, Admiral Austin K. ("Artie")
  Flew flying boats at Naval Academy in early 1930s as means of recruiting prospective aviators, pp. 15-16.

Dutton, Captain Benjamin, Jr.
  Commanding officer of USS WYOMING when she encountered hurricane during midshipman training cruise of 1931, p. 9.

Dykers, Captain Thomas M.
  As commanding officer of USS S-35 in late 1930s, pp. 49-53, 56; as originator of "Silent Service" TV program after World War II, pp. 50-53; successful CO of submarine USS JACK in World War II, p. 53; as COMSUBLANT planning officer in late 1940s, pp. 150-151.

Eddy, Captain Ian
  Loughlin's predecessor as Naval Academy director of athletics, p. 182.

Engineering experiments
  See Annapolis (Maryland) Naval Station

Enright, Lieutenant (junior grade) Joseph F.
  Served in S-boat submarines, p. 50.

Erdelatz, Eddie
  As Naval Academy head football coach in 1950s, pp. 185-191, 197, 204-205.

ESCOLAR, USS (SS-294)
  Submarine lost in Japanese minefield in autumn of 1944, p. 116.

Evans, Vice Admiral Charles
  Royal Navy officer serving as Deputy SACLANT in 1960, philosophy on offering drinks, pp. 262-263.

Ewen, Lieutenant Edward C.
  Naval aviator on board the USS NEW MEXICO in the 1930s, p. 43.

Fife, Admiral James, Jr.
  As believer in blimps for ASW, p. 92; allowed to go on submarine war patrols and got fourth star as result, pp. 113-114; description of personality and working habits, pp. 149-151; advises Loughlin about Naval Academy billet during inspection tour to Panama, pp. 161-162.

Flaherty, Captain Michael F.
  Billet changed after being ordered to command naval station at Annapolis, pp. 162-163.

Fleet, U.S.
  Impressions of fleet review at New York City in June 1934, pp. 34-35; Hawaiian Detachment in high state of readiness under Admiral J. O. Richardson in October 1940, p. 55.

Fletcher, Captain Frank Jack
  Impressions of him during period as commanding officer of USS NEW MEXICO during the late 1930s, pp. 34, 36-37.

Fluckey, Rear Admiral Eugene B.
  As commanding officer of USS BARB during wolf pack operatons in late 1944, pp. 93-97, 116-117, 119; qualities as superb naval officer, pp. 105, 217; Medal of Honor winner, p. 109; sends landing party ashore to blow up railroad tracks in Japan, p. 145; heads fund-raising drive for Naval Academy stadium in 1950s, pp. 216-217; serves tour as COMIBERLANT in Portugal, p. 284.

Foley, Commander Robert J.
  Discovers unexploded depth charge on deck of USS GATO while serving as CO in December 1944, pp. 102-103.

Football
  See athletics.

Formosa Strait
  Site of U.S. submarine wolfpack operations in late 1944 by BARB, PICUDA, and QUEENFISH, pp. 115-120.

France
  Pulls out of military participation at DeGaulle's direction in early 1960s, pp. 284-286.

Freeman, Captain Charles L. ("Larry")
  Various billets held by: S-34, USS WILLIAMSBURG, CO of Annapolis Naval Station, duty on Eisenhower's staff, pp. 161-162; requests permission to serve liquor on board REINA MERCEDES at Naval Academy, turned down, pp. 166-167.

French Frigate Shoals
  Used as site of U.S. submarine training operations in late 1930s, pp. 54-55.

French Navy
  Ships of free French fleet at Guadeloupe in World War II, p. 65.

Fyfe, Lieutenant Commander John K.
  Sinks Japanese submarines in the vicinity of Philippines while commanding USS BATFISH in February 1945, p. 109.

GATO, USS (SS-212)
  Unexploded depth charge found on deck during war patrol in December 1944, pp. 102-103.

Gatch, Rear Admiral Thomas L.
  As Navy Judge Advocate General in 1945, writes endorsement on Loughlin's AWA MARU court-martial, p. 137.

Gilmore, Morris
  Responsible for Naval Academy Athletic Association owning land in Admiral Heights section of Annapolis, p. 215.

Greig, Commander Stuart O.
  Does fine job rotating junior officers while serving as executive officer of the USS NEW MEXICO in the mid-1930s, p. 32.

Grenfell, Vice Admiral Elton W. ("Joe")
  Impressions of while serving as Commander Submarine Flotilla 1 in early 1950s, pp. 175-176; on selection board when Loughlin

made flag rank, pp. 271-272; asks Loughlin to take over ComSubFlot 6 in 1964, p. 295.

Halsey, Fleet Admiral William F.
Served as commanding officer of USS REINA MERCEDES, p. 163.

Harral, Lieutenant Commander Brooks
Makes patrol to Galapagos Islands early in World War II while commanding USS S-17, p. 67.

Hart, Rear Admiral Thomas C.
Impression of personality while serving as Naval Academy Superintendent around 1930, p. 16.

Hawk, Lieutenant Earle C.
One of only three survivors when USS S-26 was sunk in Gulf of Panama in January 1942, p. 33; acquitted at subsequent court-martial, p. 136.

Hensel, Commander Karl G.
As instructor at submarine PCO school in 1943, p. 76.

Hebert, F. Edward
Louisiana congressman seeks tickets for 1955 Sugar Bowl game, pp. 193-195.

Higgs, Lieutenant Commander Alred Henry ("Harry")
Exec of QUEENFISH under Loughlin, claimed damage to large ship, p. 146.

Hill, Rear Admiral Harry W.
As superintendent of Naval Academy in early 1950s was enthusiastic sports booster, pp. 169, 173; critical of incomplete gun salute to French president, pp. 171-172.

Hoffheins, Lieutenant Commander William L. ("Willy")
Operations officer of Coco Solo submarine base early in World War II, p. 61.

Holloway, Admiral James L., Jr.
As superintendent of Naval Academy in late 1940s, turns down request to serve liquor on board the REINA MERCEDES, pp. 166-167; as CINCNELM, commands Lebanon landing in 1958, p. 236.

Hoover, Vice Admiral John H. ("Genial John")
As Commandant 10th Naval District at San Juan at beginning of World War II, pp. 60, 62; as president of AWA MARU court-martial in 1945, pp. 129-130.

Hopkins, Midshipman Thomas W. ("Tommy")
Graduated from Naval Academy in 1932; he and sister Kitty were members of Annapolis family, p. 20.

HOUSTON, USS (CA-30)
    U.S. cruiser sunk in early 1942; when Japanese ship was sunk in
    September 1944 and POWs rescued, it was first U.S. knowledge of
    any HOUSTON survivors, p. 99.

Iberian Atlantic Command (COMIBERLANT)
    Infrastructure in place before command activated under Rear
    Admiral Fluckey, p. 284.

ICBM
    See Missile Testing.

Ingram, Admiral Jonas
    As CINCLANTFLT in 1945, counsels Loughlin on effect on career
    of AWA MARU incident, p. 135.

Irvin, Captain William D.
    As communication officer on COMSUBPAC staff in 1944-45, pp. 92,
    127.

Jacobs, Captain Randall
    Became commanding officer of USS NEW MEXICO as Loughlin was
    leaving, p. 32.

Jahncke, Midshipman Ernest Lee, Jr. ("Ernie Lee")
    Son of former Assistant Secretary of Navy, served as
    compartment cleaner on midshipman cruise, p. 9.

Japan
    Impression of by Loughlin while serving there, pp. 178-180,
    275-277.

JEAN BART
    French battleship at Guadeloupe early in World War II, p. 65.

Kane, Midshipman William R.
    Member of class of 1933 who lettered in three sports while at
    Naval Academy, p. 13.

Kauffman, Midshipman Draper L.
    Member of class of 1933 who served as compartment cleaner
    during Naval Academy midshipman cruise, p. 9.

Kelly, Colonel Sid
    Commanded Marine detachment at Annapolis in early 1950s,
    p. 164.

King, Fleet Admiral Ernest J.
    As Commander in Chief, U.S. Fleet, reaction to AWA MARU court-
    martial in 1945, pp. 126-129.

King, Commander Thomas S., II
    Assistant to executive officer of Naval Academy in 1933, arranges for Loughlin's orders to be changed to USS NEW MEXICO, p. 24.

Kivette, Vice Admiral Frederick N.
    Commander Seventh Fleet in 1959, p. 243.

Klinker, Lieutenant Commander Roy C.
    Fails to send contact report while commanding USS SEA FOX during submarine wolf pack operations in March 1945, pp. 122-123.

Kridel, Frank
    Friend of Loughlin's who was instrumental in getting Norman Vincent Peale to visit Naval Academy in mid-1950s, pp. 227-228.

Laing, Captain Frederick W.
    As commanding officer of submarine tender ORION in 1947, pp. 152-155.

Lake, Lieutenant Richard C.
    As commanding officer of submarine USS S-14 in early 1942, undergoes diving emergency, then detached, pp. 63-65.

Leahy, Frank
    Notre Dame coach briefs crew of USS QUEENFISH on football as part of USO work in World War II, p. 112.

Lebanon
    U.S. landing at Beirut in 1958, pp. 232, 236.

Lee, Commander John F.
    Submarine squadron commander at San Diego in early 1950s, p. 176.

Leeds, Midshipman John R. ("Bud")
    Company commander at Naval Academy in the early 1930s, p. 18.

LIBERTY, USS (AGTR-5)
    Intelligence ship attacked by Israelis in 1967; Loughlin conducted ceremony when skipper awarded Medal of Honor, p. 324.

Lockwood, Vice Admiral Charles A.
    Commander Submarine Force Pacific Fleet during World War II, at Pearl Harbor, p. 92; at Guam, 111-113; retired as vice admiral because not permitted to make war patrols, p. 114; reaction to sinking of Japanese AWA MARU in 1945, pp. 126-128, 133-134.

LONG BEACH, USS (CGN-9)
    First skipper, Eugene Wilkinson had great technical proficiency, p. 315.

Loughlin, Rear Admiral Elliott
  Birth in North Carolina, p. 1; father's death and subsequent hardships, p. 2; schooling at Lansdowne High School and Episcopal Academy, p. 2; great influence of brother Joseph on p. 2; West Point and early plans, p. 3; oldest living Naval Academy graduate of Sons of Deceased Veterans, p. 3; influence of athletics throughout life p. 4 ff.; State championship in tennis, p. 4; All-City basketball, p. 4; influence of family, p. 5; submarine force, p. 5; entered Naval Academy in 1929, p. 6; commission of, p. 8; playing tennis on cruise, p. 9; dual tennis matches, p. 10; national inter scholastic, inter collegiate ranking, p. 10; State tournaments, p. 12; first station after graduation, p. 16; demerits for chewing gum at football game, p. 17; ping pong as hobby, p. 18; Carvel Hall hops while at Naval Academy, p. 20; tennis games while abroad, p. 21; pranks for leaving Naval Academy base, p. 21-22; Naval Academy graduation in 1933, p. 23; Inter collegiate tennis after Naval Academy graduation, p. 24; influence of Admiral Rickover on, p. 25; marriage in 1935, p. 27; submarine school, p. 33, 44-45; birth of daughters, p. 39; submarine pin in 1938, p. 50, 52, 56; service in S-35, p. 50-56; command of S-14, pp. 57-73; first officer in his class to get a command of a submarine in 1942, p. 66; qualifying as Executive Officer on S-35, p. 56; commissioning the S-14, p. 57; during Pearl Harbor attack, 1941, p. 61; most horrifying submarine experience, pp. 62-63; problems of transit of canal in a submarine, p. 68; Lieutenant to Commander in 2 1/2 years, pp. 70-71; New Construction orders, PCO School in 1943, pp. 73-74; command of USS QUEENFISH pp. 79-127; 500-700 submarine dives, p. 85; hitting sunken ship, pp. 87-98; submarine war patrol in Formosa Strait, pp. 115-119; sinking of AWA MARU, pp. 120-126; general court martial, pp. 127 ff; training command at Pearl Harbor, p. 131; operations officer at COMSUBLANT p. 135; Navy Cross, p. 146; Presidential Citation, p. 146; Silver Star, 147; Bronze Star with "V", p. 147; Legion of Merit medal, p. 147; Naval Academy Executive Offficer to Larry Freeman, 1949, p. 161; commanding officer of USS REINA MERCEDES, p. 162; Commanding Officer of Naval Station Annapolis, p. 163; community ties in Annapolis, p. 173; Chief of Staff in Submarine Flotilla 1, p. 175; made Captain in 1952, p. 177; Director of Athletics, USNA, pp. 184-239; headaches as Director of Athletics at Naval Academy, p. 190; Sugar Bowl game of 1955, p. 193; duty at Pentagon, p. 227; command of MISSISSINEWA, p. 228; command of USS TOLEDO, pp. 242-250; entering Saigon, pp. 245-246; Director of Plans, SAC LANT, pp. 258-271, 290-295; selection as Rear Admiral, p. 271; Command of Cruiser-Destroyer Flotilla 9, pp. 272-279; gout attack in Japan, p. 277; command of Submarine Flotilla 6 in 1964, pp. 295-317; continued interest in personnel and morale, pp. 302-304; Commandant, Naval District Washington, pp. 319-325; area coordination duties, p. 320; retirement from Navy, p. 325-326; Head of Naval Academy Foundation, pp. 326-355; briefly accepts position with Marine Corps Residents Foundation at Vinson Hall, then declines, pp. 326-327; house on Cumberland Court, p. 328.

Loughlin, Ednee (first wife)
  Marriage to Elliott Loughlin in 1935, p. 27; prevented from sailing to Panama because of Pearl Harbor attack, p. 74.

Loughlin, Eleanor (King)
  Mother of Elliott Loughlin was born in Pennsylvania, p. 1; hardship on family after death of husband, p. 2-3; King family, p. 2; following sons, pp. 5-6; death of, p. 6.

Loughlin Joseph J., Sr. (father of Eliott Loughlin)
  Military background, pp. 1-2, career in Army, pp. 1-2; death in World War I, p. 2; rank, p. 2; Officer Candidate School, p. 3.

Loughlin, Lieutenant (junior grade) Joseph J., Jr. (brother of Elliott Loughlin)
  Early influence on Loughlin, pp. 2-3, influence on Loughlin to enter the Naval Academy, pp. 2-4; athletics, p. 4; varsity wrestling team, p. 5; flight training, p. 5; death in 1937, p. 5; career as aviator, p. 15; as Loughlin's platoon commander, p. 18; on INDIANAPOLIS, p. 35.

Loughlin, Marjorie (second wife)
  With new baby at Pearl Harbor at time of AWA MARU court-martial in 1945, p. 134; makes friends in civilian community, associated with Hammond-Harwood House in Annapolis, p. 173; her help to Loughlin in being selected for Naval Academy Athletic Director, p. 183-184; burden of entertaining when Loughlin was Commandant of Naval District, Washington, p. 322.

Lowrance, Vice Admiral Vernon L. ("Rebel")
  As COMSUBLANT in 1966, provides ballistic missile submarine for Loughlin's COMSUBFLOT 6 change of command, p. 30.

Luzon Strait
  U.S. wolf pack operations there in late 1944 by submarines BARB, PICUDA, and QUEENFISH, pp. 93-99.

MACKEREL, USS, (SS-204)
  Small submarine used for tactical training of prospective COs at New London during World War II, p. 75.

Magic Carpet
  Operation after World War II to return ships and men to the United States, pp. 140-142.

MARLIN, USS (SS-205)
  Small submarine used for tactical training of prospective COs at New London during World War II, p. 75.

Martin, Benjamin S.
  Topflight football coach who left Naval Academy because he couldn't work with Eddie Erdelatz, pp. 204-205.

McCandless, Lieutenant Commander Bruce
  Received Medal of Honor for bringing back cruiser SAN
  FRANCISCO when damaged at Guadalcanal in 1942, p. 84.

McKee, Captain Andrew I.
  Recognized as best submarine designer in world; got results for
  submarine skippers while at Portsmouth Navy Yard in World War
  II, pp. 80-81.

Messina, Straits of
  Passage between Italy and Sicily has treacherous currents
  which make shiphandling difficult, p. 234.

Metcalf, Lieutenant Ralph M.
  Becomes skipper of USS POGY during World War II when
  predecessor has to be relieved, p. 71.

Miller, Commander Rollo
  Commanding officer of submarine in which Loughlin rides as
  division commander in late 1940s, p. 157.

Millican, Commander William John
  Skipper of submarine USS ESCOLAR when she was lost in Japanese
  minefield in October 1944, p. 116.

Missile Testing
  Firing of Polaris A-3 in 1960s, pp. 307-308; Air Force unable
  to fire ICBM for observation by space ship, p. 307.

MISSISSINEWA, USS (AO-144)
  Fleet oiler commanded by Captain Loughlin in 1957-1958,
  pp. 228-239; converted to flagship for Commander Service Force
  Sixth Fleet, pp. 229-230; shiphandling and refueling, pp. 230-
  231; Sixth Fleet ops, incuding 1958 Lebanon crisis, pp. 232-
  239; quality of officers, p. 237.

Morale
  Given boost for submariners during World War II by publication
  of submarine exploits, p. 109.

Mountbatten, Lord Louis
  Stature as a NATO commander in 1950s, highly respected, p. 264.

Mustin, Rear Admiral Lloyd M.
  Impressions of while serving in the ASW readiness section of
  OpNav in 1960, p. 253.

NATO
  Loughlin serves as Director of Plans for SACLANT in 1960-1961,
  pp. 258-271; SACLANT must be U.S. admiral, p. 259; nature of
  planning job, pp. 261-262, 265; views of top commanders:
  Mountbatten, Norstad, Dennison, pp. 264-268; difference between
  national and NATO forces, pp. 291-295. Loughlin serves as
  deputy chief of staff, SACLANT, 1962-1964, pp. 288-295.

Nauman, Lieutenant Commander Harley K.
   Exhibition of courage against the Japanese while commanding USS
   SALMON in October 1944, p. 115.

Naval Academy
   Loughlin entered in 1929, his love of the Academy, p. 6;
   Loughlin's plebe year, pp. 6-7; classes at, p. 7; Loughlin's
   class standing, p. 8; summer cruises, uselessness of in early
   days, pp. 8-9, present effectiveness of, p. 10; hazing, pp. 13-
   14; relations with Annapolis townspeople, p. 19; Loughlin's
   pranks leaving base pp. 21-22; Loughlin's graduation in 1933,
   p. 23; Recruiting players at Naval Academy, pp. 191, 328, "bird
   dog" system, p. 191, Congressional nominations, p. 334;
   Presidential and Vice Presidential nominations, p. 335; review
   board for selection, pp. 336-338; means of supporting athletics
   at, p. 200; academic challenge and competitive sports,
   pp. 209-212; field house, p. 213; stadium, p. 214; admission
   standards, pp. 222-223; major and minor sports at,
   p. 227; female midshipmen, problems of, p. 203; degree of
   integrity of students, pp. 342-344; financing scholarships,
   pp. 345-346

Naval Academy Foundation
   Existed originaly for sole purpose of helping athletes enter
   the Academy, p. 192; Loughlin as executive director from 1968
   to present; foundation serves to provide aid to prospective
   Naval Academy midshipmen, pp. 326-355.

Naval District, Washington
   Loughlin as Commandant 1966-1968, pp. 320-325; role of area
   coordinator, pp. 320-321, 324-325; relationship with OpNav,
   p. 321.

NEW MEXICO, USS (BB-40)
   Loughlin's first station after graduation, p. 24-43;
   relationship with "Lieutenant" Rickover, pp. 24-29; Commander
   Greig's interest in well-rounded education, p. 32; shakedown
   cruise in 1934, p. 34; fleet exercises on, p. 36; experience of
   williwaw in Aleutians, p. 36-38; turbine troubles, identical on
   NEW MEXICO and MISSISSIPPI, p. 37; 4 1/2 year learning process,
   p. 41; engineering "E"s, the highest engineering score, p. 43.

New York City
   Ships of U.S. Fleet make visit there in 1934; current makes
   time difficult for ships moored in Hudson River, p. 35.

Nimitz, Fleet Admiral Chester W.
   Relationship with Vice Admiral C. A. Lockwood while Nimitz was
   CINCPAC at Guam in 1945, pp. 113, 127.

Norstad, General Lauris
   Impressions of wile serving as SACEUR in NATO in early 1960s,
   pp. 264-265.

North Atlantic Treaty Organization
   See: NATO

Norway
   Impressons of, including attitude toward drinking and driving on part of Norwegians, pp. 266-267.

Nunn, Rear Admiral Ira H.
   As U.S. naval attache in Norway in early 1960s, p. 266.

O'Kane, Captain Richard H.
   Captured by Japanese after sinking of USS TANG in World War II; held vehement anti-Japanese feelings in 1950s, pp. 178-179.

OKLAHOMA CITY, USS (CG-6)
   Served as flagship of Commander Cruiser-Destroyer Flotilla 9 and Commander Seventh Fleet during early 1960s, pp. 273-274.

Olympic Games of 1932
   Naval Academy athletes involved, p. 13.

OPNAV
   Loughlin serves in as Deputy for Antisubmarine Warfare in Readiness Section, 1959-1960, pp. 250-256.

ORION, USS (AS-18)
   Submarine tender in which Loughlin served as executive officer in 1947-1948, pp. 67, 152-156; operated out of Panama and made a trip to Peru, pp. 67, 152-156.

PAMPANITO, USS (SS-383)
   Rescues Allied prisoners of war after sinking of Japanese transport in September 1944, pp. 96-97.

Panama
   Defensive patrols conducted in vicinity of canal by U.S. submarines early in World War II, p. 66; precautions to protect canal, pp. 67-68; transits of canal by submarines during World War II, pp. 69-70; experiences polio epidemic in late 1940s, pp. 157-158.

Parks, Captain Lewis S.
   Ran training school for new submarine skippers at Portsmouth Navy Yard in World War II, p. 79; member of Loughlin's cortmartial for sinking AWA MARU, p. 129.

Patterson, Commander George W., Jr.
   As officer in charge of PCO school for submariners at New London in 1943, p. 74.

PCO School
   Training for prospective submarine skippers at New London in 1943, pp. 74-77.

PERTH, HMAS
   Australian cruiser sunk in 1942, some survivors rescued as POWs in 1944, p. 99.

Peters, Lieutenant Thomas V.
   Classmate who influences Loughlin to go to submarine school in 1937, p. 32; dies in the sinking of USS S-26 in Jauary 1942, p. 33.

PICUDA, USS (SS-382)
   Operates in wolf pack with USS BARB and USS QUEENFISH in late 1944 in Formosa Strait, pp. 115-119.

Pierce, Commander George E.
   As skipper of submarine TUNNY when she was hit by bombs on 1 September 1944 during wolf pack operations, pp. 93-94.

Pirie, Captain Robert B.
   As Naval Academy's commandant of midshipmen in 1951, reluctantly decides to let plebes play varsity basketball, pp. 169-171.

POGY, USS (SS-266)
   Skipper George Wales gets pneumonia, so Ralph Metcalf relieves him in 1942 and takes boat to Pearl, p. 71.

Polaris Submarine Force
   Became operational in early 1960s, p. 287; allies rankled because Polaris FBMs never included in NATO plans, pp. 287-288; four squadrons, p. 297; quality of crew of, p. 297; operational problems of, pp. 298-299; safety record of, pp. 300-301; education in, pp. 301-302; description of Blue and Gold arrangement and schedule of time, pp. 311-312.

Polio epidemic
   Among crews of U.S. naval vessels in Panama in late 1940s, p. 157.

Portsmouth (New Hampshire) Navy Yard
   Outfitting of submarine QUEENFISH there in 1943-1944, pp. 79-81.

Post, Commander William S., Jr.
   As skipper of USS SPOT in submarine wolf pack operations with QUEENFISH and SEA FOX in March 1945, pp. 122-123.

Prep School, Naval Academy
   Contribution to education, p. 343.

QUEENFISH, USS (SS-393)
  Building of at Portsmouth Navy Yard, pp. 79-80; sonar capabilities, pp. 82-83; use of SJ radar for communication, pp. 83-84; put in commisson by Loughlin in March 1944, p. 87; shakedown training for crew, pp. 87-91; submarine wolf pack operations in Luzon Strait in late 1944, pp. 93-98; war patrol in wolf pack in Yellow Sea at end of 1944, pp. 101-110; sinking of AKITSU MARU, pp. 106-107; wolf pack operations in Formosa Strait with USS BARB and USS PICUDA in early 1945, pp. 115-120; wolf pack patrol during which QUEENFISH sank AWA MARU, spring 1945, pp. 120-126; inspection of by Rear Admiral Freeland Daubin at New London prior to war patrols, pp. 148-149; number of torpedoes carried, p. 313.

Radar
  Rundown of radar systems on board USS QUEENFISH when commissioned in 1944, SJ radar used for communicating in Morse Code, p. 83.

Ramage, Commander Lawson P. ("Red")
  Medal of Honor winner tells of subsequent patrol, p. 77; news story on Medal of Honor patrol, p. 109.

Reich, Lieutenant Commander Eli T.
  As skipper of submarine SEALION when members of crew attacked on Guam in late 1944, p. 111.

REINA MERCEDES, USS (IX-25)
  Station ship at Annapolis, commanded by CDR William Halsey, p. 163; commanded by Loughlin, 1951-1952, pp. 163-166; request to serve liquor on board denied, pp. 166-167.

Rickover, Admiral Hyman G.
  As assistant chief engineer in battleship NEW MEXICO in late 1930s, pp. 24-30, 37; Loughlin's impressions of, pp. 25, 256, 316; generosity, pp. 27-28; fuel conservation methods, p. 29; as a friend of Loughlin in 1960s, pp. 30-32; and diesel submarines, p. 160; and submarine safety record, pp. 297-298; interested only in nuclear plants, not patrol procedures, p. 302.

Rickover, Mrs. Ruth Masters
  Loughlin's impressions of, p. 30.

Roosevelt, Mrs. Eleanor
  Impression of her when attending Naval Academy graduation in 1933, p. 23.

Roosevelt, President Franklin D.
  At Naval Academy graduation in 1933, p. 23.

Rota, Spain
  Location of U.S. base for FBM submarines, pp. 290, 309-312.

ROYONA
   First Naval Academy Class-A boat to win the Bermuda Race, p. 188.

S-14, USS (SS-119)
   Submarine put back into commission by Loughlin at Philadelphia in 1940, p. 57; operations in hurricane, pp. 58-59; operations in Caribbean and around Panama early in World War II, pp. 60-73; problems with diving because of stern planes, pp. 62-63; Loughlin takes command of, p. 65; leaves Canal Zone for New London, p. 73.

S-17, USS (SS-122)
   Makes patrol to Galapagos Islands early in World War II, p. 67.

S-26, USS (SS-131)
   Sinks off Panama in January 1942 with only three survivors, p. 33.

S-35, USS (SS-140)
   Loughlin serves in from 1938 to 1940 with Lieutenant Tommy Dykers as skipper, pp. 49-57; Loughlin becomes exec, p. 50.

Sabin, Vice Admiral Lorenzo S.
   As SACLANT chief of staff, p. 262, 268.

SACEUR
   As multinational commander, p. 292; responsible for NATO objectives, p. 293.

SACLANT
   See: NATO

Saigon, South Vietnam
   Visit to by heavy cruiser USS TOLEDO in 1959, pp. 245-247.

Sailing
   See: Athletics.

ST. PAUL, USS (CA-73)
   Heavy cruiser as Loughlin's CRUDESFLOT 9 flagship, p. 275; collision with USS CORAL SEA, pp. 278-279.

St. Thomas, Virgin Islands
   U.S. submarine base there quite effective in World War II, pp. 59-60.

SALMON, USS (SS-1820
   Courageously commanded by Lieutenant Commander H. K. Nauman in action aganst Japanese in October 1944, p. 115.

SAN FRANCISCO, USS (CA-38)
   Damaged at Guadalcanal in November 1942, p. 84.

Santmyers, Midshipman Selby
   Active as golfer while at Naval Academy, p. 39.

Scanland, Captain F. W.
   Base commander at Pearl Harbor, father of submariner, p. 54.

Schneider, Lieutenant Commander Earle Caffrey ("Penrod")
   Lost on board USS DORADO in October 1943, p. 91.

SCORPION, USS (SSN-589)
   Lost off Azores in 1968, pp. 298, 300-301.

SEA FOX, USS (SS-402)
   During submarine wolf pack operations in March 1945, pp. 122-123.

SEALION, USS (SS-315)
   Rescues POWs in Luzon Strait in September 1944, p. 97; crewmen killed while at rest camp on Guam, p. 111.

Shafner, Lieutenant Colonel Austin
   Marine attache in Peru in late 1940s, p. 156.

Shear, Captain Harold E.
   Would not notify NATO allies of location of U.S. fleet ballistic missile submarines while serving on Admiral Dennison's staff in early 1960s, pp. 287-288.

Smedberg, Rear Admiral William R. III ("Smeddy")
   As Naval Academy superintendent during stadium fund-raising drive of mid-1950s, pp. 216-217; paid some expenses himself while Academy department head and superintendent, pp. 226-227; description of personality, p. 241; helps Loughlin toward flag rank by getting him a good job, pp. 241-242.

Smith, Commander William Ward ("Poco")
   Executive officer of Naval Academy puts Loughlin on report for chewing gum at football game in 1932, pp. 16-17.

Snyder, Captain Charles P.
   Commandant of midshipmen at Naval Academy in 1930s, has beautiful daughter, Jane, p. 16.

Soule, Captain Charles C., Jr. ("Savvy")
   Tough but fair as skipper of USS NEW MEXICO in mid-1930s, p. 34.

Sports
   See: Athletics.

SPOT, USS (SS-413)
   In submarine wolf pack operations with USS QUEENFISH and SEA FOX in March 1945, pp. 122-123.

Stephan, Lieutenant Edward C.
   Executive officer of S-35 when Loughlin reported, p. 50.

Street, Lieutenant Commander George L.
   Information transmitted about his Medal of Honor war patrol in World War II, p. 109.

Submariners
   Are in their prime in early 30s, tend to get more cautious as they grow older, pp. 48-49; Loughlin sees them at beginning and end of FBM patrols while serving as ComSubFlot 6 in mid-1960s, pp. 302-304; quality of personnel in FBM submarines, pp. 304-305, 314-319; use of non-volunteers in nuclear power program, pp. 318-319.

Submarines
   Submarine school at New London in late 1930s, pp. 44-49; service in U.S. Navy's S-boats in late 1930s and early 1940s, pp. 49-71; command of USS QUEENFISH by Loughlin during World War II, pp. 78-127; German Type 21s brought to United States after World War II, pp. 140-141; decommissioning of U.S. submarines after war, pp. 142-143; use of bathythermograph to stay on station without using power, pp. 158-159, information held tightly on deployment patterns of U.S. ballistic missile submarines, pp. 287-290; Loughlin gets heavily involved with missile submarines during tour as ComSubFlot 6 from 1964 to 1966, pp. 296-319.

Submarine Flotilla 1
   Loughlin as chief of staff in 1952-1953, pp. 175-176.

Submarine Flotilla 6
   Commanded by Loughlin in 1964-1966, pp. 295-319.

Submarine Force Atlantic (SUBLANT)
   Loughlin as staff operations officer from 1945 to 1947, pp. 139-144.

Submarine School, New London, Connecticut
   While Loughlin was student there in late 1930s, pp. 44-49.

Sugar Bowl
   Football game in 1955 in which Navy beat Mississippi, pp. 193-199.

Swanston, Lieutenant William A. ("Square Shooting Bill)
   Officer at Naval Academy who punished Loughlin for rules infraction as midshipman, pp. 17-19.

Tennis
   See: Athletics.

Thompson, Midshipman Raymond W.
Naval Academy athlete who swam in the 1932 Olympic Games,
p. 13.

THRESHER, USS (SSN-593)
Loss of in 1963, pp. 298-299.

TOLEDO, USS (CA-133)
Heavy cruiser commanded by Loughlin, 1958-1959, pp. 237-240,
242-250; state visit to Saigon, pp. 245-247.

Torpedoes
Loughlin is skipper of USS QUEENFISH in 1944 when Mark XXIII
torpedo introduced for use against ASW vessels, pp. 81-82; Mark
XVIII electric torpedoes left no wake, p. 82; possible flaw in
tender preparation of torpedoes which didn't explode during
1944 wolf pack operations on part of QUEENFISH, pp. 117-118,
120.

Training
Submarine school in late 1930s, pp. 44-50.

TUNNY, USS (SS-282)
Submarine hit by bombs during wolf pack operations in Luzon
Strait in September 1944, pp. 93-94.

ULTRA
Dispatches, 86, 116; usefulness to Loughlin as submarine
skipper in World War II, pp. 86, 116.

Vinson Hall
Loughlin briefly accepts, then declines position as head of
Marine Corps Residents Foundation in 1968 after retirement from
active duty, p. 326.

Voge, Captain Richard G.
Operations officer for COMSUBPAC, p. 92; fine officer who ran
show for Admiral Lockwood, p. 113; testimony on behalf of
Loughlin at AWA MARU court-martial in 1945, p. 132; jealousy of
Voge's role by other officers led to reorganization of
submarine staffs, pp. 143-144.

Wakelin, James
As Assistant Secretary of the Navy for Research and Development
in early 1960s, pp. 253, 255.

Ward, Rear Admiral Alfred G. ("Corky")
As Commander Cruiser Division 1 in 1959, involved in exercises
around Japan, p. 243; makes state visit to Saigon in USS
TOLEDO, pp. 245-247.

Watkins, Captain Frank
   While serving in Bureau of Personnel in 1945, gives Loughlin
   letter of admonition for AWA MARU sinking, pp. 134-135.

Weather, Heavy
   Hurricane experienced by USS WYOMING during midshipman cruise
   in 1931, p. 9; Loughlin says submariners prefer to ride out
   a hurricane on the surface rather than submerged, pp. 58-59.

Wilkinson, Captain Eugene P.
   First skipper of cruiser LONG BEACH had great technical
   ability, p. 315.

Wilkins, Commander Charles W. ("Weary")
   Submarine division commander when Loughlin hit submerged hulk
   while in QUEENFISH, p. 88.

HENRY B. WILSON, USS (DDG-7)
   Guided missile destroyer which Loughlin used as flagship while
   COMCRUDESFLOT 9 in 1961-1962 during transits to and from
   Western Pacific, pp. 274-275, 279.

Withers, Rear Admiral Thomas, Jr.
   Very helpful to Loughlin as Commander Portsmouth Navy Yard
   during World War II, p. 80.

Women
   Receipt of assistance from Naval Academy Foundation, p. 351.

Wylie, Captain Joseph C., Jr. ("Bill")
   As topflight planner on SACLANT staff around 1960, pp. 267-268.

WYOMING, USS (BB-32)
   Undergoes hurricane while on Naval Academy midshipman training
   cruise of 1931, p. 9.

Yeager, Rear Admiral Howard A. ("Red")
   Loughlin's impressons of him while working in OP-03 on
   antisubmarine readiness in 1959-1960, pp. 250-253.

Yokosuka (Japan) Naval Base
   Anti-U.S. demonstrations there by Japanese people around 1960,
   p. 180.

www.ingramcontent.com/pod-product-compliance
Lightning Source LLC
Chambersburg PA
CBHW080621170426
43209CB00007B/1482